The

Character

of

Old Russia

SERGEI M. SOLOVIEV

The Character of Old Russia

Edited, Translated, and With an
Introduction by

Alexander V. Muller

Academic International Press

1987

This book is a paperback reprint of Volume 24 of The Academic
International Press Edition of S.M. Soloviev's *History of Russia
from Earliest Times* in fifty volumes.

Volume 24. *The Character of Old Russia*. Unabridged translation
of Volume 13, Chapter 1, of S.M. Soloviev's *Istoriia Rossii s drevneishikh vremen* as found in Volume VII of this work published
in Moscow in 1962, with added annotation by Alexander V. Muller.

Library of Congress Catalog Card Number: 75–11085
ISBN O-87569-095-5 (paper edition)

Printed in the United States of America

A list of volumes published by Academic International Press is
found at the end of this volume.

ACADEMIC INTERNATIONAL PRESS
POB 1111 Gulf Breeze FL 32561 USA

CONTENTS

Historical Geography—Divergent Destinies—The Eastern Slavs—First Stirrings of Russian History—Disintegration of Early Tribal Organization—Transition to Political and Ecclesiastical Unification—Princes and Retinues—Formation of Towns and Cities—Influence of the Clergy—Elements of Historical Retardation and Progress—Princes and Cities—Reorientation from Southwest to Northeast—Rise of Moscow—Consolidation of the Grand Principality of Moscow—The Clergy and the Grand Prince of Moscow —Decline of Novgorod—Symptoms of Economic Weakness—Merchants, Money and Moscow—The Cities at a New Stage of Importance—Land, Men and Work—Cossacks

Geography of Eastern Europe—Moscow and the Kremlin—The Great Sovereign—Pomp and Circumstance—Domestic Celebrations and Palace Feasts—Courtiers and Palace Officials—The Courtiers' Interests—System of Precedence—Sessions in Council and Special Assemblies—New Service Requirements and Social Change—Land, Men, and War—New Military Units—Cossacks and Musketeers—Summary of Early Military Reforms—Maintenance of the Military Forces—Central and Palace Administration—Service Posts Outside Moscow—The Russian City—Regional and Local Administration—Townspeople, Taxes, and Troubles—Taxes and Extraordinary Imposts—Duties of Townspeople—Support of Local Officials—Conflicts Between Communities and Local Officials—Measures Against Abuses—Ordin-Nashchokin's Reform Efforts—The New Commercial Statute—Tensions Between Urban Taxpayers and Service People—Conditions in Town and Country—Relations Between Peasants and Townspeople—Local Peasant Elections—Sources of Social Upheaval

WEIGHTS AND MEASURES

Linear Measure

Verst: 500 sazhen, 1166 yards and 2 feet, .663 miles, 1.0668 km
Sazhen: 3 arshins, 7 feet, 2.133 m
Arshin: 16 vershoks, 28 in. (diuims), 72.12 cm
Chetvert: ¼ arshin
Fut: 12 diuims, 1 foot, 30.48 cm
Vershok: 1.75 in., 4.445 cm, 1/16 arshin
Diuim: 1 inch, 2.54 cm
Desiatina: 2400 square sazhens, 2.7 acres, 1.0925 hectare
Chetvert (quarter): ½ desiatina, 1.35 acre (sometimes 1.5 desiatinas or ca. 4.1 acres)

Liquid Measure

Vedro (pail): 3.25 gallons, 12.3 liters
Bochka (barrel): 40 vedros, 121 gallons, 492 liters
Chetvert (quarter): ¼ bochka, 32.5 gallons

Weights

Berkovets: 361 lbs., 10 puds
Pud: 40 funts, 36.113 lbs. (US), 40 lbs. (Russian), 16.38 kg
Funt: 96 zolotniks, .903 lb.
Korob (basket): 7 puds, 252 lbs.
Rad: 14 puds, 505.58 lbs.
Chetvert (quarter: basic grain dry measure): ¼ rad, 3.5 puds, 126.39 lbs.
Chetverik (grain measure dating from 16th century): 1/8 chetvert, 15.8 lbs.
Zolotnik: 1/96 lb., 4.26 grams

Money (15th and 16th centuries)

Muscovite Denga: 200 equals 1 ruble
Novgorod Denga: 100 equals 1 ruble
Altyn: 6 Muscovite dengas
Grivna: 20 Muscovite dengas, 10 grivnas equals 1 ruble
Poltina: ½ ruble
Poltora: 1½ rubles
Peniaz: 10 equals one grosh (Lithuania)
Kopa grosh: 60 groshas, one Muscovite poltina
Chetvertak: silver coin equal to 25 kopecks or ¼ ruble (18-19th centuries)
Kopeck: two Muscovite dengas

Note: Weights and measures often changed values over time and sometimes held more than one value at the same time. For details consult Sergei G. Pushkarev, *Dictionary of Russian Historical Terms from the Eleventh Century to 1917* (Yale, 1970).

Muscovite State

IN THE MID–17th CENTURY

Annexations in the reign of Tsar Alexis

0   200   400 miles

PREFACE

The present work is a translation of Chapter 1, Volume 13 (originally published in 1863) of Sergei M. Soloviev's *Istoriia Rossii s drevneishikh vremen* [History of Russia from Earliest Times] (29 vols., St. Petersburg, 1851-1879). The text used for this translation is from the latest edition, in 15 books (Moscow, 1959-1966), in which the original volumes 13 and 14 have been combined and in which the aforementioned chapter appears as Chapter 1 of Book 7 (published in 1962).

The Cyrillic alphabet has been transposed into Latin characters in keeping with the rules of the Library of Congress system of transliteration, subject to the following modifications: (1) all ligatures and diacritical marks have been omitted; (2) the forms "ia" and "iu" at the beginning of words (though not internally or at the end) have been rendered as "ya" and "yu" (for example, "Yaroslav" and "Yury" instead of "Iaroslav" and "Iury"); (3) the forms "-ii" and "-yi" at the end of words have been replaced by "-y" ("Dmitry Poliansky" and "inozemny" instead of "Dmitrii Polianskii" and "inozemnyi"), and the form "-oi" has been replaced by "-oy" ("Donskoy" instead of "Donskoi"); (4) the use of an apostrophe (') to signify a soft sign has been omitted, though the soft sign is sometimes indicated by an "i" (as in "Soloviev"); and (5) the final "-iia" in feminine personal names has been shortened to "-ia" ("Maria" and "Evdokia" instead of "Mariia" and "Evdokiia").

Russian personal names are preserved in their Russian form (Ivan, Timofei, Andrei, Afanasy, etc.). The only exceptions to this are the names Alexander, Alexis, Michael, Nicholas, and Peter (which English usage has made familiar with regard to historical Russian figures) and the names of important ecclesiastics, which largely have been recast into their corresponding Latin or Greek equivalents. In instances where personal names refer to non-Russians, the native forms are used. However, in view of editorial restrictions on the use of diacritics, Russianized versions of certain foreign names have been adopted (e.g., Yury Krizhanich instead of Juraj Križanić, etc.). Common Christian names follow generally recognized English forms wherever possible. The names of geographical locations also conform to commonly accepted English usage (Moscow, Bethlehem, Wallachia, Rome, etc.).

No attempt has been made to transliterate Russian words which have recognized equivalents in English and particularly words for which anglicized versions are contained in *Webster's Third New International Dictionary*. They include: archimandrite, bogatyr, boyar (and though not in *Webster's,* the feminine counterpart, "boyarina"), hegumen, muzhik, protopope, the steppe, verst, voivode, etc. An exception applies with regard to the names for liquid measures. Thus, the word "vedro" (which *Webster's* defines as "a Russian unit of liquid capacity equal to 3.25 U.S. gallons") is translated as "bucket." English equivalents are provided for dry measures.

Units of money are indicated in two ways: (1) in their anglicized version, where such units are commonly encountered in English (as with "ruble"); or (2) in the nominative singular of the Russian form (as with "efimok"), in which case the plural number is obtained by adding the conventional English suffix "-s" ("efimoks") rather than adhering to the Russian plural form (*efimki*). A monetary conversion table is provided in Appendix I.

This translation is not intended to be a verbatim rendering of the original. Soloviev's style would often make for stilted and unnecessarily difficult English prose. Lengthy paragraphs have been broken up and convoluted periodic sentences simplified. Ejaculatory words or phrases have been cast into comparable English expressions, without, it is hoped, either distorting them or blunting their emotive thrust. The main purpose has been to strive always for clarity and accuracy. Where a statement in the original may be obscure (as with a person or event treated more fully by Soloviev elsewhere in the *History*), an explanatory word or phrase enclosed by brackets is incorporated into the text or a footnote provided by way of longer clarification. All passages enclosed by parentheses are Soloviev's. The division of the work into three distinctly labeled parts is not to be found in the original. Here, it has been carried out in strict adherence to Soloviev's arrangement of the material, which in no way has been altered.

Most of the subtitles in the translation are derived from topic headings at the beginning of the chapter in the Russian edition. (Such topical clusters customarily precede each chapter of the *History*.) In this translation the topic headings have been moved into the body of the text and incorporated as chapter subtitles with a view to facilitating the transition from one subject to another. To even the frequency of breaks in the text, new subtitles have been devised and added, particularly in Chapter I, where only a small number of topic headings exist in the original.

Soloviev's own footnotes to this part of his work (179 in all) consist mostly of references to Russian sources. As such, they are of interest mainly to specialists. They have been largely omitted in this translation and replaced by explanatory footnotes, whose purpose is to furnish background information to readers with a general interest in Russian history. In the few cases where Soloviev's footnotes have been retained, they are identified as such.

It is a pleasure to express my appreciation to David Fuller in the Geography Department at California State University, Northridge, for his work in producing the map that accompanies this translation and to Robert Nichols of Saint Olaf College for his sound suggestions concerning both content and style. To Helen, Alex, and Tanya, my affectionate gratitude.

Alexander V. Muller

California State University, Northridge

INTRODUCTION

Sergei M. Soloviev was born in Moscow on 5 May 1820 into the family of a priest belonging to the "white," or married, clergy of the Russian Orthodox Church. While still in his formative years, young Soloviev cultivated the interest that would lead to his lifelong vocation. He read several times through what was then the standard work on Russian history, Nicholas Karamzin's *History of the Russian State*. Published in twelve volumes between 1816 and 1829, with the last volume appearing posthumously, it carried events to the year 1611. The work was not the product of original scholarship. It relied principally on the researches of others. Karamzin took and worked over existing historical writings, which in keeping with the manner of those days consisted largely of long, undigested passages transcribed verbatim from primary sources. He meticulously polished the language, toned down archaisms, smoothed out complicated syntax, and gave an interpretive bent to the whole. The result was a history that quickly acquired an unprecedented popularity with the reading public. Karamzin's extensive notes, many taken from documents that were subsequently lost, gained the reputation of being a treasure trove for historians. Some critics alleged that the notes alone imparted the only value possessed by the work. Soloviev himself, after becoming established as a historian, decried Karamzin's preoccupation with an attractive literary format as dilettantish adherence to "artistic" history. Still, Karamzin's comprehensive work, though it be a popularization, embodies the legacy bequeathed to Russian historical writing by the eighteenth century. It stands, moreover, as the immediate predecessor of Soloviev's own multivolume history.

Karamzin's main thesis held that autocracy, the sovereign rule of an absolute monarch, played a dominant and positive role in the unification and consolidation of the Russian state. This assertion assured the work of an enthusiastic reception by the government. Thus it enjoyed both official approval and wide appeal with the reading public. In stressing the historical formation of the state, Karamzin followed in the footsteps of earlier historians, for whom national life centered on the actions of prominent figures whose main sphere of action lay in the political field, including foreign relations. History meant primarily political and dynastic history, often incorporating the ecclesiastical component as an adjunct. With the progressive refinement of historical studies, and in response to new arguments arising in the 1840s between Slavophiles and Westernizers over the question of national identity and Russia's future, historians were spurred on to expand their field of inquiry. Attention was devoted to such subjects as the organic growth of social forms and the historical effects of geographical factors. The development of legal codes and institutions was treated with revived interest. The move toward new vistas did not mean that the older historical orientation was to be discarded or forgotten altogether. It continued to be felt in the works of subsequent historians, and Karamzin's influence in particular thus penetrated into the writings of Soloviev.

In 1838 Soloviev entered the University of Moscow. Among the influential writers he studied there were the Italian philosopher Giovanni Battista Vico, who in *The New Science* described the "ideal eternal history" through which each nation passes in a series of distinct and orderly stages. He also read the English historian Edward Gibbon, who in *The Decline and Fall of the Roman Empire* castigated with anticlerical zeal the role played by Christianity in bringing about the downfall of Rome, and the Swiss historian and economist Jean Sismondi, author of a history of Italy (in 16 volumes) and of France (in 31 volumes), who was an early champion of state control of capitalistic competition in bringing about the permanent establishment of small-scale commodity production.

At the University of Moscow Soloviev also was influenced by his contact with Hegelian philosophy, which helped to structure his overarching view of history as a dynamic process revealing itself in the progress of mankind. In terms of Soloviev's own vision of history, two points should be made with regard to Hegel's concept of progress. First, the movement of history was seen by Hegel as being an entirely rational process. It follows the logical progression of thought through the stages of the dialectic: thesis, antithesis, and synthesis. In this evolution of mind or spirit, a paramount role is ascribed to the state, in and through which the spirit is manifested. The will of the state becomes the highest expression of reason. The process moves forward through the actions of select individuals, the great men of history, who are not so much begetters as midwives of the momentous events associated with their names. It is their function to stand at the forefront for the vast masses of humanity to follow. Second, progress reveals itself in the history of different nations which are deemed to be "historical," as opposed to those which remain unadmitted into the process and are therefore relegated to the category of "unhistorical" nations. This unilineal movement of history along the Hegelian "royal road" in the unfolding of world civilization restricts the final stage in the revelation of progress to the Germanic-Latin culture.

Adhering to Hegel's idea of history as a processual and patterned movement which is capable of being known, some Russian historians were prompted to attach major value to the state and to legal institutions. For obvious reasons they did not subscribe to Hegel's exaltation of Prussia as the particular state which brought to a climax the passage of history. It was the broader parameters of Hegel's system that proved to be more fruitful. Working within them, historians like Soloviev were induced to develop an interest in the comparative method and to undertake the study of the "westernization" of Russia.

In formulating his historical conceptions while at the University of Moscow, Soloviev was deeply impressed by the views of Timofei Granovsky, professor of general history. Although himself the product of a Hegelian academic background through training received at the University of Berlin, Granovsky was able nonetheless to generate a measure of autonomy in defining his own position. He acknowledged the presence of weaknesses in Hegel's historical design and criticized Hegel for the creation of "an arbitrary conception of general history." Even so, Granovsky gave indication of his continued immersion in the historical essentials of Hegelianism. He adhered faithfully to a nomothetic conception of history, that is, he regarded history as a process strictly governed by invariable laws. In his lectures he pointed out how Western Europe had passed through different clearly defined and orderly stages in keeping with such laws, and he insisted that this line of regular development was far superior to the manner in which the Russian past had unfolded. For Granovsky, then, the superiority of the West lay not merely in a few specific areas, but in the whole course of historical evolution. It is not without significance that in his teaching and writing Granovsky focused on European rather than Russian history. Soloviev, drawn by the attraction of an expanded view of history in a "universal" (European) context, moved away in the course of time from his earlier Slavophile attitude toward the Westernizing position expounded by Granovsky, with whom he continued to maintain ties long after his student days.

While yet at the University of Moscow, Soloviev was exposed also to the writings of J.P.G. Ewers, professor of Russian history at the University of Dorpat (the German name for the east Estonian city of Tartu, which became Russian in 1704). Ewers' main interest lay with the

history of legal institutions. In studying them he adopted a broadly evo-
lutionary point of view. He also articulated the so-called "gens theory."
The gens (*rod* in Russian) was viewed as a type of patrilineal clan, or expanded family, whose origin could be calculated from a single male an-
cestor. The theory held that a political state grows directly out of the
primitive social organization of the gens, which is formed by a people
during the early stages of their history. Ewers' statement of his views
appeared in 1826 in a book entitled *The Earliest Russian Law in Its
Historical Development*. The theory was picked up by Soloviev and
came to occupy a pivotal position in his explanation for the emergence
of the Russian state.

Soloviev completed his undergraduate studies at the University of
Moscow in 1842. He then found employment as tutor for the children
of Count A.P. Stroganov. His new situation opened to him a propitious
opportunity for traveling abroad and taking advantage of what turned
out to be a most rewarding experience in expanding the horizons of his
historical outlook.

In Berlin, Soloviev attended the lectures of Karl Ritter, a founder of
modern scientific geography, who demonstrated the existence of a link
between man and his natural environment and stressed the role of geographical factors in the course of historical events. Another scholar
whom Soloviev heard was Friedrich von Raumer, whose writings covered
a multitude of subjects, including economics, law, literature, and history. Also in Berlin, Soloviev had the opportunity of listening to the
brightest star in the galaxy of the German historical school, Leopold
von Ranke, who as a teacher imbued generations of historians with the
ideal of abiding by the principle of objectivity as a standard of supreme
importance and who insisted upon the value of historical criticism. In
Heidelberg, Soloviev sat in on the lectures of Friedrich Schlosser, who
was then just in the process of seeing published the first of an eventual
nineteen volumes on world history, completed in 1857.

After arriving in Paris, Soloviev attended lectures given by Jules
Michelet, professor of history at the Collège de France. In the preceding
decade Michelet had begun publication of his history of France, in
which he gave vivid and picturesque treatment to the historical role of
the masses. To the writing of this work Michelet devoted himself, while
also undertaking a host of other books, until its completion in nineteen
volumes in 1867. Soloviev also became attracted to the historical works
and political stance of François Guizot, who at the time of Soloviev's
visit was the leading cabinet minister in the French government. Before
his rise to that position Guizot had produced historical studies on the

origins of representative government, on the Puritan revolution in England, and on civilization in France and in Europe. In his notes Soloviev described himself as being a "worshipper" of Guizot's writings. He also expressed his open admiration for the principles espoused by this spokesman of middle-class values in the regime of Louis-Philippe, declaring that he was "an adherent of the Orleanist dynasty and the ministry of Guizot." While in Paris Soloviev was prompted to start writing on a theme that was to occupy a prominent part in his panoramic assessment of historical evolution: the formation of the state from its earliest stage and its origins in the emergence of an incipient political force, the retinue (*druzhina*), out of the primitive tribal organization of peoples in Europe and Asia. Soloviev would return to this idea frequently and include elements of his developed view of it in the work that is here translated.

Finally, during his journey abroad, Soloviev had the chance to hear the official historiographer of Bohemia, František Palacký, who in 1836 issued the first of five volumes on the history of the Bohemian people, a study based on a painstaking pursuit of source materials in the archives of his native country and in the leading libraries of Europe. These and other contacts, as well as the numerous examples of personally-authored, multivolumed, comprehensive histories either in print or in various stages of completion, were to have a lasting effect in shaping Soloviev's historical perspectives, adding to his depth of social and geographical understanding, and influencing the form of his major written work.

On the basis of his maturing historical sophistication, Soloviev submitted in 1845 his master's thesis, "On the Relations of Novgorod with the Grand Princes." He had earlier that year, upon successfully passing his master's examinations, begun to deliver lectures in Russian history at the University of Moscow. Thus he established himself, at the age of twenty-five, as successor to Michael Pogodin, whose last major work, *Early Russian History Before the Mongol Yoke,* appeared in three volumes in 1871 as the culmination of the author's efforts to endow the course of Russian history with a providential design and sense of mission. This aspect of Pogodin's work was less successful than his actual delving into source materials, which brought forth items of considerable importance and furnished a model for Soloviev and others to follow in their own researches. Soloviev later berated Pogodin for his publicistic activity and "historical dilettantism." Yet, Pogodin's methodological example stood before him as a sound approach to the presentation of historical research. Combined with his own prolific writing ability, this soon yielded rich results. In 1847 Soloviev published a monograph, "The

History of the Relations Among the Princes of the House of Riurik," which he then defended as his doctoral dissertation. That same year, together with his doctorate, he was granted a professorial appointment at the University of Moscow.

In 1851 appeared the first volume of Soloviev's monumental work, *The History of Russia from Earliest Times*. He worked steadily on this project, at the rate of one volume every year, while also authoring a number of articles and essays. By a fortunate circumstance the government opened some invaluable archives to which he was the first historian granted access. With enormous patience and perseverance, Soloviev turned this stroke of luck to full advantage. The *History* is replete with material that he gleaned from his archival investigations. From 1864 to 1870 Soloviev served as dean of the historical and philological department at the University of Moscow, and in 1871 he was made rector of the university. During the last years of his life he presided as chairman of the prestigious Imperial Society of History and Russian Antiquities, and held the directorship of the historical museum, the Armory Chamber, in the Kremlin. In 1877 he found it necessary to go into retirement because of a dispute with the authorities over preservation of university autonomy. By the time of his death on 4 October 1879 he had not yet completed the *History,* having reached the events of the year 1774 in volume 29, which was published posthumously in the year of his death.

Soloviev sought in his *History* to portray Russia's past in terms of an organic process whose principles can be traced back to earliest times. This insistence upon characterizing the historical origins in their most elementary aspects meant for Soloviev the necessity of considering geographical factors and the manner in which initial settlement began on the east European plain. The incorporation of these topics in a work on Russian history was in itself a historiographical milestone. Still, the introduction of the fundamentals of geography and settlement fell short, in and of themselves, of providing the critical ingredient that could furnish the dynamic for a consistent theory of historical evolution.

In searching for the missing element, Soloviev turned to the gens theory. With this as a point of departure, he was able to envision the basic law of Russian history as being manifested in a dialectic opposition between the principle of the gens and that of the state. The operation of the law took the form of an inevitable and progressive movement in which the gens was superseded in the course of a long transitional period by a powerful unitary state and a distinct form of national existence. The transitional period itself was marked by the transfer of historical development from the south of Russia to the north and the emergence there of new princely cities as opposed to the old cities dominated by popular urban assemblies. The whole complex process was brought to its conclusion in the reign of Peter the Great.

Soloviev's first steps toward his personal exposition of this general theme can be traced back to his Paris days. The elaboration of it was advanced in his master's thesis and doctoral dissertation, as well as other writings. And he incorporated a developed statement of it in the first volume of his *History*. Its main features are also clearly discernible in that chapter of the *History* (Chapter 1 of the original Volume 13) which is here rendered into English. Entitled "Russia Before the Epoch of Reform," the chapter occupies a unique position relative to the overall arrangement of the work. For it constitutes in effect a recapitulation by Soloviev of the major events and dominant trends which he regarded as significant for the earlier periods and which he suffused in the earlier volumes with an enormous wealth of detail. If so great an abundance of narration and description, coupled with copious citations drawn directly from primary sources, can distract from the main lines of interpretation, then the advantage of a summary statement is obvious. It permits an author to express his general propositions with clarity while at the same time fitting together in one place just those specifics that he himself judges to be most pertinent to his exposition. Soloviev evidently appreciated this, for in the present work he constructed almost an outline of his central ideas.

Even the placement Soloviev gave this chapter within the *History* gives an insight into his thinking about the periods into which Russian history ought to be divided, their relative importance, and their connections. Positioned at approximately midpoint in the *History*, its coverage ends just short of the beginning of Peter the Great's reign. It moves from the earliest period of Russian history to the end of the reign of Tsar Alexis in 1676. By then the presence, activity, and influence of foreigners other than clergymen or monks unmistakably foreshadowed, in the favorable response accorded them by a growing number of important Russians, the type of secularization and modernization inspired by the West that would become prevalent under Peter. In Soloviev's theoretical scheme the period of the Petrine reforms was conclusively decisive because, as mentioned earlier, it constituted the final stage in a long line of historical development. Hence, in the portion of the *History* which is here translated, Soloviev was able to sketch that entire line of development from its inception.

Using as his starting point, or thesis, the primal conditions of Russian life, which he envisioned as centered on the predominance of clan relationships, whose collectivity engulfed the individuality of its members, he demonstrates how the development passed through the stage of antithesis, in which the individuality of the princes challenged and eventually destroyed the collectivity of the gens, and he brings the work to a close at the threshhold of the final synthesis, in which the personality of the prince firmly stabilized a new political collectivity, brought to realization in the absolutism of the eighteenth century. Thus, the historical process is seen as having advanced through all the stages of a Hegelian-type dialectic, at the end of which the triad is complete.

Soloviev's use of abstract concepts in combination with historical details is a masterful interplay between the general and particular. Theoretical constructs are judiciously and coherently supported by factual data. Some idea of the vast documantation which fills the pages of the *History* can be gained from the quantity and diversity of material in the present work. But the end result is far more than just the sum of such material. Soloviev's *History* represents the first broadly inclusive effort at employing rigorously precise and disciplined scholarship to produce a large-scale view of Russian history as an organic process governed by universally applicable historical principles. This feature of the *History* can clearly be seen in that part of it which is translated here.

To be sure, criticism can be, and has been, leveled at Soloviev in a number of areas. His adoption of the theory of the gens (which in its original form has been largely discounted), the treatment of feudalism, the description of relations between social classes, the transfer of attention from south to north, the sharp and artificial distinction between old and new cities, the creation of historical stereotypes (bogatyrs, women, etc.) based on the use of literary sources—on all these counts, and others, he can be faulted. Moreover, the application of a dialectic scheme as an interpretive device seems to have deprived Soloviev of a controlling idea for the second half of the *History,* treating the period after which synthesis presumably had been achieved in the creation of the state. Yet, none of this diminishes the fact that Soloviev's guiding principles were put to use most effectively in the first half, as reflected in the summary chapter translated here. If Soloviev's frame of reference appears dated, it must be recognized that his own impressive historical reconstruction often provoked the very questions and reinterpretations which followed him. Readers will find much to reward them in the *History.* A rich store of documentation, it continues to enjoy a meritorious reputation as a work of enduring historiographical interest and as an outstanding portrayal of the Russian past.

History of Russia

Volume 24

The Character of Old Russia

I

EARLY RUSSIAN HISTORY

HISTORICAL GEOGRAPHY

Upon first glance at a map of Europe one is struck by the difference between its two unequal parts, western and eastern. In the west, a region of many separate nations and states, the land is varied. It consists of islands, peninsulas, and mountains. In the east there exists a continuous plain of enormous dimensions under the control of a single huge state. Based on these differences, one can easily conclude, even if only on the most surface of impressions, that the two parts of Europe must have had a very dissimilar history.

It is well known that certain factors are beneficial to the expeditious development of social life. These include such features as proximity to the sea, a long coastline, clearly delimited boundaries encompassing a state of moderate size, ease of internal communications, a variety of geographical formations, the absence of anything in oppressively large size, and a healthful atmosphere without African heat or Asian cold. The possession of these advantages, which is the distinctive hallmark of Europe, has been cited as the reason for the brilliant advancement of the European nations and their dominance over other peoples throughout the world. It should not be overlooked, however, that the enjoyment of these advantages pertains only to Western Europe, since Eastern Europe does not have them. Towards the people of Western Europe, Nature acted like a mother; towards the people who were fated to dwell in Eastern Europe, she was a stepmother.

If the aforementioned advantages do indeed facilitate the early and solid achievements of civilization, then it becomes clear why the southern peninsulas of Europe were the first to appear on the historical scene and why in Europe the ancient civilized world (the Roman Empire) came to include the southern peninsulas, Gaul, and Britain, or in other words, the southern and western peripheries. It was after this that central and northwestern Europe, Germany and Scandinavia, became joined to the Greco-Roman civilization of the Roman world. This attachment was followed by the inclusion of the western Slavic tribes. Then, only very late, was claim finally laid to European civilization by the state that embraced within its confines the territory of Eastern Europe. There can thus be seen in the history of the diffusion of European civilization a gradual movement that proceeded, in accordance with natural dictates, from west to east. For it was in the west that were concentrated the most propitious conditions capable of producing the early achievements of civilization. These conditions, prominent in Western Europe, gradually diminish in the direction of the east.

In this regard it is interesting to note the limits in Europe to which penetrated the flood of savage Asiatic hordes, people with primitive social structures. Here is evident the same gradualness. The advance of the Huns was halted on the Catalaunian Plains of Gaul; the Avars were barred any further access after reaching Germany; the Magyars settled farther to the east, in Pannonia; the Tatars were unable to stay even there, but poured into the eastern plain, into which earlier had streamed other people like them. All these nomadic tribes, whom our ancestors referred to collectively as pagans [*pogan*] disappeared eventually eastward, relinquishing the eastern half of Europe. Many centuries, however, passed between the defeat of Attila at Châlons and the conquest of the Crimea under Catherine the Great, from which event can be dated the final extrication of European soil from the suzerainty of Asians.[1] It was by that number of centuries that history allowed Western Europe to proceed in advance of Eastern Europe.

It should be noted that the southwestern extremities of Europe were subject during the Middle Ages to invasion by inhabitants of the Asian and African deserts—the Arabs, who long held sway on the Iberian Peninsula. In this connection, the fate of the southwestern extremity of Europe can be seen quite readily to bear a certain resemblance to the fate of its eastern borderlands, in that the fate of Spain corresponded to the fate of Russia, and Ferdinand the Catholic,[2] who put an end to the rule of the Arabs in Spain, was a contemporary of Ivan III,[3] under whom took place final Russian liberation from the Tatar yoke. Yet what a difference there was in what the Spanish Visigoths and other Europeans acquired from the civilized Arab and what the Russians could adopt from the Tatar and his cohorts—the Bashkir, Chuvash, Cheremis, etc.![4]

DIVERGENT DESTINIES

It was stern history that forced one of the early European nations to undertake a movement from west to east and to populate those regions where Nature is a stepmother to mankind. In the beginning of the new

Christian-European era, two nations assumed a predominant position, and they have kept it for themselves ever after. These were the Germans and the Slavs, nations related to each other through their common Indo-European background. These two nations divided Europe between them. In this original division the Germans moved from northeast to southwest, into the regions of the Roman Empire, where a solid foundation of European civilization already had been established. The Slavs, on the other hand, proceeded in the reverse direction, from southwest to northeast, into virgin expanses fashioned by nature. This opposite movement lies at the heart of the difference in all the subsequent history of both nations.

There exists no justification for drawing conclusions about any early distinction in the character of these two nations, about the superiority in this regard of one of them over the other, and about the influence this may have had upon history. The only thing that can be said is that one of these nations functioned from the very outset under the most favorable circumstances and the other, under the most unfavorable. Of course it is very tempting for a Slav (which is to say, mostly for a Russian) to be of the opinion that a nation which, under the most unfavorable conditions, was able to stand its ground while surrounded by barbarism, which could safeguard its Christian-European form, which successfully founded a powerful state, and which eventually prevailed in subjecting Asia to Europe—that such a nation displayed a remarkable strength of spirit. Quite naturally the question arises: Could the German nation, similarly placed in unfavorable circumstances, have done the same? But such distasteful praise of one's own nationality, in which German writers allow themselves to indulge, cannot induce Russians to follow their example.

THE EASTERN SLAVS

In the great eastern plain of Europe Slavic settlements were to be found along the Dnieper river and its tributaries; they were likewise located along the Dniester, the Western Dvina, the Oka, and along the water system associated with Lake Ilmen. The Slavs lived in separate tribal divisions that traced descent in the male line. Each such division, a patrilineal clan or gens,[5] was subordinate to its own chieftain. Other Slavs lived in cities. But this conspicuous word "city" should not give rise to confusion by raising the question of an apparent contradiction between the existence of cities and a way of life developed around a particular form of tribal division. The name "city" [gorod] was applied to all kinds of strongholds and enclosures. A brief historical comparison can help clarify the matter. When Russian military units in the seventeenth century were extending the tsar's authority through northern Asia, they found natives living in separate tribal divisions, each under the authority of its chieftain. But the habitations of the families constituting a clan usually consisted of strongholds surrounded by fortified walls, which the Russians sometimes had to capture with bloodshed. Inside the fortifications were to be found as many as fourteen circular domed tents, or yurts, each of which was large enough to accommodate up to ten families.

To the north and northeast of the Slavs lived Finnish tribes, who adhered to a mode of life like that of their neighbors. In the south and southeast swarmed rapacious nomads who, through the exertion of constant pressure, displaced one another from successive locations. Sometimes the Slavs suffered terribly from them. Unable to protect cities that had been cut off and rendered vulnerable because of their isolation, the Slavs would find their defenses breached and the plunderer harnessing the Slavic women to his wagon. But such storms passed, and then everything again would become as quiet and monotonous as before. The plunderers of the steppe would disappear, leaving behind only the saying, "They vanished like the Avars."[6] The vigor of the people was not aroused by the continuous presence of an enemy, as was the case with the Germans, whose mettle was constantly being tested by the hostile movements of the Romans. In any event, how was it possible for any vitality to be summoned when the various scattered Slavic tribes were lost over an enormous expanse of territory? It would be entirely unrealistic to imagine that those tribes were composed of numerous people who densely filled that expanse. The fact that the population was sparse can be readily confirmed. Was this area densely populated during the many centuries following the period of time being described? Even today the eastern plain remains one of the thinly populated parts of Europe. What must it have been like over a thousand years ago?

FIRST STIRRINGS OF RUSSIAN HISTORY

The moment came when historical life was to begin for Eastern Europe also. Along the water route that stretched with only brief interruption or portage from the Baltic to the Black Sea, boats appeared, filled with armed men. In the boats was the prince of Novgorod with his retinue. "Pay to us the tribute!" he repeated in every settlement and every fortified stronghold of the Slavs. Such demands were not unfamiliar, and so the Slavs brought furs, if only to rid themselves more quickly of these guests. But this time the newcomers did not disappear like the Avars; they did not leave for the steppe along the rivers Don and Volga, as had the Khazars.[7] Instead, on the high west bank of the Dnieper, a city began to rise. This was the capital city of princes, the mother of cities, Kiev. The prince situated himself there with his retinue, and for the neighboring tribes there was no longer any peace. Along all the rivers and streams the prince traveled with his retinue, collecting tribute. Wherever the prince himself did not come, the prince's man would appear with his own retinue after the tribute.

The Slavs watched what was happening about them. They saw towns being constructed and newcomers settling in them. The newcomers also installed themselves in those of the old cities which were larger and offered greater advantages. They announced to the surrounding countryside that whoever desired to settle near the cities would enjoy protection and privilege, that whoever knew an essential trade would stand to make a profit. And since they were unable to do everything for themselves, they were willing to pay well for those who bore arms. Cities started to gain in population, commerce originated in them, people gathered from everywhere, and the outlying villages grew empty. The former princely chieftains were no longer able to account for all their people. All those who left were among the able ones, suited for every kind of work.

More people continued to desert the villages as new announcements were made, that the prince was undertaking an expedition and all who were able should assemble in his service. The young men arose, cut down trees for boats, and departed. For a long while, no word of them was heard. And then, at long last, when they returned, they were different people! They had traveled as far as Constantinople itself, and what marvels they had beheld there! What wonderful things they had brought back with them! They had beaten the Greeks in spite of all their cleverness, and had compelled them to pay tribute. Whoever had distinguished himself in battle was admitted into the retinue of the prince or of a boyar.[8] And life in the retinue was marvelous—feasting, hunting, and fishing from morning till night. The prince had much of everything and did not begrudge his retinue any of it. And what prestige!

Thus, the history of Russia, like the history of other states, began with a heroic period. In other words, as the consequence of a certain movement, which in the sprawling plain of Eastern Europe saw the appearance of Varangian-Russian princes and their retinues,[9] the obscure, undifferentiated mass of the population was aroused. There split away from the mass those who were, according to the standards of the day, the best people. By this was meant the bravest men, those who were endowed with the greatest physical strength and who felt the necessity of exercising it. An old Russian song describes very well such a person, a bogatyr[10] or hero, whose qualities were considered to be most admirable: "Laden with power, as though weighted with vigor, strength through his veins flows free with each heartbeat." These were the foremost men, men of pre-eminence, while the rest remained in their eyes half-men, little men, muzhiks.[11]

It is with the exploits of the foremost men, or bogatyrs, that history begins. Through those deeds their people acquired recognition among foreigners, while the people themselves made such deeds the subject for their songs, which became the first historical sources. The imagination of the people was kindled by the heroes' feats, their victories over enemies abroad and the changes that they brought about through their actions at home. All of this, it would appear, became exaggerated, being perceived in overblown proportions. The people, culturally still at an early stage of development, ascribed everything that departed from the ordinary routine of daily life to the influence of higher powers. Because the heroes naturally appeared as beings who stood above ordinary mortals, divine origination became ascribed to them.

In Russia, where mythological development was not extensive and where the influence of Christianity spread rapidly, the warrior did not acquire the characteristics of a divinity. He was nonetheless viewed as a sorcerer. Prince Oleg,[12] who fired the popular imagination with his successful campaign against Constantinople and with the wealth be brought back from there, appeared inevitably as a sorcerer, to whose name was popularly attached the epithet "Wise." Even the tale of the bogatyr-sorcerer acquired a miraculous aspect. The very sea is stilled when the song of the hero is intoned.

> Now shall be told the tale of ancient times,
> Of the times of Dobrynia:
> Told shall it be for the calming of the blue sea,
> Told shall it be for the hearing of all you good people.[13]

This ancient formulaic introduction demonstrates that the epic songs of the bogatyrs were sung first on those boats from which the Black Sea was called Russian.

DISINTEGRATION OF EARLY TRIBAL ORGANIZATION

The bogatyrs thus exercised their strength, with which they were abundantly endowed. But what happened as a consequence of this in the great eastern plain? It has been shown that, in the midst of the Slavic tribes, there appeared a city with new characteristics, a city that became the seat for a new kind of authority, that of a dominant princely ruler. Not long afterwards other princes, the sons or brothers of the foremost prince in Kiev, also arrived in various leading cities. With them came their retinues, which would not permit the tribes to retain their independence or refrain from paying the princely tribute. Moreover, the best people were leaving their tribes, some to enter service in the retinues, others to join the commercial population of the cities and become merchants. The people of the eastern plain thus ceased to be divided into tribes.

There was created a new social structure consisting of three classes. Above all the rest stood the warriors, who as members of the retinue constituted the leading people. Below them were ranked the nonmilitary population, consisting of persons known variously as the common people, free agriculturists, and peasants. But this latter group was further divided into two categories, the urban business class and the villagers. Having lost their finest elements, the villagers became weakened and accordingly were relegated to last place. The Chronicle[14] naturally speaks only about those who, being active, drew attention to themselves and compelled others also to be active in bringing about changes. It is for this reason that the Chronicle makes reference principally to the princes and their retinues, since it is primarily they who were engaged in activity. Also mentioned occasionally in the Chronicle are the urban people whenever they were able to assert themselves after they had acquired sufficient wealth and strength, and after they found themselves in a position to take advantage of princely feuds, divisions, and weaknesses. At that historical juncture the people of the cities likewise began to be active and bring about changes through their activity. But about the villagers the Chronicle remains silent, for the countryside was quiet, with no perceptible movement.

The tribes disappeared during the heroic period of the bogatyrs. In their place appeared principalities, whose names were derived not from the tribes, but from the chief cities, the administrative centers that had attracted the neighboring population. Grand Prince Yaroslav[15] distributed to his sons principalities and cities, but not tribes.

This disappearance of tribal names serves as the clearest evidence of the weakness of Russian tribal origins. In German history there are frequently encountered Saxons, Thuringians, Franconians, Swabians, Bavarians, etc. Reflected in the prevalence of such names is the existence of tribal particularism, independence, and strength, from which arose the impossibility of establishing German unity. It is this situation which German patriots now bemoan. The strength of tribal affiliation as a tendency toward particularism and independence is not manifested merely in differences of dialect. Nor does the influence of the tribal principle in history appear only in the form of different mores and customs, derived from the circumstance that one group of people lived, for example, in a swampy region while another inhabited a dry area, or that some persons lived in forests and others in the steppe.

The tribal principle becomes influential in history only when a tribe is numerous, when it has been unified under a single authority, and when it has received by way of historical activity an awareness of its own independence and distinctiveness as regards other tribes through the acquisition of particular interests. With respect to these conditions, it is legitimate to ask whether anything approximating them can be discerned as existing among the Slavic tribes before or after the arrival of Riurik.[16] It is true that, in cases where tribes never before had paid an annual princely tribute, they were known to refuse to pay it. It is also true that one of the tribes, the Derevlians, after losing patience with the rapacity of the prince of Kiev, rebelled against him.[17] But can these events be considered comparable to the struggle of the Saxons against the leader of the Franks, Charlemagne?

Scattered in various places throughout the eastern plain, the Slavs lost their tribal names, meaning that they lost their awareness of tribal distinctions and tribal alliances. From this, the conclusion can be drawn that whatever distinguishing characteristics existed among them must have been unremarkable and that the tribes either did not have any alliances or that such alliances as they did have were merely occasional. The way of life of those tribes, divided into separate clans, was subjected to radical transformation when, as activity began, they were drawn into the historical process. The beginnings of that process coincided with the arrival of the prince, with his retinue, and of the townspeople, who had split away from the population of the villages.

Nor were the changes limited only to this. As another consequence of the heroic bogatyrs' activity, which sometimes took the form of distant campaigns against Byzantium, there came to be implanted and diffused a new faith, Christianity. With the arrival of the church, a new and distinctive part of the population came into existence. This was the clergy. An unprecedented and serious blow was applied to the former tribal chieftain, the elder, who lost his priestly significance. Appearing now beside him was a different spiritual leader, the Christian priest, and this new authority gravitated towards the city because it was there the bishop resided.

It is obvious, however, that all this upheaval in the life of the Slavs of the eastern plain could not be completed during the initial heroic period, extending from Riurik to the death of Yaroslav I. The roots of Christianity, for example, had taken only feeble hold in their new setting by the end of that period and for a long time thereafter, as is evident by the success of an idolatrous priest in restoring almost all of Novgorod to primitive paganism.[18]

The military activity of the first princes affected all the tribes, leading each one to feel the aforementioned changes in greater or lesser degree. Yet, just as weakness is a biological characteristic of both very young and very old bodies, so also is there an apparent political similarity between states which have been newly created and states which have lapsed into disintegration. They are both unable to preserve their unity by maintaining direct connections among all their parts. The decaying Roman Empire ended its existence in division, while it was with division that the new European states began their history. The newly-formed Russian state could not but submit to this general law. Still, can a historian, on the basis of superficial observation, simply stop his inquiry without proceeding further and be satisfied merely with accepting this as a valid conclusion? Of course not. He must, rather, focus attention on those factors which did not permit the continuation of separatist divergencies and which, in the face of external division, facilitated the maintenance of internal unity. Emphasis should be placed on how the interconnections between different areas became gradually strengthened and how the unification of the state was achieved. It is the task of the historian to trace the growth of the state together with the development of the people by way of the progressive clarification of the awareness of themselves as a unitary whole.

TRANSITION TO POLITICAL AND ECCLESIASTICAL UNIFICATION

As was said earlier, the Slavic tribes were in no condition to oppose the strengthening of political unification. The greatest obstacle to such unification might have been posed by the enormous geographical size of the political area carved out by the first princes of the Riurik dynasty through force of arms. With the slackening of the military activity that marks the beginning of the historical life of a people, or else with the diversion of that activity in a different direction, the unity between the region of Kiev as a distinct entity and the principalities located at a distance from it could have been weakened at the very outset of Russian history. The rulers of those principalities, because of their remoteness, could have opted for independence, especially if the leading prince among them, the grand prince of Kiev, had sought to impose on them the fulfillment of heavy obligations through the payment of a sizable tribute from their principalities. In that case the interests of the people in those areas would have fallen into accord with the interests of the local ruler, and there would have developed a general tendency in the direction of independence.

To keep all the parts united, it was imperative that the activity marking the first, heroic period should not come to an end, that the representatives of the historical movement, the prince and the retinue, should not halt their activity, but should ceaselessly travel across the expanses of the eastern plain. Thus, without affording the outlying principalities the opportunity of going their separate ways, they continually could freshen the conditions necessary for nurturing a community of interests. It was precisely this situation which prevailed from the death of Yaroslav I until the emergence of northern Russia on the main scene of action. In this intense and continuous movement the princes and their retinues trekked from one principality to another. Because of internal conflict and internecine warfare, the entire force of the activity was concentrated within the Russian regions and did not pass beyond their borders. There were many princes during this period who were no worse warriors than Grand Prince Sviatoslav[19] had been earlier. But not one of them ventured beyond the Danube.

The activity of the princes was regulated by the clan relations existing among them. The princes branched out into different principalities, some even quite far away. But the unity of the clan remained. The most important throne belonged to the eldest in the entire clan, while the other principalities were distributed according to a hierarchy of seniority. Hence, the princes were only temporary rulers of their principalities. All their attention was devoted to retaining the seniority that would assure them the right of succession to a better principality. Their gaze was constantly toward Kiev, and instead of harboring a desire for separation, they considered it their greatest misfortune if they found themselves excluded from the general activity of the clan.

It is apparent that, if the entire attention of the princes was directed toward a single common objective, if they all possessed a single common interest, if everyone gravitated toward Kiev, then both the principalities and the people in them could not remain isolated from each other. The people of Rostov and Chernigov, of Vladimir in Volynia and of Smolensk, had to pay constant attention to Kiev and Pereiaslavl. For any changes occurring there inevitably would have telling repercussions in their own regions as well. It might happen that some prince would leave his former principality and another take his place, or a civil war might start in which a prince and the people themselves would have to take part. In this way, through the princely clan relations, through the incessant movement of princes and their retinues from one region to another, the people of even the most remote areas could not isolate themselves from the general course of life in common. They constantly nurtured mutual interests and became imbued with an awareness of the indivisibility of the Russian land. It stands to reason that the frequent shifting about of princes, because of changes in clan standing, and the civil wars resulting from the confusion in determining their genealogical relations, could not but have unhappy.consequences for the people of the various regions. Yet, it was impossible to compel a prince to reject the principle of clan unity. The people of Novgorod tried to acquire a permanent prince for themselves, but they were unsuccessful. At least the connection with Kiev did not cost the regions anything in another sense. They did not have to pay anything to Kiev and were completely independent of it.

To political unity based on clan relations among princes came to be added an ecclesiastical unity when the leading primate of the church, the metropolitan, took up residence in Kiev. Toward him were drawn the bishops of the entire Russian land and toward Kiev was drawn all of Russian Christianity, which spread with the passage of time through the eastern plain, driving out the Slavic and Finnish paganism. To be sure, Russian Christianity did not gravitate toward Kiev solely because the church administration was concentrated there. Rather, it was because Christianity was spread everywhere from Kiev. At first, this occurred in consequence of the zeal of the princes and their travels with the retinues in the various regions. But later from Kiev came monks bearing the gospel of Christianity, and bishops were sent everywhere from the Kiev Monastery of the Caves.[20] The religious attraction that Kiev has today for all parts of the Russian land, the custom of going on pilgrimages to the sacred shrines of Kiev, is not just a recent phenomenon.

Hence, the very period that at first appears to be filled with division, dissension, and princely feuds is actually a time when there was established a broad base for national and state unity. During the interval between the "invitation of the princes" and the death of Yaroslav,[21] the tribes were propelled, willingly or no, toward a common life. Their way of life was subjected to change. Yet this was just the start. In order that these beginnings might develop and grow strong, it was necessary that there be a continuation of the same intense activity of the princes and their retinues, an activity concentrated in the region staked out by the weapons of the first princes.

It was just such activity that did indeed appear, taking place in consequence of the clan relationship among the princes and the unity this imparted to them. The period from the death of Yaroslav to that of Andrei Bogoliubsky[22] constitutes a continuation of that heroic period of activity which had for its purpose the awakening of historical life. The princes, as before, possessed the attributes of bogatyrs, moving constantly from one place to another. To settle in one place that they might establish something stable and permanent was not in their character. A good prince was not supposed to accumulate or save anything. He was expected to distribute everything to the retinue, through the use of which he was able to obtain anything that he himself wanted. A prince held in view the prospect of moving endlessly from one throne to another until such time as he should deposit his mortal remains in hallowed Kiev, next to the sepulchers of his sires and grandsires. One such princely bogatyr, Vladimir Monomakh, whose legacy of glory exceeded that of all the rest, left to posterity a personal account of his own activity.[23] The activity of such princes consisted of incessant journeying, of uninterrupted campaigns from one region to another. A glance at the map of Russia and its wide expanse of territory in the eleventh and twelfth centuries will reveal the significance of Monomakh and of this constant roaming activity, by which were supported the beginnings of historical life in all respects. There was maintained everywhere thereby an awareness of the unity of the Russian land.

Before the invitation of the princes there existed separate tribes, which through their homogeneity were capable of belonging to a single nationality. With the arrival of the princes and the beginning of historical progress, the tribes underwent a unification that was primarily external. A transformation in their way of life began to take place. But it was only because of conditions which characterized the period from the death of Yaroslav to the end of the twelfth century that there emerged a Russian people.

PRINCES AND RETINUES

Important for Russia was the continuation of the aforementioned movement in the east European plain associated with the heroic period of the bogatyrs. For it was under conditions of incessant activity that history began to unfold throughout the vast extent of the unspoiled land. Now, attention should be given to the results of all that activity. When thought

is given to such constant movement, it is difficult to conceive of anything durable and fixed. In Western Europe, at the time of the formation of new states, there can be seen the movement of Germanic bands
under their leaders in the provinces of the Roman Empire and their
armed occupation of those provinces. But after the newcomers had
taken possession of the land and settled on it, the most important leaders among them allocated selected portions of their own large landed
holdings for the use of others under conditions of definite obligation.
Landed holdings given in temporary possession became, for various reasons, hereditary property. A weak landowner, desiring to gain the protection of a powerful neighbor, would give his land to him and then
receive it in return, with the addition of certain obligations to the seign-
ior. Accordingly there developed in the West on the basis of land relations a connection between landholders which is called feudalism. This
was a bond which, during the period of weakness in the state organism,
contributed in exactly the same way to the preservation of the unity of
the country as did the princely clan relations among the Russians. It is
land and the relations based on land that constituted the essence of the
feudal system. This system, according to the apt expression of one historian, was like a religion of land. Immovable property, land, was the
governing principle, and only later, after the rise of industry and trade,
did cities begin to flourish. At that point there appeared also a moneyed
aristocracy next to the aristocracy of the land.

In the east European plain there can be observed no similar phenomenon. Even the most careful search of the Chronicle fails to reveal
any evidence of a relationship based on land among members of the
retinue. This state of affairs can be easily explained by once again directing attention to the main condition under which Russian history originated and had its development, namely, the vastness of the territory and
the small size of the population. There was abundant land but it had no
value in the absence of manpower to cultivate it. The chief source of
princely revenue, which apparently went primarily for the maintenance
of his retainers, was derived from the tribute that the prince collected
from the tribes and later sold in Greece. In the beginning, if the prince
did not go forth to collect the tribute, his retinue became impoverished.
"The servitors of Sveneld are adorned with weapons and fine raiment,
but we are naked. Go forth with us, Prince, after tribute!" Thus did his
retinue fatefully goad Prince Igor to a more vigorous collection of
tribute.[24]

This is a valuable piece of information, for it suggests the proper view
to take of the matter. Those constituting the retinues did not settle on

landed estates apportioned to them as independent landholders who depended for their livelihood on revenue from those lands. As companions-in-arms and followers of the prince, they remained as before in complete dependence on him for their maintenance. It was to the person of the prince, their leader, who provided them with food and clothing, that they were attached. If he carried out these functions badly, they complained. If a prince heeded their complaints, as did Vladimir, who at a feast had silver spoons laid out before his retinue to replace less costly ones made out of wood, then all went well.[25] But if a prince did not accede to their wishes and their grievances remained unremedied, then the retainers would leave to enter the service of another prince who gave promise of greater generosity.

It may be argued that this state of affairs was typical only of the early period in Russian history. Could it be that the relations between the prince and his retainers changed afterwards? Not at all. There is information pertaining to the later period which indicates that the retainers were supported not from the land, but by a monetary salary they received from the prince. The chronicler, lamenting a growing preoccupation with luxury, writes that the earlier retainers did not permit their wives to indulge in excessive extravagance and had thus been satisfied with one hundred grivnas[26] as payment from the prince. But he goes on to note that, at the time he was writing, the retainers were given to say, "One hundred grivnas, Prince, is too little for me!"—for their wives now adorned themselves with gold instead of silver.

Things could not have been any different under a system of princely relations based on the clan principle. Lacking a strong authority in his principality, but striving to attain the senior throne by ascending step by step through the clan structure, a prince moved about from one principality to another, followed by his retinue. Should a prince be ejected by hostile kinsmen, the same misfortune likewise awaited his retinue. In the face of such migrations, could the principle of immovable landed property have had any important significance?

Hence the retinue, after its appearance in the eastern plain and through the course of several centuries, did not settle down. It preserved its original character as a fraternal military society following its leader in search of adventure and profit. Under its prince a retinue lived happily and well. The prince was regarded as the eldest comrade or brother, and not as a sovereign. He did not withdraw himself from his retinue, which was always aware of his every thought. He did not spare anything in the way of food or drink to insure the welfare of the retinue. He hoarded nothing for himself, distributing everything among his retainers. If, however, the prince should not be a good one, if he kept his thoughts from the retinue, withheld his wealth from them, or cultivated a favorite, then the retainers would leave him.

A retinue could take such action with ease, since there existed no bond between it and the territory of the prince whom it abandoned. The members of the retinues were Russians, and the Russian land was vast, with numerous princes who were only too glad to accept the services of an intrepid warrior. Thus, through the course of entire centuries, those who made up the princely retinues became accustomed to live in this primitive form of military fraternity. They moved on their own volition from principality to principality in the immeasurable vastness, retaining their original freedom of departure and the right of serving any prince they chose. They learned to live without responsibility, without any thought of tomorrow, without the consciousness of any pressure from above, without awareness of any need to unite their strength for opposition in the defense of their rights. They became accustomed to avoid every sort of unpleasantness, to react to everything that was troublesome not with resistance, but with withdrawal. They fell into the habit of being guided by their individual interests instead of the interests of their class.

In speaking about the princely clan relations and the vital consequences of those relations for the retinue, sight must not be lost of one exceptionally important circumstance: the rapid proliferation of the princely dynasty of Riurik. The situation mentioned earlier, in which retainers become landowners, is not the only condition that leads to the development of a strong aristocracy within a country. An aristocracy also can arise when a prince places the administration of cities and entire regions in the hands of his attendants, who naturally gain an important distinction and pass it on to their posterity. It was in this way that the Polish nobility developed. Very quickly it began to struggle against and restrict the king's authority. But in Russia the members of the princely dynasty multiplied rapidly, for which reason all the regions and all the cities, however slight in importance, came to be governed by princes. Consequently the boyars found their path blocked to the development of a powerful aristocracy like that of the Poles. The foremost places were occupied by the princes with their clan relations and activities, and with their internecine struggles arising out of those relations. The retinue, carried away by the hurricane force of those activities, did not have time to acquire any kind of significance of its own. This circumstance furnishes an explanation as to why, during the period under consideration, it was almost exclusively the princes who filled the entire historical scene. The Chronicle, in speaking about the princes, became a princely chronicle. Their names alone appear endlessly before the reader's eyes with tiresome monotony.

THE FORMATION OF TOWNS AND CITIES

A closer examination reveals that, next to the unsettled princes and their retinues, moving about from one region to another in the manner characteristic of a primitive society, there is evident another interesting phenomenon. It is a phenomenon which, disclosing a social organization just in the process of coming into being, would have been impossible in a society that was in the least degree mature or developed. The Chronicle speaks of the bogatyrs, persons of unusual physical strength and courage who did not enter into the composition of the princely retinue. They constituted a distinct force, giving their help to one or another of the princes. History can still note in the virgin eastern plain the process in which power comes to be elicited from the people after they have been stimulated into action.

The Russian society about which we are concerned is referred to as primitive in relation to European society, which was distinguished by the complexity of its organization and, being more complete, occupied a higher position than other societies. Nevertheless, if a comparison is made between Russian society in the eleventh and twelfth centuries and that of neighboring peoples to the east, then how high will the Russians be seen to stand! Next to the steppe, with its nomadic inhabitants, a transformation was taking place from a nomadic to a settled way of life. Between the wild nomads of the steppe and the settlements of early Russia there developed people who were half nomadic and half settled. Semi-independent, they had their own princelings. Although they presumably recognized the superior authority of the Russian princes, yet they frequently withdrew this allegiance in favor of supporting their savage brethren.

When in the eastern plain the princes and retainers still preserved their original character of bogatyrs, when they had not yet abandoned their far-flung travels or attached themselves to the holding of land, as in the West, it was inevitable that the cities, owing to favorable circumstances fostering their growth through industry and trade, would gain in importance precisely because the other centers of power, the prince and retinue, exemplified mobility and change while the cities represented the principle of permanence and stability. The minor principalities and lands, together with the lesser towns, were at first drawn to the senior city because the prince lived there. As princes began to change and argue with one another, it became difficult to determine which of them was right. Minor towns and entire principalities would then look, quite naturally and in accordance with ancient custom, to the senior city. What would it say? As it decided, so would all others decide.

The residents of the senior cities, gathered together in an assembly of the heads of households,[27] assumed in this way a position of authority. Whatever the senior cities decided, the surrounding towns would support. As the number of princes grew, together with their quarrels and internal wars, the cities naturally strove to attain the same prerogative which the retinue had acquired for itself, the capability of changing an unbearable prince for a better one. Shortly after the death of Yaroslav, when several princes came to the fore simultaneously, the people of Kiev expelled a prince who proved unable to defend them from the Polovetsians, and availed themselves of another who had been his prisoner.[28] Thereafter such incidents took place with greater or lesser regularity, but most often in Great Novgorod.

It was natural that certain contractual conditions or agreements between the princes and cities should arise under these circumstances. It is only the contractual agreements concluded by Novgorod that have come down to the present time. As for the other cities, one would not be justified in assuming that the contracts they executed had much in the way of defining the independence of their urban administration. Just as a member of the princely retinue who had gained for himself as an individual the right of free departure did not have reason to formulate other definitions relative to his rights as member of a class, so likewise the city encountered an obstacle in developing with precision any definition of its way of life exactly because of the opportunity it enjoyed to change an unacceptable ruler and judge. The citizens could summon an acceptable candidate and come to an agreement with him, stipulating that he should in all instances appoint as administrators and judges subordinates who were suitable to them. Thereupon everything would proceed smoothly.

In the West a proprietor lived permanently on his property. He remained always a landowner. A city did not have any means to resist his oppression other than of taking an oath "to stand as one" (*jurer la commune*) so that with the aid of the highest authority it might compel the oppressor to define forever his relations with the city. But it was a different matter in early Russia. No need existed for a guarantee against an acceptable and weak prince. Should a strong prince replace him, he would not pay attention to the contractual agreement of his predecessor, for he was not bound to him in anything and frequently indeed was his enemy. There was no higher authority that might confirm the rights of a city as regards its prince. All the princes were equal on their thrones and did not recognize any other as superior. Finally, the best evidence for the lack of developed self-government in the early Russian cities appears from the circumstance that when several of them fell under the sway of Lithuania, they accepted foreign forms of self-government, namely, the Germanic Magdeburg Law. Foreign forms are voluntarily adopted when there are no native ones.

INFLUENCE OF THE CLERGY

The leading figures among the clergy, the bishops, often came from abroad. Nevertheless, having taken up permanent residence among their flock, they could not but exert a great influence upon the affairs of their region and its relations with the prince. On every important occasion it was the bishop who occupied a place of distinction. However, in the midst of the constantly moving princes, fighting with each other, in the midst of the retinues, moving about with their princes, in the midst of the principalities, shaken and wavering by reason of this movement and struggle, only the metropolitan of Kiev and all Russia could acquire anything more than local significance. This was the one permanent force to stand firmly in the midst of other shifting, and therefore weaker, forces. But this metropolitan was usually a Greek, a foreigner. Lacking communication with the people, he remained without influence.

ELEMENTS OF HISTORICAL RETARDATION AND PROGRESS

During the century following the death of Yaroslav I it is evident that, mostly because of the continuation of the aforementioned activity, all the elements as they originally appeared lagged behind in their development: the wandering retinues, whose members freely transferred from one prince to another; the tireless princely bogatyrs at the head of their retinues, moving from one principality to rule another, seeking in all lands to gain honor and not bothering to think of anything else that smacked of permanence—princes with nothing of their own, but holding everything jointly in a community founded on the clan; the urban assembly, with its primitive form of organization and function, which did not have any definition of its rights or jurisdiction; and on the borderlands, the nomads who were becoming transformed into half-settlers, and not much farther, in the steppe, the pure nomads with their tents. Everything in the eastern plain bespoke a primitive world, of society existing as though in a fluid condition. It is impossible to foresee yet in what relationship to each other these social elements would stand when the time came to pass from this indeterminate condition to one that is consolidated, stabilized, and more definite.

Exactly when and where and under what conditions did a new system of relations begin to evolve? On the resolution of these questions depends the understanding of the entire subsequent course of history. It has been shown that history in the beginning always selected the very best lands, and it is from there that commenced the gradual progression of historical movement in Europe from south to north or from southwest to northeast. The same thing was to be found in the eastern plain. History began there in the west, along the water route from the Baltic to the Black Sea.[29] It began in the northwest. But already the second prince[30] moved from north to south, to the central area of the upper Dnieper region. There it was in early times, amidst the better lands, that Russia began. The area in the western part of the plain along the great water route formed the main historical stage for the first princes, and it remained so for a hundred years after the death of Grand Prince Yaroslav.

As mentioned earlier it fell to the lot of the Slavs in the very beginning to move northeast, into the east European plain, where the lands were rendered increasingly barren by nature. At an unknown time in the past, some powerful enemy ejected the Slavs from the Danube and forced part of them to settle along the rivers of the eastern plain.[31] But even there, in the richer southwestern part of the plain, they could not long remain in peace. This was true even after the Russian princes united them and stood at the head of retinues as protectors of the Russian land. The princes built towns along the borders facing the steppe. Yet neither the Russian princes with their retinues nor the Russian towns could hold back the flood of nomads. Cities and villages lay empty and desolate. The ploughman did not dare leave for work. The tents of the Polovetsians became filled with Russian slaves, and the forays of the princes into the vastness of the steppe to defeat the predators brought only momentary respite. The prince of Chernigov at one point announced that his principality was depopulated and that his cities harbored only hunters or Polovetsians. Other principalities bordering the steppe did not find themselves any better off. Moreover the princely civil wars took place mostly in these very same regions, and it was among the Polovetsians that the princes searched for allies.

Such an unfortunate state of affairs in the southwestern borderlands of necessity forced part of its inhabitants to seek more peaceful climes. Areas of this kind were to be found precisely in the distant Russian principalities of the northeast. It was to the region of the upper Volga, harsh in climate and lacking a sizable population, that the princes attempted to attract settlers. In seeking to overcome the scarcity of peo- they offered immunity from taxation and built cities.

What were the conditions of the people in this new country? If tribal divisions in the old Russia of the west or southwest had but little histori- cal importance, in the new Russia of the northeast there is scarcely any mention made of tribes at all. The Chronicle points to the existence there of Finnish tribes prior to the arrival of the Varangian-Russian princes. But by the middle of the twelfth century it is to a Slavic-Russian population that attention must be paid. The arrival of only the Russian princes and their retinues could not have slavicized the natives. It is known that usually a ruling prince will keep one nationality, while the lower population will retain another. For the slavicization of northeast- ern Russia to occur, a strong influx of Slavs into the cities and villages was essential. That immigration was accomplished not by the collective movement of tribes, but by individual effort. People gathered together either one by one or in small groups from various places. Coming into contact with persons from tribes other than their own, they lacked the opportunity to form a strong union. Finally, upon arriving, they were keenly aware of their weakness and dependence.

In the western regions the Slavs were longtime settlers and proprie- tors. It was the princes who were newcomers. In the east, to the con- trary, the Slavic settlers appeared in a country where the prince was al- ready established as proprietor, having constructed the cities, summoned the settlers, and given them immunities. The settlers, living on the prince's land and in his cities, were in everything obligated to the prince and were in everything dependent on him. It was these relations between the population and the prince that lay at the heart of that strong de- velopment of princely authority which was to be seen in the north.

To be sure, much depended on whether the princes would put to use the leverage afforded them by their advantageous relations with the new population and with their own new cities, and whether they would en- counter strong opposition in other parts of the population. There ap- peared precisely such a prince as could not have taken better advantage of his auspicious position over the people. This was Andrei Bogoliubsky. He moved his residence from the old city of Rostov the Great to new Vladimir on the Kliazma, where there was no urban assembly and where the princely authority would meet no obstacles. Andrei understood very well the meaning of the words "mine" and "property." He did not de- sire to identify with the south, where princes knew only the principle of common clan rule. Andrei, like an early bogatyr, understood the power that derived from the land into whose possession he had come and upon which he had become established forever. He remained on that land and did not move to Kiev when the city became his in accordance with the customary rights of the clan and by right of conquest. This first example of a settled way of life and of attachment to something distinctly one's own in the way of personal possession became a sacred tradition for all the northern princes. It constituted the starting point for a new state of affairs.

PRINCES AND CITIES

When these new conditions were being first established, as has been said, much depended on whether the princes would take advantage of their favorable situation and whether they would encounter opposition from other quarters. Things did not proceed without a struggle. The southern princely bogatyrs, accustomed from youth to fear none but God alone, rose up when they saw that Andrei, the northern sovereign, began to deal with them not as before, not as with kinsmen, but as with subordinates. They destroyed a large army that Andrei sent against them to the south. But with this defensive action of the princes the matter was brought to a conclusion in the south. The north, with its newly-emerging regime, remained untouched. Novgorod the Great, under a brave prince who came there from the south, repulsed Andrei's regiments and witnessed their flight from its walls. But with this defensive action on the part of the most powerful independent city in Russia, the matter ended.[32] Novgorod the Great did not come to the aid of Rostov the Great, which Andrei according to the expression of the day, "struck with his heel." He then established his residence in Vladimir, one of the minor surrounding towns, furbishing it as his capital city to spite old Rostov.

It was said earlier that members of the princely retinues had become accustomed to live with a prince not as a ruler, but as a senior companion and leader whom they served through their freely given loyalty and whom they could leave upon their first dissatisfaction with him. Andrei did not tolerate these customary pretensions of the retinue and drove out of his principality the old boyars of his predecessors. And what did the boyars in other Russian regions do? Did they stand up against this injury to their compeers? Not at all.

Everywhere the offensive actions of the northern sovereign were met only with defense. He remained unaffected in his own principality. Still, even there the struggle was not over. Andrei fell victim to the new order of things which he himself had introduced. It was the boyars who killed him. But this stealthy nighttime murder of a stern master demonstrated more than could anything else the weakness of the people who perpetrated the criminal act. However, there remained no longer any man who compressed everything together within his powerful hand. Consequently everything that had only been contracted, but not permanently bent, could now expand and become straight. There arose once more the old city of Rostov, with its strong urban assembly. It intended to depose the insolent minor city of Vladimir, which had seized primacy through the will of the prince. On account of their common interests, the boyars joined with the old city. But victory belonged to the surrounding towns. Rostov lost its importance once and for all, and the princes entrenched themselves in the newer towns where there was no urban assembly and their authority was not restricted by anything. The conclusion of the struggle between the old and new cities had a decisive effect on the further course of events in the north and, ultimately, in all of Russia. For the north acquired a distinct importance.

It has been shown that, because of the clan relations among the princes, their activities, and their civil wars, princely authority appeared as temporary and changing. To the degree that it became weakened on account of this, to that degree triumphed the importance of the old city and principality, representing permanent authority. Hence, next to the authority of the princes there existed another. As princes succeeded one another in a given area with greater frequency and as their efforts to claim the throne of a principality grew ever weaker, so accordingly was raised the importance of permanent urban authority.

Thus the city of Novgorod the Great as a corporate entity attained in its title the status of "lord," even though it retained a prince and hence did not exclude the princely authority. It preserved the form of a historically developed dyarchy and did not undertake to formulate a more precise juridical definition. This kind of dyarchy existed to a greater or lesser degree in other regions during the prevalence of princely clan relations. But as soon as the prince made the first attempt to establish himself in the north and to become a permanent authority, naturally he had to come into conflict first of all with the authority of the senior city. It was easy to foresee the outcome of the collision in the north, where the prince was ruler of the country and builder of the cities. There the prince had created for himself a power base upon which he could depend and with which he could begin the activities that characterized the career of Andrei Bogoliubsky.

Andrei, incidentally, did not enter into open warfare with the old city of Rostov. He merely deserted it and formed for himself a capital in the minor neighboring town of Vladimir. He acted the same way with Kiev, the most senior city of the entire Russian land. His nephew Prince Yaroslav[33] wished to follow the same policy with regard to Novgorod when he abandoned it and established his residence in the neighboring town of Torzhok. Only when, after the death of Bogoliubsky, the inhabitants of Rostov announced their demands did an open struggle break out between them and Andrei's brothers, ending in the defeat of Rostov. It is not surprising that the struggle was shortlived. For it would be difficult to suppose that Rostov was a strong city in terms of having a large population based on extensive commercial activity. This city, built by the Finnish Merians, was hidden away from the lively river routes, and particularly the Volga. Located next to a melancholy and lifeless lake, it could hardly have been expected to enjoy as thriving an existence as Novgorod, Smolensk, or Polotsk.

As the old type of city with an urban assembly was deposed, there developed in the north a general uniformity. All the cities were new and inconsequential. Rostov became deserted. Vladimir had scarcely risen to its position as capital of a grand principality when it was devastated by the Tatars and also deserted. The grand princes lived in their own separate, hereditary domains,[34] such as Pereiaslavl, Tver, Kostroma, and Moscow. One cannot fail to see in Russian history a certain imbalance that led to important consequences. In the western part, which was the main historical scene during the early period, there could be found many important cities, flourishing because they stood on the road "from the Varangians to the Greeks," that is, from northern to southern Europe. In the northeastern part, which now became prominent under different and less favorable natural conditions, there were no important cities. Consequently they exerted no influence on the course of events occurring apart from them. The cities were principally large, enclosed villages, and the political organization that was created and established there had principally the character of an agricultural state.

REORIENTATION FROM SOUTHWEST TO NORTHEAST

In general, the movement of Russian history from southwest to northeast was from better regions to worse, into environmental conditions that were less favorable than before. History moved out of a land that was advantageous in terms of its natural situation, out of a land that constituted a path from northern to southern Europe, out of a land which, accordingly, was capable of maintaining constant contact with the Christian European nations and which functioned as a commercial intermediary between them. But as soon as the course of historical life turned eastward to the regions of the upper Volga the connection with Europe and the West inevitably became weakened. It was severed not because of any supposed influence of the Tatar yoke, but because of powerful natural influences.

Everything came to be oriented eastwards, in the direction toward which flowed the Volga, the main river of the new political region. Under these circumstances what was to be the future of western Russia, an area left behind with no possibility of moving east? Having lost its importance western Russia became deprived of the capacity for further material, political, and moral development, and of the means for exerting an influence upon eastern Russia through its contacts with European nations. Mention already has been made of the fate that befell western Russia in consequence of its proximity to the steppe and the predatory nomads, the Polovetsians, who foraged there. The final destruction of western Russia was left to the Tatars and Lithuanians. Kiev, in earlier days a second Byzantium, was described by a traveler as a sorry little town, whose environs resembled nothing other than a cemetery.[35]

Depopulated, divested of power, and broken in pieces, the Russian southwest fell under the authority of Lithuanian princes. Galicia, a fortunate corner where were concentrated the last energies of southwest Russia, rapidly rose and flourished. But it quickly fell, owing to its isolation from the rest of Russia, that is, Great Russia, where life still remained. For Little Russia in the period under consideration could not be called alive. The political connection between eastern and western Russia fell apart. Moreover, there arose hostility on account of the rivalry of the rulers, who attempted to destroy the former ecclesiastical unity. Consequently, different metropolitans appeared, one in Kiev and the other in Moscow.

The union of blood relations was ruined as brothers broke away from each other to go their own ways. It is useless to talk about the extent of material loss that occurred through this separation. There is a proverb that says, "Money is a matter of gainful living." This is generally true when speaking of material resources. Yet, how much moral and spiritual wealth was lost because of this division and long period of separation! A Russian who arrived in the northeast did so "without seeds for planting," in all the unhappy meaning conveyed by that phrase in olden days. Alone, thrown into a world of barbarians, a Russian in the northeast was the last, most distant representative of the Christian European family.

Having broken away from his own brothers, he was forgotten by them, just as he himself, many miles distant, forgot about them. He was foreordained to travel for entire centuries still farther and farther into the wilds of the East, living in isolation from western communities. If the development of the capacities of individual persons or entire nations requires communication with other people and other countries, if only to allow a possibility for disseminating ideas and expanding one's own sphere of activity, then it becomes understandable what consequences would ensue for the Russian people in the absence of such interaction.

Other favorable circumstances might have compensated, at least in part, for the lack of the primary condition necessary for the successful development of national life. For example, an equable climate, a fruitful land, and a large population in a spacious and variegated country might have made possible the division of labor, extensive internal trade, uninterrupted communications between various localities, and the development of large cities. Nothing of this sort could come about in northeastern Russia. Depressing, severe, monotonous nature could not act vitally upon the human spirit, fostering in it a feeling of beauty or a desire to enrich life. It could not elevate a person above the daily routine of existence or bring him to a joyous state of mind indispensable for the renewal of vital energies. The small population was scattered across an enormous wilderness which grew interminably without a corresponding increase in the population. All this meant poverty and weakness, without the possibility of independent existence or defense against whatever enemy might appear.

It is instructive to examine what happened when occasionally an event of some magnitude did occur. The typical reaction of the inhabitants was to hide. They drew tight the shutters of their houses and locked up their shops. Into the city might come the steward of a wealthy landlord in the neighborhood. Surrounded by a horde of peasants under his authority, he would give himself all manner of airs among the townspeople. This sort of weakness in the separate regions induced all of them to turn to Moscow in everything. To it they sent their complaints and from it they expected protection.

The strength of a people and their breadth of outlook, the consciousness they have of their own situation and their resultant effective motivation to defend with tenacity one thing and reject another, depend upon the concentration of large masses with a vigorous and diversified range of activity in a single geographical area. When a people are united internally by way of a sufficient number of inhabitants in relation to the geographical size of the country, when they are joined by the diversity of their labors, which brings together the different regions and different parts of the population into inseparable union and dependency upon one another, when these regions and parts of the population are to be found in uninterrupted communication with each other and bound by mutual interests, so that they take an active part in the fortunes of each other—in a word, when they consciously live a common life—then such an internal unity or bond offers an opportunity for decentralization, an opportunity for the separate parts to govern themselves without damage to the political integrity of the whole. Whenever the injured member of an organism has healed internally, then external bandages and splints are no longer required.

On the other hand, when the different parts of a population, spread out over enormous expanses of land, live separate lives, not bound by the diversity of their labor, when there are no large cities bustling with a variety of activities, when communications are difficult and there exists no awareness of common interests—then the many scattered parts are made to undergo unification. They are drawn together by the process of state centralization, the strength of which increases as internal organic unity grows weaker. Centralization compensates for the inadequacy of an internal bond. The process is accommodated by this inadequacy. It is, apparently, a beneficial and necessary phenomenon, for without it everything would disintegrate and be dissipated. However, this is a surgical bandage applied to the exterior of a sick organ that has suffered the loss of internal ties and unity.

THE RISE OF MOSCOW

Mention has been made of the favorable situation in which the prince in the northeast found himself from the very start and how he took advantage of his opportunities. The successors of Bogoliubsky, his brother Vsevolod III[36] and the latter's descendants, were unswervingly faithful to the tradition which passed to them from the first sovereign. A prince who was installed according to his place in the clan as the grand, or senior, prince no longer left his own hereditary principality to take up residence in the capital city of Vladimir. Hence, after the Tatars' devastation, the grand principality did not have a chance to recover, gain in importance, or take a role in princely quarrels and feuds. Its role was passive. It remained without any initiative of its own. Each grand prince strove now to utilize his importance and power to expand his personal hereditary principality and possessions at the expense of other principalities. In the new Russia of the northeast, in contrast to the former movement from one principality to another that existed in early southwestern

Russia, the princes did not venture from their principalities. A prince and his principality developed mutual ties as their interests became identical. The princely feuds assumed a different character in that they had a different goal, namely, the strengthening of one principality at the expense of all the rest. With such an objective, the former clan relations inevitably crumbled. For he who felt himself strong did not give heed to them any longer. One principality in particular eventually overcame all the rest and came to form the Muscovite state.

In this process the prince of Moscow, who was to become sovereign of all Russia, consolidated the advantageous position which had been enjoyed by the first northern princes. In keeping with the relationship by virtue of which people in the north appeared from the start in a subordinate capacity to the prince as their lord, founder of the land, and builder of cities—in keeping with that relationship a free man in the Muscovite state referred to himself as "the grand prince's man." But what of the retinue? Throughout the entire time that a state was forming in the north the retinue preserved its former character. One prerogative dating back to old Russia it guarded jealously. This was the right of free departure from one prince to another: "Liberty to the boyars and free servitors." Consequently the prince took the lead away from the retinue. At the time that he began to establish a new order of things, having first sunk roots in the land and, like a bogatyr, having drawn new strength from it, the retinue still continued to roam and wander about on the assumption that this capacity to move was its sole right or guarantee of all other rights. Thus the retinue fell considerably behind the prince. It fell behind by an entire period. If some retainers did settle down and gain power as a result, the movement of the rest interfered with their further entrenchment and definition of relations.

It was advantageous to be in the service of the most powerful prince. In accordance with the right of free departure, members of other princely retinues streamed from all sides to Moscow. Among them were boyars with many holdings in the depopulated south. To borrow an expression from the "system of precedence,"[37] the new arrivals outranked the old Moscow boyars. The latter had, up to that time, been the principal princely servitors, and a struggle began. In these feuds within the boyar class, if one of the boyars should grow unduly strong and dangerous, the prince could always find a defense against him among his rivals. In this way perished the boyar Alexis Khvost from the enmity of his own peers. When the important post of commander of the city militia at one point threatened to become dangerous through heritability in a single notable family, Dmitry Donskoy[38] abolished the office. In vain did the son of the last commander of the Moscow city militia, Vasily Veliaminov, resort to submitting a petition in Tver and before the Horde,[39] raising a threatening storm against the prince of Moscow.[40] Yet, at home, his only zealous ally was a wealthy Muscovite merchant. No one from among the boyars came to his aid. Then, when Veliaminov's head fell under the executioner's axe at Kuchkovo Field, the people wept. But the Chronicle contains not a single word about the boyars' having shown the least concern for the fate of one who was from their own class. In precisely the same way, under Donskoy's grandson,[41] did there come to an unsuccessful conclusion the rebellion of the boyar Ivan Vsevolozhsky.

During this important time, then, when the prince of Moscow was gathering together the Russian land and was becoming the sovereign, autocratic ruler of all northeastern Russia, there could be found instances of attempted resistance by powerful individuals or families in the service of the grand prince. But in the collision and struggle with the grand prince's authority, the relative strength of the contestants was far from equal. A rebellious boyar acted only in the name of his own personal interest. Unsupported internally by any of his peers, he acted with the aid of other princes or the khan. The retinue remained, as before, committed to the maxim "Liberty to the boyars and free servitors!"

THE CONSOLIDATION OF THE GRAND PRINCIPALITY OF MOSCOW

Toward the end of the first half of the fifteenth century the court of the grand prince of Moscow became filled with arrivals of a new sort. These were princes, offspring of Riurik and Gedimin,[42] whose genealogy entitled them to stand in first place. Their presence aroused the hostility of the boyars, who now were relegated to a secondary position. Consequently, instead of an increase in the power of the retinue from the influx of princes, there was instead a decrease because of a disjunction of interests. Moreover the princes arrived in Moscow merely with pretensions of importance, and without the means to uphold them. Some of them kept the titles they had held in their former principalities, but they did not in fact remain rulers of those principalities. This meant that they did not possess any base of independent support, for they no longer had any importance in the regions where their fathers once ruled. They did not live there, and soon were forgotten. Their new place was in Moscow, as retainers who were never far from the grand prince. They did keep possession of some patrimonial estates, but these split up as they were divided and bequeathed to all the sons. A part of them also passed to the monasteries as donations for the commemoration of souls.

All the boyars, the entire nobility, found themselves in the same situation with regard to material means. All of them possessed only meager resources. The princes and boyars were impoverished while the grand prince was enormously wealthy, having acquired for himself a considerable quantity of land. In the formative period of the Muscovite state, an agricultural country with undeveloped industry and trade, it was land which constituted the only wealth and means of support. Landed wealth furnished the grand prince with the means to consolidate his power firmly and at the same time obstruct the pretensions of the princes and nobility. The device used to accomplish these ends was the service estate [pomestie] —a military tenure, or a tract of land granted by the grand prince in exchange for the performance of military service. By distributing such tracts as temporary tenant holdings in return for service, the grand prince created for himself a large military force dependent wholly upon him for its maintenance.

The princes and boyars did not possess large regions, cities, or even fortified castles where they might live more or less independently. Since early times the retainers, who did not receive in Russia the status of landowners, had become accustomed to live near the prince. Now the boyars, lords-in-waiting,[43] and councillors,[44] as well as the recently arrived princes who entered their ranks, lived constantly in Moscow, always crowding together in the palace. In the fifteenth, sixteenth, and seventeenth centuries the relations remained the same as they had been in the tenth and eleventh centuries. It is said of the kings of Spain and France that they strengthened their authority and importance by drawing the aristocracy out of their castles into their own courts. In Russia such a development could not have taken place, for there never existed in Russian history a period when the nobility lived independently in their own castles. The retinue always kept its original character and direct relationship to the prince, from whom it did not part. With the formation of the Muscovite state the servitor princes and nobles could not ordinarily bestow lands upon others who had no material means, for they themselves were impoverished. Hence, they were unable to form a military force of their own or even establish separate courts. The grand prince alone had the capacity to distribute lands and by this means to form his own army. The consequences are not difficult to comprehend. People who lived then had a clear appreciation of what the situation meant. The Polish magnates, when they deliberated among themselves the possibility of electing the Muscovite tsar for their king, said that this election would not benefit them because the tsar was wealthy and therefore could induce all the gentry who were in their service to come over to him.[45] This had been done earlier under Ivan III, when that grand prince, after having confiscated lands from the clergy of Novgorod, gave them in military tenure to persons entering his service from the courts of other notable personages.

The grand prince became a firmly established ruler with full authority in a country where the inhabitants referred to themselves as the grand prince's people. He exercised control over the land and organized for himself a sizable military force. But the old retinue, the nobility, at the head of which now stood the princes, continually cast their glances backward, to the old, timeworn order of things. Instead of accommodating themselves to the new conditions of stability, they desired to preserve the former character of the retinue, move about constantly, and retain for themselves this movement as a right: "Liberty to the boyars and free servitors!" It is easy to understand how this Muscovite nobility fell behind and of what it became representative, an order of things which in Western Europe had ended when the German bands arrived on Roman soil. The Muscovite nobility still lived according to the traditions of the heroic epoch. That period, however, had long since passed away in the north, in Moscow.

There, the princes had become securely grounded. Instead of many princes with equal rights, a single sovereign of all Russia rose to prominence. It became impossible to leave him and enter someone else's service. The only place left to go was to the sovereign of a foreign country. This was difficult, for it meant treason. The right of the boyars and free servitors was extinguished of its own accord, disappearing in the natural course of events. No one took it away. There ceased to be any further guarantee of the formerly advantageous conditions. The grand prince became sharply distinguished from the old retainers and rose high above them through the cultivation of his independent material resources and through the importance that he held for the rest of the people of the land.

In the midst of general poverty only he might surround himself with splendor so luxurious that it exerted an astonishing effect upon the imagination. Quite purposely the grand prince of Moscow, Ivan III, married a Greek princess who had been educated in Italy.[46] She helped her husband to set himself apart from the mass of the new serving princes and the old retainers. She helped in changing old relations and customs to the sovereign's advantage and to the detriment of the former free retainers, for whom there existed no longer any free departure. The leading nobles entered into a struggle with the shrewd Greek woman, but she succeeded in emerging as victor out of the conflict. Her son, brought up in this struggle and deeply involved in it, mounted the throne of the grand principality upon his father's death.[47] The last years of the Muscovite line of Riurik were spent in a bitter conflict with the pretensions of the nobility, which clearly remembered the free retinues of the recent past and which in the writings of one of its gifted members has left to posterity a bitter denunciation of the new order, so burdensome to it, and about the fateful Greek woman, who supposedly brought it with her into the Russian tsardom.[48]

That struggle, whose conclusion assumed a sanguinary aspect, ended as might be expected to the detriment of the Muscovite nobility, which was compelled to forget its old traditions dating back to the free retinue. Even princes of the dynasties of Riurik and Gedimin began to be called "slaves of the great sovereign" and to sign their names in shortened form, connoting self-abasement. Yet, notwithstanding their straitened circumstances and degradations, the members of this nobility maintained their foremost importance and highest places in the administration. Ivan the Terrible[49] in his bitter animosity towards them did not deprive them of position or prestige; nor did he endow new persons of lowly origin with either the one or the other. Ivan, suspecting and detesting his boyars, allowed them to retain their former status, and even risked strengthening them when he placed them at the head of the Regular Administration.[50] He did not expel the boyars, but himself fled from them, surrounding himself with a new and loyal retinue, the Extraordinary Administration.

In the beginning of the seventeenth century there began for the Muscovite boyar class a period that was even worse than the reign of Ivan the Terrible. This was the Time of Troubles.[51] There came to be established two tsars and two separate courts. Whoever could not gain the highest honors in one court would take himself off to the other. Tushino became [a second capital], filled with people of different origins who sought there an opportunity for advancement.[52] When Tushino crumbled they hastened away to the vicinity of Smolensk, offering their services to King Sigismund III [of Poland].

Later the Muscovite boyars swore allegiance to the Polish king's son, Wladyslaw, in order only to rid themselves of the cossack tsar-impostor and get out from under the rule of their own slaves. They discovered to their horror that by his majesty's grace there was appointed to sit in council with them the tradesman Andronov, who began to take charge of everything. In spite of this the boyars clung fast to Wladyslaw. But the country did not want him. It perceived that there stood to the rear of him, or even in front, the old king [his father], together with the Jesuits.

The country rose up in arms and organized a militia to do battle with the Poles and cossacks. The leaders of the militia did not belong to the highest class. Their genealogical background was undistinguished. Those who were boyars came from Tushino, while the real Muscovite boyars sat with the Poles inside the Kremlin. After the storm had passed and things began to subside, it became evident that a failing existed in those men whom the people had been accustomed to see leading the military regiments and occupying the foremost places in the council. New people appeared who did not have the traditions or importance of the earlier "pillars." Here was an opportunity for commoners to enter into the highest class, the boyars. This probably took place slowly in the beginning, with protests and stratagems on the part of the noble families. But an example was set already for the boyar class by [the careers of] Afanasy Ordin-Nashchokin[53] and Artamon Matveev.[54]

The signal was given for new and inescapable reforms. The conduct of difficult wars on a large scale demanded the same military skills that foreigners possessed. It required a new military organization and command structure. The Muscovite state no longer could adhere to its ancient practices, based on a system of clan relations, which impeded all efforts to make effective appointment of military commanders. It could no longer be satisfied with the simple structure of primitive princely organization. No longer might it be content merely with the retinue. But the reforms that took place in response to the new demands belong to a later period of history.

THE CLERGY AND THE GRAND PRINCE OF MOSCOW

The time has come to devote some attention to the clergy. What position did it have in the formation of the Muscovite state and in what situation did it encounter the period of reform?

Mention already has been made of the importance in early Russia that the single metropolitan there might have had among the numerous princes if only he had been a Russian. After the final devastation of southwestern Russia, when the country's vital forces flowed northeastward, the metropolitans also naturally began to incline in that direction. Eventually they settled there permanently. With the transfer of the metropolia to the north, where it was consequently farther removed from Greece, there immediately began to appear metropolitans who were Russian, although at first they alternated with Greeks. As evidence of the importance of this new development it should be noted that the three metropolitans whose names are associated as being most crucial in the ecclesiastical and political history of this period, were Russians: Peter, Alexis, and Jonas.[55]

Of these the most prominent place was occupied by Alexis, under whom the importance of the metropolitan dignity attained its highest level. He supported and championed with all the means at his disposal the prince of Moscow and his principality. It is not hard to appreciate what effect upon the course of subsequent events a continuation of that policy would have had if the importance of the metropolitan relative to the grand prince had been maintained at the same level by competent successors. Alexis, indeed, wished to see as his successor an individual who did have great importance for the country and a widespread reputation for piety, Sergius of Radonezh.[56] But that holy hermit was appalled at the thought and with humility refused the proffered honor. Grand Prince Dmitry desired to see his own candidate installed as Alexis' successor. Over Alexis' objections he selected a priest named Mitiai, keeper of the prince's seal. Mitiai never managed, however, to become the metropolitan. Instead, misfortune befell the metropolia with the appearance of several rival metropolitans, from among whom the grand prince could choose anyone he pleased, depending on the circumstances.

After the death of Metropolitan Alexis the metropolia became weakened through division and strife. Meanwhile the position of grand prince was held by the forceful Dmitry Donskoy. The role of the sole metropolitan of all Russia was a critical one inasmuch as he stood between the two grand princes of Moscow and Lithuania. The metropolia, however, soon became divided into two, northern and southern. Moscow retained one metropolitan, while Kiev obtained its own.[57] Finally, the metropolitan of Moscow saw his dependence upon the Byzantine patriarch brought to an end in consequence of troubles in Constantinople and its eventual capture by the Turks. All these events took place at the same time as the final consolidation of the grand prince's authority in Moscow. As a result, the situation of the metropolitan of Moscow became definitely fixed.

Between the Russian clergy and nobility there was only a scant connection. This proved to be of no vital significance to the one class as to the other. No custom existed, as did in the West, for members of the foremost families to enter the spiritual calling and attain to episcopal rank. Metropolitan Alexis, to be sure, was the son of a prominent Muscovite boyar. But the fate of Vassian Kosoy (Prince Patrikeev),[58] who involuntarily was tonsured a monk, demonstrated very clearly the consequences of uniting in a single person the attributes of a clergyman with a nobleman's origins, connections, and traditions. Vassian's antagonist, Joseph Volotsky,[59] a man of so-called respectable background, insisted that monasteries retain their possession of villages to permit the tonsuring of persons from high social positions, who would then occupy the top places in the hierarchy. The villages were, in the event, kept by the monasteries. However, Joseph's desire to see highborn persons become prominent in the church administration did not come to pass, or else occurred only rarely.[60]

As for the white clergy,[61] the requirement that they be married must from the beginning have had an enormous influence upon their situation. For they thus were afforded the opportunity of replenishing their ranks from their own midst. But there was yet another circumstance that effectively contributed to the weakening of the clergy. It is known how heavily weighed upon the government the lack of population in Russia and how valuable each individual person was in consequence. Grand Prince Vasily I[62] concluded an agreement with Metropolitan Cyprian[63] which provided that the latter would not admit into the ranks of his ecclesiastical establishment, that is, ordain into the priesthood, any servitors of the grand prince.

Despite some disadvantages in its position, the clergy of early Russia maintained an important status in that it preserved the character of an exclusive educational class. Enlightenment consisted of what was contained in church books, and it was to the clergy that belonged the interpretation of those books. The clergy itself was the only class in Russia for whom education was mandatory. A boyar did not even have to know how to read or write, but a priest could not be illiterate. To be sure, a secretary [crown official] or clerk also was expected to be literate, but their literacy served them merely as an external means for the attainment of a specific objective. A priest was required not only to be literate, he had also to be learned, and no one denied him the exclusive right to learning. Accusations did arise that the Russian clergy were insufficiently learned and that they did not conduct themselves in a manner suitable to teachers, but no one denied them the right to teach or suspected in general the purity of their teaching.

In the second half of the seventeenth century, because of a reform movement that had as one of its objectives the correction of church books, a fraction of the faithful declined to obey their pastors. The authority of the patriarch of Moscow,[64] the patriarchs of the Eastern church, and a church council did not hold with the people, to whom it appeared that they were being compelled to pray differently than had their ancestors. They declared that the bishops and priests were teaching erroneously and that it was wrong to listen to them. Some of them became thoroughly convinced of their position and refused openly to render further obedience to the clergy; others could not resolve upon such a drastic step and remained in doubt. Unable to decide where the truth lay, they became cool in their attitude toward the church. Thus the clergy acquired domestic enemies in the form of ecclesiastical rebels who stood up against the clergy's former importance and tried to demonstrate their inadequacy. These enemies fought for the past and armed themselves against the clergy because of various innovations.

There soon appeared enemies of a different sort. Among the Russian people a need came to be felt for the kind of learning that had gained prominence among foreigners. In order to acquire that knowledge, teachers were necessary. Such teachers could be only the heterodox foreigners themselves—fearsome guests! They appeared with all the authority of teachers and with complete awareness of their pre-eminence over their pupils, while the latter recognized their superiority. Thus, alongside the authority of the former teachers, a new authority arose. These were new teachers, who did not recognize the importance of their predecessors and did not omit any occasion to express this disdain in a scornful manner.

How were the prerogatives of the new teachers to be defined? How was it possible, having acknowledged the superiority of the new teachers generally, not to accept that superiority in any one specific matter? Where among the pupils was it possible to find the requisite independence and strength of mind, capacity for inquiry, and breadth of knowledge? It was in this kind of difficult situation that the clergy found themselves at the beginning of the new period of Russian history. From two sides enemies foregathered against the clergy's former importance and dignity. On one side were arrayed adherents of the past who refused to obey the church, following their own teachers and knowing no restraint in their attacks upon the clergy. On the other, enlightenment ceased to have an exclusively ecclesiastical stamp as, alongside the church teachers, there appeared foreign heterodox laymen who inevitably came into hostile collision with the church teachers once their influence began to be felt in their pupils. The pupils, finding themselves under a dual influence, became adherents of either one side or the other depending on the different conditions of their personalities, situations, and other accidental circumstances.

THE DECLINE OF NOVGOROD

The relations between the cities and the prince under which history began in the north of Russia have been examined. It has been shown how, with the first prince who desired to consolidate himself firmly in the north, there inevitably followed a collision between him and his retinue, as well as between the prince and the city, which regarded itself likewise an authority in the surrounding countryside. Andrei Bogoliubsky perished as a result of the new relations between prince and retinue. But his successors took advantage of their relations with the majority of the new northern cities and were successful in vanquishing the old city of Rostov, with its urban assembly, depriving the inhabitants of power.

Consequently, in the area of the upper Volga where emerged the Muscovite state, there appeared only the single authority of the prince. To the west, however, Novgorod the Great stood as representative of the ancient dyarchy consisting of the prince's authority and that of the city, with the city enjoying a clear predominance because of its stability, whereas the princes changed without ceasing. A struggle arose between the monarch of the north and Novgorod, representative of the ancient dyarchy. Novgorod maintained the view that it possessed sovereign authority. The grand prince demanded that he should be recognized as monarch, so that there should exist a single sovereign authority in Novgorod.

The grand prince came out of the struggle victorious, for Novgorod resembled the biblical statue with a head of gold and feet of clay. Several of the prominent, wealthy families had seized all power into their hands and filled the final period of Novgorod's history with their feuding. A split between their interests and those of the lower classes had taken place earlier, when complaints arose that the wealthy wanted to aggrandize themselves at the expense of the poor. However, the protests of the latter diminished as it became clear that their power was broken by the oligarchy. Over the urban assembly came to preside people who were salaried representatives of the oligarchy, and they vigorously pursued the settlement of matters to the benefit of their benefactors. It is not difficult to see how, in consequence of this situation, there developed a condition of extreme internal weakness. The people in whose hands reposed the power could not depend upon the lower classes, who grew increasingly indifferent to the old freedoms which no longer brought any benefit to them. It is for this reason that, in their struggle with the grand prince of Moscow, the rulers of Novgorod resorted continually to the expedient of paying for their freedom with money, a portentous recourse which better than anything else betrayed to the grand prince Novgorod's weakness and the ease with which it could be conquered.

The final hour struck. The bankruptcy of Novgorod's moral and political power was illustrated beyond possibility of doubt. The rupture between the interests of its social classes was beyond repair. Crowds of people streamed from Novgorod to Moscow—for justice! In Novgorod there was no justice, no impartial tribunal. The violence of the powerful trampled the rule of law underfoot. The old, sacred forms of life were of value only for a few. As for the rest, they carried no assurance as to their most urgent concerns. They did not satisfy the first requirements of social life. To the oppressed lower classes, the grand prince of Moscow appeared as the destroyer of the power of those people who made the weight of their power so oppressively felt. Finally, a split occurred with regard to the most important issue of all. In order to save themselves from Moscow, the oligarchy undertook to join with Lithuania. But there existed between Novgorod and Moscow an ecclesiastical connection. This gave rise to the question where the archbishop of Novgorod should be consecrated, in Moscow or Kiev. Kiev, which was under the domination of the grand prince of Lithuania, a Catholic, was the see of a metropolitan who was regarded in the north as a renegade inclining to Rome. Moscow, on the other hand, had preserved ancient Orthodoxy without defilement. Mention has been made of the kind of reaction that arose from efforts to carry out church reform. It should not come as a surprise, then, that there was engendered among a majority of the citizens of Novgorod strong opposition to any attempt at separation from the metropolitan of Moscow. In this regard it is well to keep in mind that ecclesiastical and political dependency were closely allied with one another.

SYMPTOMS OF ECONOMIC WEAKNESS

In the north, the existence of Novgorod as a rich commercial city next to an area of sluggish urban growth in the lowlands of the Suzdal territory presented a lamentable picture. It clearly indicated the kind of one-sided development that is always detrimental to the healthy growth of nations. In one corner stood a city which, because of an influx of wealth, became artificially puffed up into a state at the same time that it retained a backward and weak method of administration by way of an urban assembly. As a state it was beset by vast territories that were sprawling, noncontiguous, and mostly desolate, by the festering sore of an internal rift between different parts of the population, and by inadequate means for assuring its own defense in spite of its deceptive appearance of wealth and size.

Beyond the boundaries of Novgorod lay an immense region that was being settled under an unfavorable set of conditions. The cities there were but overgrown villages, with neither the opportunity nor the means to gain in importance. The country was poor and sparsely populated. Furthermore there was taking place internally a momentous process of gathering together the land through the concentration and unification of authority. To accomplish this, it was necessary first to accumulate the needed resources. The princes required money for the purchase of lands and holdings, and for the Horde. Finally, when a new state did become established through the gathering of land, it found itself in a most disadvantageous situation as regards its borders. The relations between Russia and Asia had not changed. Still only a short distance away was the steppe, with its predatory nomads, against whom security might be assured only by erecting a defense or paying a tribute. On the western border with Europe there likewise had to be waged continual warfare against implacable enemies.

Money was a necessity, and the burden of the financial system fell with all its weight upon the working population of the cities. This served, of course, as a hindrance to their enrichment, so that the people, unable to gain wealth, became ruined. Contributing even more to their ruin was the continuation of the primitive method for supporting the prince's officials.[65] This was carried on in a manner that once had been used for provisioning the retinue. The support of administrators serving the prince at the local level was put at the expense of the governed. The execution of crown business thus was converted into a function from which the service people were directly provided with salaries and provisions in kind. In a financial sense the situation of the cities in the Muscovite state reminds one strongly of the condition of the cities in the Roman Empire during the time of its decline. In both instances can be seen ruinous burdens and service falling upon the urban population, whom it was necessary to keep in place by force. The Muscovite princes strove, before anything else, to attach the urban people to their cities financially in order to be able to obtain a steady income from a definite number of taxable individuals.

The search for people to constitute a work force in a largely impoverished and empty country became a vitally important state activity. Should a person leave, he was to be caught and fixed to his location, where he was expected to work, produce, and pay. It is not difficult to see what the consequences of this would be.

The crown took out in pursuit of someone. It tried to fix him to one place in order to compel him to pay taxes and provide service, not only without compensation, but under heavy obligations. Such a man, prostrated by taxes and other duties, would become filled with a single overriding desire—to escape those imposts and responsibilities. The first means for doing so was flight and concealment. It was an easy matter to leave, for there was no lack of space in the Muscovite state itself. Even without that space the sparsely settled country was continually being depleted by the flight of people who increasingly spread out into northeastern Europe and later into northern Asia. Notwithstanding the impoverished economic condition of the early Russians and the opportunity thus afforded them to take everything they owned easily with them, the abandonment of their native soil and the adoption of a wandering life fraught with danger and uncertainty about the future were difficult things to do for many and impossible for everyone.

There existed other alternatives. For those who were literate there was the possibility of becoming a government official. This form of escape was very rewarding. A townsman was transformed from an individual responsible for supporting others at his own expense into one having the right to be supported by others. Understandably this kind of departure by becoming an official held a strong attraction. The crown however, looked unfavorably upon it and placed impediments in its path.

A third means of sloughing off the burdens of taxation was through pledging oneself to a state of dependence upon another.[66] The strongest personal connection existing in society through the entire period of early Russian history consisted of blood, or clan, relations. At the death of a father, his next eldest brother took his place as regards the younger brothers and nephews. He also stood as the representative of the clan before the government. No person was ever regarded as a solitary individual, but always in connection with his brothers and nephews. Despite distinctions arising from unequal distribution of property through inheritance and the proliferation of a clan, its unity nonetheless was preserved. The eldest brother or elder brothers (depending on the extent to which a clan had diverged into families) had the responsibility to watch over the conduct of its junior members, punish them for improprieties, and answer for them before the crown. A clan of this type, regardless of how many family branches it may have developed, constituted an integral unit with respect to state service. Any increase in the honor of one member of a family increased it for all members of the clan. Any dishonor suffered by one member reflected adversely upon the rest. Upon this arrangement of relations was based the famous system of precedence.[67]

Besides family relations, certain special social conditions led to the formation of other ties. The helplessness of solitary persons not belonging to large clans or families compelled them to join persons of other families and clans, forming with them a single entity through mutual agreement. Thus, together with an independent householder and his family—his children, brothers, and nephews—there lived other people who made up with them a single unit in the eyes of the crown. They bore different designations: boarders, lodgers, domestic workhands.[68] Finally, the heavy taxes that lay upon the various industries forced the working people to move away from a condition of direct subordination to the state, which required too great a sacrifice on their part, and to enter into a condition of dependence upon private individuals who could offer them protection. This is the process that was called pledging one-self to dependence.

Those who pledged themselves in this way could work without pay-ing taxes or serving, as the various categories of townspeople were re-quired to do, for they were considered dependent upon the person to whom they had pledged themselves. Obviously the interests of the pledged dependents must quickly have collided with the interests of the townspeople, who continued to remain directly subordinate to the crown. They collided likewise with the interests of the state itself. The dependents took away work from persons subject to taxation, who were unable to compete with a group enjoying freedom from the payment of taxes. The taxpayers were faced with ruin and, as such, were unable to carry out their crown obligations. Their complaints led, at the beginning of the reign of Tsar Alexis,[69] to the abolition of pledged dependence. All inhabitants of cities were obliged to enter into a direct relationship with the state. This deliverance of the townspeople weighed heavily upon the pledged dependents. They even considered the possibility of rebelling in order to regain for themselves the right to enter into a con-dition of personal dependence. More than anything else this demon-strates the low level of economic development in the Muscovite state.

MERCHANTS, MONEY, AND MOSCOW

The cities were generally poor, scattered across long distances from each other under extremely unsatisfactory conditions of communication. The wealthiest of them, those enjoying the greatest commercial activity through favorable circumstances, were notable for their sparse popula-tions. But there was one city which, because of its advantageous situa-tion and especially its political importance as capital of the tsar auto-crat, inevitably had to rise. This was Moscow.

The strong tendency toward centralization constantly attracted to Moscow from all parts of Russia crowds of people who had to spend large amounts of money in the capital. For to wend one's way through the red tape of the Muscovite bureaucracy cost a pretty sum. Just as it was the center of civil government, so Moscow was also the center of ecclesiastical administration. The nobility took up permanent residence in Moscow, near the grand prince. It is easy to appreciate that both commercial and industrial activity here could not but be significant and that there had to develop a wealthy merchant class. It is possible to obtain information about the wealth and importance of the Muscovite merchants even before the time of Ivan III. It was a merchant, Nekomat Surozhanin, who acted in concert with the noted Veliaminov, son of the last commander of the Moscow city militia.[70] The very abolition of the post of city militia commander indicates that the grand prince did not consider it convenient to appoint in Moscow a permanent military governor, who might become popular and pose a serious threat to him. Information also exists about Muscovite merchants who engaged in sedition against the grand prince and later had to leave Moscow.

These, however, were isolated instances. They took place during a period of transition, when the Muscovite principality was just in the process of formation and the new order had not yet been established firmly. It was a time when, besides the grand prince of Moscow, there were still other grand princes to whom could go those boyars and merchants who found themselves dissatisfied. When the sovereign authority became firmly planted in Moscow, episodes of this kind are no longer to be found.

In early Russian history the inhabitants of cities were sometimes in a position to exercise decisive political leverage. For, during the period of civil wars, they took part with their own distinct military regiments in battles between princes. The outcome of those engagements frequently depended on the participation of the townspeople. Even as late as the beginning of Ivan III's reign regiments from Moscow left for war under a special commander. But later, the creation of a large military force composed of military tenants allowed the state to dispense with the city regiments. The townspeople ceased to form a part of any military units and were transformed into a totally unarmed class. Thus they were recast completely into lesser men, becoming inconsequential persons as regards the "real men" or magnates, that is, those who bore arms. For according to the notions of those days, it was only the armed man, only the warrior, who was an individual with full rights.

THE CITIES AT A NEW STAGE OF IMPORTANCE

The reign of the first tsar, Ivan IV, witnessed an increase in the importance of the townspeople, especially those of Moscow. Seeing in the nobility persons with old claims extending to the time of the princely retinue and suspecting them of strong disaffection toward himself and his family, Ivan the Terrible, in accordance with a predictable line of behavior, began to seek another source of strength upon which he might rely. Ceremoniously from the tribune in Red Square[71] he made known publicly the disorders in the boyars' administration of the government during his minority. Then, leaving Moscow after having disclosed the treachery of the boyars and the indulgence shown them by the clergy, he declared that he did not harbor any resentment toward the townspeople of Moscow. Finally, he summoned the latter to a council to consider vital matters pertaining to the state. Ivan wished to grant in all of Russia self-government to urban and village councils, to remove appointed officials sent by the central government, and to replace them with judges elected locally.

The most telling evidence for the backwardness of those local councils was the fact that Ivan the Terrible's measures failed to take root. Many councils did not accept from the crown its proffered gift of self-government. Only in those places where development was stronger and the ground made ready did Ivan's reign leave a mark. Such a mark was left on the townspeople of Moscow. The extent to which their importance had grown is evident from their participation in the maneuvering that took place by various factions during the reign of Ivan's successor. Such activity was not to be seen either during Ivan's minority or the reigns of his father or grandfather. When a conflict erupted between the Shuisky family[72] and Boris Godunov,[73] the Muscovite merchants took the side of the former. They clearly understood that the situation allowed no possibility of reconciliation between the rivals. When Shuisky made an announcement to them that an understanding had been reached, they replied: "You have made peace at the price of our heads." Indeed, their heads were brought to the executioner's block. Godunov, having liquidated the best people among them, inspired fear in the rest. He destroyed in its most incipient form the importance of the townspeople of Moscow, which had come about as a result of Ivan's policies concerning them.

The Time of Troubles aroused the townspeople to independent action, and the reign of Michael[74] was notable for its national assemblies,[75] in which representatives of the urban population played a part. But if the cities even before the Time of Troubles had been insignificant and impoverished, then afterwards, under Michael, they were in a dreadful state of devastation. It became urgent to recover materially so as to be able to lend support to the state and assist the new sovereign against the Poles and cossacks. Taxation was the question of principal importance, for the taxpaying population had been shattered and uprooted. Their households were empty and no one remained who could pay. It was necessary to return the fugitives to their former places of residence and compel them to become tax-producing. But there also existed people who, though they worked, did not pay taxes: the service people, clergy, and pledged dependents. These also had to be made to produce revenues. Domestic trade was being ruined by foreign merchants, who acted in collusion with each other. The indigent Russian merchants, operating individually, could not compare to them. Finally, the military governors (voevodas)[76] and administrative officials also contributed to the devastation. Here, then, were the three fundamental questions that engrossed the Russian townspeople of the seventeenth century after the Time of Troubles. The replacement of military governors with locally elected officials did not help, since the latter also despoiled the townsmen just as the governors had done.

The complaints that accumulated in Michael's reign brought about an explosion in Moscow and other cities at the start of Alexis' reign. The crown, accordingly, took certain steps to calm the urban disturbances. It enacted the Law Code of 1649, abolished the condition of pledged dependence, and passed a measure against English merchants. There is a most curious feature about the Code of 1649. It was compiled with the assent of elected delegates who represented all classes of people, it was enacted under their signatures, it was promulgated under pressure of fear caused by urban riots, and it had for its purpose the pacification of the townspeople, making obvious concessions to their demands. Yet, this Code was demonstrably hostile to self-government by local councils. Thus it completely entrusted the administration of justice to military governors and administrative officials. According to the Code, there were no longer to sit in a court of justice the locally elected judges, court assistants, or court recorders.

Insurrections flared up in Pskov and Novgorod as isolated incidents and were extinguished because of their isolation. In those uprisings, as well as in the second uprising in Moscow,[77] there can be observed a divergence in the interests of the urban masses and the important commercial people, against whom the masses directed their resentment. It can be easily understood how this struggle between the higher and lower urban classes weakened the urban population, whose strength even without such an internal conflict was far from great. As will be seen, this ulcer was bequeathed by the seventeenth century to the eighteenth.

LAND, MEN, AND WORK

Turning now from city to village, it will be found that Russia, from the very beginnings of the Muscovite state, was primarily an agricultural

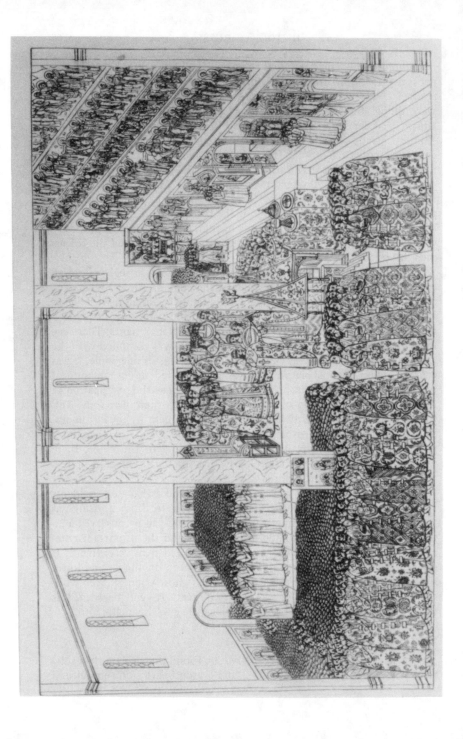

country. Even its cities bore the character of villages. The townspeople engaged in agriculture and in this way the Muscovite cities of the seventeenth century were reminiscent of ancient Russian cities, about which information is given in the account of Olga's revenge.[78] But from the prevalence of agricultural pursuits, one ought not conclude that the people attached any particular significance to them or that special protection was afforded agriculture and the persons involved in it. To the contrary, an agricultural state implies backwardness and a primitive social structure. This takes the form of relations between a part of the population which bears arms and another part, without arms, which is obliged to maintain the former and labor directly for it. This pattern could be altered were cities to develop, with their industry and trade. This would provide the country as a whole with movable wealth, lead to widespread extension of urban activity, promote enlightenment, and provide means for establishing a more suitable set of relations between the different parts of the population. As for the Muscovite state, the mass of the military forces, except for members of the old retinue and princely families, was created by the grand princes and supported by an elementary form of maintenance, namely, landed holdings from which the service people derived their livelihood so long as they continued to serve. To supplement these landed holdings the servitors also drew subsistence from the cities and rural districts, where they functioned as administrators. Thus in early Russia there existed the primitive form of relations between armed and unarmed segments of the population, between magnates and muzhiks, with the magnates being directly supported at the expense of the latter.

There can be little doubt but that primary consideration was given to the question of maintaining the military establishment. It constituted the foundation of the internal strength of the country and was essential to defense and expansion under conditions of interminable warfare in the east and west. Together with that problem, the question of land possession and use also rose to a position of paramount consideration. In order to have the capacity to preserve and augment its military force, the crown must have at its disposal as great a quantity of land as possible. The land had to lie not far from the capital or from those frontiers to the south and west that particularly were threatened by enemies. The sizeable lands which the state might have utilized in the north and east could not serve this purpose. They were too far away to be military tenures, and they lacked sufficient population. Therefore, notwithstanding the

CORONATION OF TSAR MICHAEL IN 1613

apparent enormity of the area under the control of the crown, the government met with difficulty in establishing military tenures.

Out of this emerged an inevitable collision with the material interests of the church, which owned vast stretches of land in the central region and continually added to them through purchase and donation for the commemoration of souls. In this respect, land was almost the only form in which donations for any purpose were made to the church. This was necessitated by the scarcity of money in an undeveloped country. The crown paid the salary of its servitors in land, and the private person made donations in land to a monastery for the eternal remembrance of his parents' souls. It becomes obvious from this why the question whether monasteries ought to own populated lands received such conspicuous attention in the fifteenth and sixteenth centuries, and why it became associated with every ecclesiastical and political problem. In view of the prevailing notions of those days, it would be too much to expect that this question could have been definitively resolved. The imperative requirements of the state could lead, and indeed did lead, only to compromises, to moderate measures, to a limitation only on the further expansion of ecclesiastical landownership.

The matter could not end there. The conduct of exhausting wars waged by the Muscovite state in the reign of Ivan the Terrible sapped the resources of the service people. Complaints arose about the inadequacy of maintenance obtained from the military tenures under conditions of heavy and prolonged service that required lengthy absences of military tenants from home. The source of this inadequacy was attributed to the small number of workhands. Moreover, the majority of those who constituted the army, the small military servitors, found themselves at odds with those among the wealthy landowners who, by the promise of substantial immunities, attracted peasants to their estates from the tracts of the small landholders, the military tenants. The latter, unable to work their own lands, could not carry out the responsibilities of military service, which had now become of prolonged duration. If maintaining the well-being of the mass of the army always had been a matter of first importance, it became essential to attend to the complaints of the military servitors at the time of Ivan the Terrible's death, when a fearful war was threatening to break out with a most dangerous enemy, the like of which the Muscovite state theretofore had not encountered and whose strength had but recently been tested.[79]

At first an attempt was made to reduce the movement of peasants by equalizing all lands with respect to immunities and eliminating immunities on church lands. But this measure did not last long. It was followed

by a measure prohibiting the movement of peasants from one landholder
to another. This law, it would appear, could not be strictly enforced.
Throughout the entire seventeenth century there were heard constant
complaints from the small landholders against their wealthy neighbors,
that the latter were enticing and concealing their fugitive peasants. The
hunt for people, for manpower, was carried on in massive proportions
throughout the whole of Muscovy. It was a hunt that was conducted for
townspeople who fled wherever they could from the burden of taxation,
who took themselves into hiding, who pledged themselves in dependence
upon others, and who broke their way into the ranks of minor government officials. It was also a hunt for peasants who one by one took leave
of heavy taxes and fled in droves beyond the Ural mountains. The military tenants chased after them as they moved away to other landholders,
fled to Little Russia, or sought refuge among the cossacks.

THE COSSACKS

In the seventeenth century, just as in the tenth, there came to be distinguished in society persons who went to roam in the fields and plains.
The bogatyrs of old came to be known now as cossacks. The way of life
and exploits of the early bogatyrs were comparable to those of the cossacks. The popular imagination correctly identified these two phenomena, which were distinguishable in name only. Even here the songs of the
people erased any difference, referring for instance to the bogatyr Ilia
Muromets as an "old cossack."[80]

During early periods of political formation the process of singling out
such people and creating out of them military fraternities, or retinues
with elected leaders, leads usually to the establishment of a state, the
commencement of historical life, and the progress of a nation. Out of
such individuals there develops an elite group of armed persons, which
in one way or another determines its relations with the remaining unarmed mass of people. But if a state already has been formed and, because
of special circumstances usually of a local character, the process still
persists of singling out persons of this type and creating military societies out of them alongside the state, this concomitant development
obviously must lead to important consequences. First of all, the country
and the nation are enfeebled because of the separation and exodus of
these people. Russia, spread out as it was over an enormous area, was
especially weakened in this respect since it had been lacking in population even without their departure. On the other hand, the separation of
restless energies facilitated the unimpeded progress of the government
toward centralization. But if governmental activity was made easier,

internally by the departure of the bogatyrs to roam the steppe, the formation by them of parallel military fraternities could not fail to be of concern to the crown.

Having gone to the steppe for freedom, the cossacks were in a position to owe only nominal allegiance to the crown and carry out government orders only when it was advantageous to them. At the first inkling of any divergence between their interests and those of the state, the cossacks made it abundantly apparent that they were free men. They could not live peacefully. They had to exercise their strength, with which they were heavily laden. They had to procure for themselves the means of subsistence, "to pick up a coat or two," as they used to call their pillaging expeditions. The older cossacks generally preferred to maintain a connection with the crown and fulfill government requirements. But the cossack population was subject to a steady influx of new young people who wanted to roam far and wide and "pick up a coat or two" for themselves. The caution of the old cossacks, the elders, did not appeal to them. And so, on occasion, quite independently of the older cossacks, there would appear among the audacious "seekers of coats" their own new leader, noted for his daring *(dux ex virtute)*, who would lead his band either against strangers or his own people.

Obviously the formation of such communities on the borders of a state could not but lead to constant warfare. If a state happened to be weak, the onslaught of roaming bands against it would be successful. The circumstances under which ended the destiny of the Roman Empire in consequence of pressure brought to bear against it by Germanic bands are well known. They entered the provinces of the empire and formed there the highest class, that is, the military class. In the seventeenth century in Eastern Europe a similar phenomenon took place. Because of the weakness of the Polish government and in reaction to the persecution of the Russian faith, the cossacks were able after a long struggle to gain the upper hand, destroy or eject the previous landholders in the Ukraine, and set their own chieftains up as a new upper class in the country. As for the other country in the eastern plain, the Russian or Muscovite state, though the conflict was fierce and desperate, the struggle ended in quite a different fashion for the cossacks. In the sixteenth century the Russian tsar captured Kazan and Astrakhan. The entire Volga was then in Russian hands. Furthermore the empty area along the Volga's western tributaries and their interwoven links with the tributaries of the Don thus were secured. But in place of the Tatars, the cossacks very soon appeared there. Ivan the Terrible took strong measures against those bogatyrs. As was usually the case whenever the cossacks were prevented from roaming along their accustomed paths, they hurled themselves in some other direction toward some distant enterprise. So it was here. Having been driven from the Volga the cossack bands flung themselves toward the Kama, and from there carved their way beyond the Ural mountains where they conquered the capital of Khan Kuchum, the so-called khanate of Siberia.[81]

Under the son of Ivan the Terrible the cossacks again grew stronger along the Don, and their relations with the crown held no promise of peace in the direction of the steppe. In the reign of Boris Godunov the state once more took preparatory steps for decisive action against the cossacks. But there appeared on the scene the Impostor.[82] With that began the Time of Troubles and the creation of a cossack tsardom. The struggle soon assumed its true character as a conflict between the landed people of Muscovy and the cossacks, who were "fiercer than the Lithuanians or the Germans" and sought to assure their supremacy by elevating to the throne of Moscow their own leader as tsar.

The question at issue was clear. The boyars and all Muscovites of high rank swore allegiance to the son of the Polish king lest they become subject to their former cossack slaves upon the triumph of the "little tsar" from Kaluga.[83] The arousal of religious sentiments which followed in the wake of schemes conceived by the king of Poland, Sigismund, provided a symbol and rallying point for the inhabitants of Muscovy. It gave them the opportunity to overcome their lack of coordination so that they could accomplish a common task, and it gave them a unity that was not merely national or political, but religious—the common baptismal font in which all had been christened into the Orthodox faith. This religious enthusiasm served for the most part as a focal point against the cossacks. The liberation of the country from the Poles became simultaneously a liberation from the cossacks. Thus the cossacks proved unable to exploit a set of favorable circumstances, and it was the crown that emerged victorious.

Still, the cossacks did not refuse to do battle. Closed off from the mouths of the Don by the Turks, they awaited a bold and promising leader to slash their way elsewhere. And, indeed, a charismatic bogatyr did appear. This was Stenka Razin.[84] His throngs flung themselves in the direction of the Volga and the Yaik, and to the Caspian Sea, where they pillaged the Persian shores. But Persia was stronger than the Siberian capital of Khan Kuchum, and Razin was unable to offer a captured Persia to Tsar Alexis as the cossack Ermak[85] had offered Siberia to Ivan the Terrible. Forced to return from the Caspian and without hope that the Muscovite state would allow them free passage to the mouth of the

Volga, Razin's hordes turned themselves against the crown, inciting the lower classes of the population against the authorities, as had been done in the Time of Troubles. The crown however, despite its exhaustion, was stronger than the cossacks, and Razin perished on the executioner's block in Moscow. Nevertheless, Razin's rebellion was not to be the last act in the conflict between crown and cossacks. In a later period of Russian history there would appear the figures of Bulavin and Pugachev.[86]

II

MUSCOVY

THE GEOGRAPHY OF EASTERN EUROPE

In general terms such was the historical development of early Russia. It is time now to consider its way of life at closer range, especially during the period when the first signs of reforming activity made an appearance.

References are often made to Western and Eastern Europe. These terms have given rise to much study and considerable interpretation concerning the differences between them and the resultant consequences of those differences. But if a traveler should journey from Western to Eastern Europe, or vice versa, look at their differences from a fresh point of view, and give himself an accounting based on those immediate impressions, he would first of all conclude that Europe consists of two distinct parts. The western part is the Europe of rock or stone; the eastern part is the Europe of wood or forest.

Among early Russians the name for mountains was "rocks." It was such rocks that broke up Western Europe into numerous states and created the boundaries of many nations. It was out of stone that western nobles built their nests, from which they lorded over their peasants. It was stone that provided them with independence. But it was not long before the peasants also built fortifications made out of stone for themselves, achieving freedom and independence. Everything was solid and well-defined, thanks to stone. Because of stone, man-made mountains arose in the form of enormous, long-lasting buildings.

In the eastern plain there is no stone. Everything is level, with no diversification of people. There came into being, consequently, a state unprecedented in size. Nowhere was there a place for the magnates to construct stone nests for themselves. They did not live apart and independent, but as members of a prince's retinue, and they moved about eternally through the wide vastness of the land. The cities had no firm relations with them. In the absence of diversity and sharply delineated local boundaries there did not develop any marked local differences among the people, such as would have made it difficult for them to emigrate, leaving behind their native soil. There were no permanent dwellings in which entire generations had lived and from which it would have been difficult to part. The cities were masses of wooden huts, which but a single spark readily transformed into a pile of ashes. Nor was this any great tragedy. There was so little movable property that it was a simple matter to cart it off. Moreover, because building materials were cheap, it cost nothing to construct a new house. It was with the greatest of ease, then, that the Russian of old would leave his house and his native city or village. He would pack up and part company with the Tatar, the Lithuanian, heavy taxes, a mean military governor or corrupt government clerk. To wander alone was not a matter of life and death, for everywhere one would find the same thing. Wherever one went there was the familiar flavor of Russia. From this arose among the people the custom of moving away. From this also stemmed the tendency of the government to catch them, put them in place, and fix them there.

Together with this general difference which distinguishes the Western Europe of stone from the Eastern Europe of wood, there is also to be found in the eastern plain a difference of forms which is imbued with historical importance. Two forms preponderate there, the forest and the field—the latter being the steppe. Out of the juxtaposition of these two forms, existing next to each other, there derived a historical opposition marked by a struggle between the people of the two parts. The steppe was from the beginning the home of marauding nomadic peoples. It was against them that Russia, having come into existence along the edge of the steppe, waged her first battles. Despite the valor of the princes and their retinues, that conflict ended with the triumph of the steppe people, who persistently preyed on the Russian land under the Polovetsians and finally devastated it under the Tatars.

Only at a distance from the steppe could stabilization take place. A state capable of fighting off the steppe people could only be developed and secured in the inaccessible forests of the north, where nomadic predators found it hard to penetrate. It was precisely in that region that the Muscovite state was formed. Through expansion, however, it soon came into contact with the steppe where there was created the borderland region of the steppe, as it was known in those days. This was an area which thereafter had to cope continually with the proximity of the steppe. It was now only the borderland region. Yet, during the early period of Russian history the capital city of the grand princes [Kiev], and with it the main scene of action, had been located in the very heart of that area.

The Muscovite state conducted constant warfare against the people of the steppe. With the weakening of the nomadic hordes, no end to the struggle still appeared in sight. For in the steppe there arose a singular kind of people, the cossacks. The conflict that pitted the landholders and the crown against the cossacks was, as regards natural geographic features, a struggle between field and forest. This was especially evident during the Time of Troubles and in subsequent cossack movements, when Russia was divided in the spirit and character of her people into a northern part, composed of landholders, and a southern part along the edges of the steppe, consisting of cossacks. The steppe facilitated the cossacks' style of life, with its primitive form of wandering and roving. The forest on the contrary, tended more to restrict, shut in, and bring a person to rest, making of him a settled landholder in contrast to the freely roaming cossack. From this came the quieter, steadier, and hence more effective activity of the northern Russian. From it also, among other reasons, came the precarious condition of the southern Russian.

MOSCOW AND THE KREMLIN

For the most part, then, the Muscovite state was a country of forests. To travelers the whole land looked like a vast forest, cleared away here and there near dwellings and meadows. Some travelers could not restrain their delight at the sight Muscovy afforded them in springtime, when it appeared like an enormous, bright-green garden, filled with an innumerable multitude of songbirds, in contrast to the forests of the American New World, where the birds create by their movement a considerable rustling and noise, but are little given to song. Yet, no matter how grand was the springtime view of sylvan Muscovy, this predominance of the forest had its drawbacks. It contributed to the severity of the climate, the dampness, and the surfeit of water and swamp, so detrimental to summer travel and necessitating arduous toil to pave the roads with logs. Near the capital travelers during summer nights had to light bonfires to protect themselves from the swarms of mosquitoes and insects. Besides this unpleasantness there lurked danger from wild animals living in the forest and even more from people who were able readily to conceal in the woods their vicious schemes.

In the midst of the vast wilderness, where it appeared that human beings only recently had begun to bend nature to their will and where only rarely were encountered small villages, hamlets, and large fortified villages or towns, the Western traveler awaited with impatience the sight of that famed city which lent its name to the entire country and in which resided its absolute master. Suddenly, Moscow loomed before him. From a distance it created a powerful and attractive impression. On a measureless expanse of land stood an enormous black mass of

houses. But above them ascended countless numbers of church domes
and bell towers. Highest of all rose the Kremlin, residence of the grand
prince, with its walls of white stone enclosing churches of white stone
with golden domes. In their center stood a tall white edifice with a
golden cupola, the belfry of Ivan the Great, a gigantic structure in comparison to the modest height of the other buildings.[1] The sheer whiteness of the Kremlin wall and of the churches, in sharp contrast to the
mass of black wooden houses, and the existence of so many stone buildings in comparison with other cities, gave rise to the famous designation
by which the city remains known even to this day, White-Stoned Moscow.

Especially in the summer, Moscow from a distance excited the viewer
with its magnificence and beauty. Then the splendid variety of the
churches was complemented by the verdure of numerous gardens. But
this impression changed once the traveler entered the sprawling city.
There he was struck by the wretchedness of the dwellings, with their
isinglass windows, the shabbiness and small size of those same churches
which from a distance had created such a pleasant impression, the large
vacant areas, and the filth of the dirty streets, even though paved here
and there with hewn logs. Glowing from a distance with the splendor of
Jerusalem, Moscow at a closer distance looked more like scrubby Bethlehem. Such was the observation of one traveler.

THE GREAT SOVEREIGN

By its very appearance Moscow was thoroughly representative of the
country whose capital it was. Into the unlimited open spaces it stretched
out, along its rivers and over hills and meadows, with the simplicity and
unpretentiousness of a wooden dwelling surrounded by a large yard and
garden. Moscow continued to retain this village character as the capital
city of a primitive, agricultural state. Earlier the city had been even
larger in size and there had lived a greater number of people in it. But
Moscow had undergone the same painful history that affected the rest
of the country and left behind deep traces. Moscow rose conspicuously
over all other cities in the period of the final gathering together of the
country and the concentration of power in the hands of the great sovereign.[2] From all directions streamed new residents, either willingly, attracted by the advantages of the capital, or unwillingly, having been
evicted from Novgorod and Pskov at the command of the grand prince.
Moscow surged upwards, or perhaps it is better to say grew outwards,
and filled with people particularly during the reigns of Ivan III and his
son Vasily III.

Moscow became the chief city of Russia at a time when the Russian people in their historical development began to turn away from the East to the West, from the steppe to the sea. This turning point, although only just begun and slow in evolving, nevertheless made its appearance in Moscow as the reflection of the light which had started to burn brightly in Western Europe during the Renaissance. In Moscow there rose beautiful and relatively large and lasting buildings—a palace, churches, and towers—constructed by Western architects. This construction activity in Moscow in the fifteenth and sixteenth centuries was important for Russian history in that, by elevating the capital and making it an object of reverential awe for the Russian people, it enhanced the importance of the grand prince of Moscow and contributed to his becoming the great sovereign, great lord, and autocrat by setting him apart in a most visible manner, through the magnificence of his surroundings, from the mass of princes and boyars, in comparison with whom he had not enjoyed much distinction owing to the simplicity of his former style of life. Thus the Italian artists who decorated Moscow were carrying out the same task as the half-Greek and half-Latin Sophia Paleologue, educated in Italy in the milieu that also produced Macchiavelli, Catherine de Médicis, and Queen Bona Sforza, wife of Sigismund I of Poland.

If Moscow became the most important city of Russia when that country began to turn from East to West, it did so at a time when Russia had to carry on heavy warfare in two directions in defense of itself from both East and West, from Islam and Latinism. The barbaric world of the steppe weakened. This permitted Russia to commence an offensive movement, though sometimes the steppe sent forth large robber bands that carried on pillaging expeditions to Russia's very capital. On the other side, in the west, Russia collided with Poland and locked with it in ferocious struggle.

It cost Moscow much to defend Russia from Islam and Latinism. Under Ivan the Terrible, grandson of Ivan III, two Tatar hordes were defeated before Moscow. The entire Moslem world grew worried about this strong military showing of the Christians. Thereupon the khan of the last horde located on European soil, the Crimean Tatar Devlet-Girei, forced his way as far as Moscow and consigned it to the flames.[3] Moscow had not time to recover from this catastrophe when a great agitation stirred the cossacks, marking the start of the Time of Troubles. The Poles came, sensing disaster for Russia. The boyars, trapped between two fires and fearing the cossacks with their fraudulent cossack tsar, admitted the Poles into Moscow. Before the Russians could drive these visitors out of the Kremlin, Moscow again was burned and sacked, and its population dispersed. Through the rest of the century after this misfortune Moscow recovered with difficulty, as did the rest of the country, beset by new struggles and tensions. The capital city in the seventeenth century did not attain the size or contain the number of people it had in the sixteenth. Yet, the time was already fast approaching when Russia must finally make its way to the sea, and the marshy shores at the mouth of the Neva would become the site for the capital of an empire.[4]

Like other old Russian cities, the largest of them, the capital, was cast in the mold of early Russian history when religious interests held sway not only predominantly, but one might say, exclusively. Western Europe, having passed through the period when religious interests prevailed during the so-called Middle Ages, left behind a memorial of that experience in the form of enormous churches, intricately embellished in stonework. In Western Europe the necessary material, stone, was ready to hand. There, before the eyes of the people, stood the necessary models, the mountains, whose natural altars lifted their peaks to heaven. Most important, there could be harnessed the force capable of erecting such huge monuments, even though it did not always bring them to completion. This was the social force centered on large and populated cities whose inhabitants, accustomed to working at common tasks, were conscious of constituting a single entity. It was such cities that constructed splendid religious monuments for the benefit and beautification of the entire community. It is obvious that there could not have been many such monuments, and all of them bore the sign of concerted social activity.

As for the eastern plain, in what kind of monuments could the exclusive dominance of religious interests find expression? In the eastern plain there was no hard material—stone. There were no mountains to stimulate human creativity in competition with nature. There was no unification of common effort. It has been mentioned that conditions in the eastern plain tended to support a process of separation and dispersion throughout the limitless expanse of territory. There existed no wealthy or populous cities, and social life unfolded for the most part in an isolated and secluded environment. It should not come as a surprise, then, to see the poor man bringing to church his icon, lighting a candle and praying before it, while the rich man constructs his own church near his home. It is obvious that churches constructed by individuals could not possibly be noted for their massive proportions and lofty splendor. But there were many of them. Their number has been calculated at approximately two thousand, or roughly one church for every five houses.

The churches, then, were usually small. But in various places there were to be found some of quite substantial size, surrounded by other smaller ones, and fortified by walls. These were the monasteries, of which there were many in Moscow. They stood principally along the edge of the city or marked the boundaries of the city's districts. They served to indicate the history of the city's growth, for monasteries in the center of the city had once stood on its outskirts. There were several suburban monasteries which were surrounded by strong stone walls and tall towers, surrounding Moscow like a line of fortifications.

Lay landholders in Russia, even the wealthiest, never possessed fortified castles. It was pointed out earlier that the Russian nobility never lost the character of a retinue, and their dwellings clung near to the residence of the sovereign. Not far removed from the lay landholders, the secular nobility, who were relatively poor and weak in comparison with the wealth and might of the great sovereign, there existed landholders of another sort—the rich, powerful, and independent monasteries. Mention has been made of the long lived tradition of the bogatyr in Russia and how, with the strengthening of the crown that tradition continued to exist among the cossacks. The people as a whole, however, endowed with the rich instincts of life, tended invariably to seek a balance of forces. Next to the bogatyrs, heavily laden with physical strength, there existed energetic bogatyrs of a different kind. These were the spiritual bogatyrs, who represented the moral strength of the people. They were leaders of spiritual retinues, founders of monastic brotherhoods and monasteries.

Far away in the backwoods, but usually in a commanding and beautiful place, they built their monasteries. The spiritual resources harbored there invariably attracted material resources within a short time. The holy founder celebrated religious services in old, dyed vestments. His successors vested themselves in gold. No amount of reasoning or reckoning could halt the tendency to make the most expensive material donations for adorning that which was spiritually so precious and holy. Monasteries became wealthy landowners, whose property was never alienated or divided. Only one affluent type of landowner, the monasteries, lived a separate and independent life. Only they were capable with their own means of constructing castles and fortifications, enclosing them with firm stone walls, raising towers, mounting artillery, and acquiring the ability to defend themselves against an enemy. Thus, during these centuries of predominantly unspecialized forms of labor, the spiritual forces of the country invariably were combined with the material forces. In the Time of Troubles it was Holy Trinity monastery that administered the strongest repulse to a hostile army. On that occasion the country's spiritual and material forces did indeed combine.[5]

The inseparability of the moral and material forces in early Russia was expressed in the old Kremlin in Moscow. If the array of suburban monasteries appeared as a line of fortifications near the city, the Kremlin, castle of the tsar and residence of the great sovereign, resembled a huge monastery. It was filled with large, beautiful churches. In their midst, like the quarters of an abbot in a monastery, stood the tsar's palace, an assorted collection of buildings varying widely in size, scattered about without symmetry, and constructed only in conformity to the standard of convenience. If churches constituted the only form of social monument and if every person of means possessed a strong desire to leave behind such a monument, it is understandable that the individual with the most resources in the country, the great sovereign himself, must have been distinguished by his zeal for the construction and adornment of churches. In this sense he maintained the role of an all-Russian churchwarden.

POMP AND CIRCUMSTANCE

One can easily appreciate why so many churches should have been located near the tsar's residence. Nor is it surprising that the tsar was often to be found inside those churches, and that magnificent royal processions wound their way to monasteries near and far.

At church services the tsar was in attendance with his entire court. On the first of September, the feast day of St. Simeon, the church and the entire country observed the traditional start of the Russian new year. The crowds streamed into the Kremlin from early morning. There, in the open square between the cathedrals of the Annunciation and the Archangel, a prayer service was held in the tsar's presence. Then the bishops, high court dignitaries, crown officials, and foremost merchants offered their greetings to the great sovereign. One of the boyars delivered a speech, whereupon the tsar left to attend the divine liturgy.

During winter, just before Christmas, there was celebrated in Moscow on 21 December an important feast day in commemoration of St. Peter the Miracle-Worker, the first metropolitan who took up residence in Moscow and sanctified its greatness. This feast day was observed personally by Peter's successor, the patriarch of Moscow. As early as the nineteenth of the month the patriarch appeared at the palace to invite the great sovereign and his eldest son to the celebration and to dine. Also invited were all the nobility. After the divine liturgy in the cathedral of the Dormition, the tsar went to the patriarch's for the repast. Custom required that the host administer a blessing to the guest and bestow rich gifts upon him. These usually consisted of goblets, brocades of gold and silver, velvets, satins, silks, and sable furs.

On the morning of the day preceding Christmas, four hours before sunrise, the sovereign departed for the Prison Yard and the English Court. He distributed alms with his own hands to the convicts in the Prison Yard, and to the Polish, German, and Ukrainian captives in the English Court. Along the way, the sovereign provided alms to wounded soldiers and beggars. At the same time, the tsar's alms were dispensed also in Red Square and at the tribune. Altogether, more than a thousand rubles would be given away. Sometimes the sovereign also went to an invalid and presented him with a gift.

On Christmas Eve a loud singing resounded in front of the palace. The protopopes, priests, and deacons from all the cathedrals stood praising the name of Christ. After the cathedral clergy, the choirs made their appearance. Five companies of the sovereign's choristers and seven patriarchal companies alternated in their singing. When they finished, the sovereign ordered refreshments to be ladled out to them.

On Christmas Day itself, after the divine liturgy, the sovereign's entire table was delivered from the palace to the patriarch. Two prepared dishes, with goblets, were sent as gifts to each of the boyars, lords-in-waiting, service gentry of the council, and chancellors of the council, as well as as bishops, archimandrites, and the tsar's confessor.

On January 6 was celebrated at the Moscow river the feast of the Theophany, commemorating the baptism of Christ in the Jordan. Along the riverbank and in the Kremlin were formed twelve regiments of armed musketeers[6] in dress uniform. The great sovereign appeared in full robes of state, assisted by table attendants and privy councillors. After the sovereign followed the lord of the bedchamber, escorting the regalia being borne by the crown agents, some of whom also carried a towel, chair, and pedestal. Then came a mass of courtiers, leading military commanders, and foremost merchants. The more important courtiers were dressed in furs, and the rest, in cloth of gold. The military officers wore long tunics and uniforms, while the merchants were attired in cloth of gold

Just before the Great Fast preceding Easter the tsaritsa led her small sons to the cathedrals and monasteries of the Kremlin, accompanied by relatives, governesses, the highest boyarinas, and treasurers. All this time, however, the Kremlin was closed, and no one was admitted inside.

On the last Sunday before the Great Fast, known as Forgiveness Sunday, the tsar proceeded with the boyars and councillors directly from the cathedral of the Dormition to the patriarch, who already had assembled all the ecclesiastical dignitaries, the bishops and archimandrites. With the sovereign there arrived from the palace the stewards and cupbearers, with all manner of delicious refreshments. There followed a mutual exchange of hospitality. The patriarch brought before the sovereign various foreign wines and many different kinds of honey. He then had goblets served to the boyars and members of the boyar council. The sovereign, in his turn, ordered that goblets be served to the ecclesiastical dignitaries. Upon his return to the palace the sovereign received the heads of the various chancelleries and heard their reports about the prisoners in their custody. They described those who had been incarcerated for many years and others who had been imprisoned for only minor offenses. These the sovereign ordered to be released. At the same time, in the palace, the tsaritsa received her father, brothers, relatives on both sides of the family, governesses, principal boyarinas, treasurers of the household, ladies of the bedchamber, and craftswomen.

With the arrival of the Great Fast, there came to Moscow guests of a special kind. From all the monasteries thronged monks, bringing to the tsar and the patriarch bread, cabbage, and kvass.[7]

On Palm Sunday the tsar took part in a religious ceremony of a kind that Russia in a later period would not have the opportunity to witness. From the cathedral of the Dormition to the Savior Gate of the Kremlin moved a solemn procession. Preceded by the holy icons and clergy came the table attendants, crown agents, service gentry, and chancellors in cloth of gold, followed by the sovereign himself, the boyars, lords-in-waiting, councillors, and foremost merchants. On both sides of the street, near the tsar, advanced the colonels [of Western-style military units] and regimental commanders of musketeers. After observing the holy day (in one of the satellite sanctuaries of the cathedral of the Intercession), the sovereign left for Red Square, where the patriarch presented him and the boyars with willow branches.[8] When the Holy Gospel had been read the patriarch took in his right hand a cross and in his left, the Gospel. He sent away for a donkey to be unhitched and brought to the steps of the tribune, upon which stood both he and the tsar. The donkey was brought forth, and the patriarch mounted it. The tsar then led the donkey by the reins of the bridle, while nearby were borne the tsar's baton, willow, candle, and towel. The tsarevich and one of the boyars held the donkey by the middle of the reins, while a patriarchal boyar and treasurer guided it at the bit. On both sides the musketeers carried bright pieces of cloth and spread it along the path. In front came an enormous decorated willow placed in a red sledge, which was hitched to six dark-grey horses, caparisoned in colorful velvet and adorned with feathered plumes. The route led directly back to the cathedral of the Dormition.

The great day of the solemn feast of the Resurrection drew near. At the approach of midnight prior to Easter morning the sovereign went to the cathedral of the Dormition, followed by the boyars, lords-in-waiting, councillors, table attendants, crown agents, service gentry, and chancellors. The cathedral thronged with people dressed in cloth of gold. At the Easter morning service, after the singing of the laudatory paschal canticles, the tsar reverenced the holy icons and exchanged the kiss of peace with the patriarch and bishops. All of them presented Easter eggs to each other. The rest of the clergy then were permitted to approach the tsar. As they did so they were given eggs. After the clergy, the tsar greeted all the laymen who had entered after him into church.

After the Easter morning service the tsar went to the Ascension monastery to do reverence before the sepulcher of his mother, and then to the cathedral of the Archangel to repeat the ceremony before his father's tomb. In the cathedral of the Annunciation, he exchanged the paschal kiss with his confessor. The tsar then returned to the cathedral of the Dormition for the divine liturgy.

On the first day of the feast all the ecclesiastical dignitaries and secular nobility presented themselves before the tsar and tsaritsa. The tsaritsa granted them permission to offer their respects. Approaching the sovereign with gifts came the distinguished and wealthy merchant, Danila Stroganov, followed by the foremost merchants of Moscow and those from other cities. The next day the patriarch again came with the ecclesiastical dignitaries, this time bringing icons and cloth of gold as a gift. On the third day the court servitors, secretaries of the workshop in the tsaritsa's quarters, her fire tenders and their wives, precentors, choristers, tutors of the tsar's sons, and palace chamber guards were admitted to the tsar's presence and given Easter eggs. On the fourth day the tsar admitted to his presence the battalion and company commanders, foreign doctors and native physicians, and the artisans of the Gold, Silver, and Armory chambers.

On Trinity Day [Pentecost], the sovereign attended the divine liturgy in the cathedral of the Dormition. Before him the table attendants carried leaves and bouquets of flowers. In church, table attendants held the regalia: the baton, pedestal, and bowl. Sometimes they also bore a trunk with the tsar's robes of state. On the feast of the Dormition [15 August], the feast day of the main cathedral church in Moscow, the tsar dined with the patriarch, who presented gifts to his guests just as on the day of Metropolitan Peter.[9] Nor did Tsar Alexis omit to observe the feast day of Metropolitan Alexis, celebrated in the Miracles monastery on 20 May. If he happened to be in [his village of] Preobrazhenskoe

ALEXEI — MICHAÉLOVITS
Czaar et Grand Duc de Moscouie   Conseruateur de toutles Russes
et Dominateur de Plus.res terres   et Seigneuries, & Fils de Michael
Foëderouits Czaar et Grand   Duc de Moscouie Auquel Il a
Succede en L'anneé 1645. le 12.e   Juillet estant Age pour lors de 15.
Ans Il a Espouse en L'anneé 1647. la fille d'Illia Danilouits Miloslausky. &

[outside the capital] at the time, he made a special effort to return to Moscow for the celebration. If he did not travel to Holy Trinity monastery for the feast of St. Sergius, he attended the divine liturgy in that monastery's church inside the Kremlin. On the feast day of his own saint, celebrated on 17 March, he attended vespers and the divine liturgy in St. Alexis' monastery. In front came musketeers with rods, followed by the lord of the bedchamber and crown agents with the regalia. Behind them approached the tsar himself, in a gold coat trimmed with lace and decorations, and wearing a cap of costly fur. He was transported in a sledge of highest state, along whose runners stood boyars, while stationed on guard along the shaves were table attendants and privy councillors. On foot, next to the sledge, marched the regimental and battalion commanders of musketeers. On 17 November, the feast of St. Gregory of Neocaesarea, Tsar Alexis went to attend the divine liturgy in the suburb of Sadova, where resided his confessor.

Besides attending church services and ceremonies on feast days, the great sovereign also traveled to other cities on pilgrimages: Mozhaisk, Borovsk, Zvenigorod, Kashin, Uglich, and the monastery of St. Nicholas-on-the-Ugresha. While en route to the Holy Trinity-St. Sergius monastery, where the tsar customarily went on the feast day of St. Sergius, 25 September, he was greeted with offerings of bread and fish at way stations in the villages of Tainskoe, Bratovshchina, and Vozdvizhenskoe by the townspeople of Yaroslavl, Rostov, Pereiaslavl, and Uglich. The tsar's pilgrimages also included the monasteries near Moscow. The arrival of the great sovereign always was regarded as an event for joyful celebration by the brethren, and the guest invariably bestowed his gracious bounty upon the monastery. Finally, besides monasteries, the sovereign also visited all the hospitals.

The sovereign's travels had other aims as well. Tsar Alexis often enjoyed going to various villages outside Moscow, where he sometimes remained for quite a long time. These villages were Kolomenskoe, Golenishchevo, Pokrovskoe, Khoroshevo, Vorobievo, Semenovskoe, Izmailovo, Nikolskoe, Vsevidnoe, Ostrov, Sokolovo, Alekseevskoe, and Diakovo. Because these trips were more than of a single day's duration, the procession included the special enclosed carriage equipped with sleeping accommodations. On such occasions it was escorted by the lord of the bedchamber and a crown agent carrying the key. With them were 300 palace attendants, arranged three in a row, colorfully attired and mounted on horses. They were armed with a wide assortment of weapons.

TSAR ALEXIS

After the palace attendants followed 300 mounted musketeers, riding five abreast. Behind them were 500 reiters, or cavalry soldiers, and twelve sharpshooters armed with long guns. The marksmen were succeeded by a chancellor from the Chancellery of the Horse, who supervised the passage of the sovereign's saddles, stallions, tall and expensive Asiatic steeds, trotters and pacers—40 saddled mounts magnificently caparisoned, with chains and reins loudly jingling, and saddles covered with bright coverlets and golden carpets. To the front of the sovereign's coach rode a boyar, while nearby on the right hand side was posted a mounted lord-in-waiting. The tsar himself was seated in an English coach-and-six. The horses were bedecked with European feathers, while the coachmen wore velvet caftans and velvet caps trimmed with sable and feathers. Inside the coach with the sovereign rode four boyars. The tsarevich rode in a smaller closed carriage, also drawn by six horses. He was accompanied by his uncle and a lord-in-waiting, and was followed by boyars, lords-in-waiting, table attendants, and crown agents. Near the carriage were stationed musketeers. After the tsarevich came the tsaritsa, her mother, and boyarinas in a heavy closed carriage of twelve horses. Thereupon followed the elder and younger daughters of the tsaritsa, also in heavy closed carriages, surrounded by musketeers and followed by the leading boyarinas, treasurers of the household, dwarfs, and ladies of the bedchamber. In all, there were fifty heavy closed carriages. The chief aim of such travels out of town was Tsar Alexis' favorite diversion— hunting. He went to the fields to amuse himself with the birds, though he also took pleasure in hunting bears.

DOMESTIC CELEBRATIONS AND PALACE FEASTS

The way in which the sovereign celebrated various church feast days has been described. Some attention should now be given to his family observances, both joyful and sorrowful.

It was a matter of universal rejoicing when a son was born to the tsar. The patriarch, leading ecclesiastics, boyars, lords-in-waiting, councillors, and table attendants went with gifts to the newborn child. The tsar ordered a bounteous table prepared for the occasion. The patriarch himself, assisted by the foremost clergymen, christened the tsarevich in either the Miracles monastery or the cathedral of the Dormition. By ancient custom the godfather would be the archimandrite of St. Sergius-Holy Trinity monastery or the tsarevich's elder brother, if he was of age. Peter, the youngest son of Tsar Alexis, had as godfather his eldest brother, the tsarevich Fedor, while the godmother was Peter's aunt. For the baptismal ceremony the patriarch received 1500 zolotoys; the metropolitans, 300 each; the archbishops, 200 each; the bishops, 100

each; the archimandrite of the Miracles monastery, 80 rubles; the protopope of the cathedral of the Annunciation (the tsar's confessor), 100
rubles; the protopope of the cathedral of the Dormition, 50 rubles; the
protodeacon, 40 rubles; and the sacristans, 30 each. The total expenditure amounted to 3800 zolotoys and 330 rubles. In observance of this
joyful event, the sovereign had meals served in his antechamber for those
brethren who were destitute and bestowed his bounty upon them.

A tsarevich who died was interred the same day. On memorial anni-
versaries the patriarch and leading members of the clergy officiated at
services in the requiem chapel. Also, a large banquet was prepared. The
sovereign first entered the requiem chapel. He then withdrew to serve
food and drink to the patriarch and bishops. The patriarch accepted the
plate and goblet offered him, and extended them in return to the sovereign, who passed them to a lord-in-waiting in attendance nearby. After
the feast the sovereign came again into the requiem chapel for the com-
memorative service. At its conclusion he escorted the patriarch as far as
the cathedral of the Annunciation.

On church feast days and other occasions when the tsar held a celebration, elaborate banquets were prepared, to which were invited the
patriarch, boyars, lords-in-waiting, service gentry of the council and
chancellors, crown agents, service gentry of Moscow, palace attendants,
and townspeople from all the city districts. Moreover, stately banquets
also were arranged to mark the reception of foreign princes and important ambassadors. In the Hall of Facets,[10] where the feast was held,
there were gathered rare and expensive items to be put on display for
the guests. On one window ledge stood four silver clocks on golden velvet, while beside it stood a silver candleholder. Along a second window
stood a massive silver tray, flanked by tall vessels. The third window
ledge held a large silver bowl on a coverlet of golden velvet, as well as a
silver cask finished in gold. Opposite the sovereign's place at the table
stood a covered dais with carpeted steps. Near the table stood a side-
board, on which were arranged utensils of gold, silver, Sardian stone,
crystal, and jasper. Foreign ambassadors made note that these utensils
were not especially outstanding for their cleanliness.

COURTIERS AND PALACE OFFICIALS

Whenever an ambassador arrived on an important diplomatic mission it
was necessary to formulate considered replies to his proposals. With
whom did the great sovereign ordinarily hold consultations about all
sorts of questions, both military and civil? It was a long time since the
senior prince of the princely clan had become the sovereign tsar of

Moscow and all Russia. But the simplicity of his original relations with those around him, his close advisers, had not disappeared. Close by the great sovereign's palace lived noblemen of different ranks, who enjoyed positions of greater or lesser familiarity with the tsar. At first they had resided inside the Kremlin. In time they moved to other of the better parts of Moscow, such as Kitai-gorod[11] and White City.[12] There, surrounded by poor relations, acquaintances, and numerous serf households, they resided in houses grander than their neighbors'.

This was the old princely retinue. The name had disappeared, but its basic military character remained. All of them were military men, senior and junior members of the retinue. To them were delegated, as of old, different civil responsibilities. Still, they never lost their permanent military character. Early Russia never had achieved a separation of military and civil service. The original marks of a military retinue remained with those who surrounded the tsar. However, the relationship between the retinue and its leader had changed. The members of the formerly free retinue, who once were able to leave their prince for another, became attached to the single great sovereign, the tsar and autocrat. In the course of this development, they had become his slaves.[13]

This entire group of servitors was obliged to be constantly in attendance on the great sovereign. From early in the morning, they prepared to make an appearance at court. The old men rode in carriages, or in sledges during winter. The young men among them arrived on horseback. At a point beyond the tsar's courtyard, at a distance from the portico, they got out of their carriages or dismounted from their horses and walked on foot toward the portico.

If one were to follow them into the palace, he would find that there appeared among them a distinction based on their noble rank and closeness to the tsar. The crowd did not walk far. They halted when they reached the portico of the bedchamber and there, on its large floor, they awaited word of any orders. These were the junior, or less distinguished, noblemen. Here were to be found the table attendants. They were children of fathers who held noble rank but who were not of highest noble standing by virtue of birth. They numbered about five hundred people. The main kind of service they performed was in the palace, from which they received their name. At solemn feasts they carried food to the tsar's table. Also, they were dispatched as ambassadors to foreign courts. Some were appointed to be military governors in cities, while others were assigned to the chancelleries. The table attendants of the portico were called *ploshchadnye* in contrast to those of the throne room, *komnatnye,* who were children of fathers with higher rank and closer to the tsar. Waiting together with the table attendants on the portico were the crown agents. Mention of them was made earlier in regard to their court functions during the tsar's ceremonial appearances. The crown agents, numbering about eight hundred people, also were sent on various missions, though of lesser importance. A crown agent would not be appointed the military governor of a city or an ambassador to a foreign country.

One other group of notables also went only as far as the portico. These were the service gentry of Moscow. They were persons who assumed a position of pre-eminence ahead of the gentry in the outlying regions that had become annexed to the principality of Moscow. They had no functions at court. During wartime they held command positions in the regiments. In peacetime they were given assignments as military governors of cities, ambassadors, investigators, and bureaucratic officials. But experience long ago had shown that the man who wields a sword makes a clumsy pen pusher. And so there had sprung into existence a special class of people whose duties were concerned precisely with the execution of written matters. They were divided into senior and junior officials, into chancellors and clerks. Without them, a boyar who was appointed by the sovereign to supervise one or another of the state chancelleries in Moscow was helpless. Without them a member of the service gentry who received an appointment as military governor of a city or ambassador to a foreign country could do nothing. The crown official who was concerned with written matters acquired increasing importance as against the military man, who in early times had been responsible for carrying out civil duties. A man in a secretarial position was no longer subordinate to him, no longer merely one who put into words the opinions, orders, and decisions of his superior. The chancellor was now his associate both in the state chancelleries and on ambassadorial missions. Thus, together with the table attendants, crown agents, and service gentry, there also gathered on the palace portico the chancellors. Back and forth scurried the palace attendants. This was a force of some two thousand young men, children of the service gentry, chancellors, and clerks. Some forty of them lodged during the night at court.

On the floor of the portico things were not always quiet. Not always were there to be heard only peaceful conversations. Sometimes there would suddenly reverberate the sound of loud voices. Two enemies or adversaries over some matter in dispute might meet. Unable to restrain themselves, they would begin fighting. It is enough to utter only a single barbed word, and the tongue begins to lose all control. There is no holding it back. From comments about the individual, references come to be made about one's father, mother, sisters, and other relatives, both far and near. No one is spared. Everything is resurrected—old and recent history, gossip, rumors. Everything now will be repeated, and with such embellishments as a heedless heart may dictate. A table attendant might get into a fracas with another table attendant over a slave, whom they try to snatch from each other. Then one of them makes an insinuation about the slave and the unmarried sisters and mother of his rival. Strong words and noise might not bring the affair to an end. One of the protagonists might pass from strong words and noise to chasing his enemy along the portico. Such a pursuit sometimes ended when one of the rivals had his skull crushed by a brick.

The crowd of young men who stood waiting on the portico moved incessantly one way and another to clear a path for the old boyars, lords-in-waiting, and members of the council. These did not halt on the portico, but went farther, into the antechamber. The antechamber held a greater importance than the portico. One palace attendant, in recounting his services, submitted the following petition to the tsar: "For the sake of the great miracle-worker, the metropolitan Alexis, and for the longlasting health of your son, the tsarevich, be gracious unto me, your slave, for my humble services. Suffer me to be admitted, Sovereign, to your illustrious majesty's presence in the antechamber. My kinsmen have been granted such permission to serve there."

Here, in the antechamber, halted the boyars, lords-in-waiting, and members of the council. These were persons of the three highest ranks of crown service in old Russia. The name "boyar" appears in the very first pages of the old Russian Chronicle, where it has the meaning of a senior member of the retinue and an indispensable adviser to the prince. This close connection between the two meanings—boyar and princely adviser—was expressed in the epithet "boyar councillor."

During the time when the princely authority was being established, the lords-in-waiting served chiefly as courtiers. They had charge of court ceremonials and the reception of ambassadors. Whenever the sovereign undertook a journey, they traveled ahead and took care of necessary preparations at the way stations. Later the dignity became a titular one, no longer associated with service. The name was retained to designate noblemen of the second rank, just below the boyars.

Finally, since early times, there existed among members of the retinue persons who had not yet attained to the rank of either boyar or lord-in-waiting, but who "resided in council," that is, participated in the council of the grand prince. From this arose a third rank, that of the "service gentry of the council."

Besides these three ranks, which participated in the tsar's council, there were also the chancellors of the council. There were no more than four of these leading functionaries, who held the highest position to which a non-military person, a man of the pen, might aspire. Working directly in the presence of the sovereign, who directly availed himself of their skill with the pen, their expertise, and their experience, the chancellors of the council acquired a signal importance. They became especially powerful in the time of Ivan the Terrible. Suspecting the nobility of iniquitous schemes, Ivan placed his trust principally in the chancellors as persons not of noble birth who only lately had attained to positions of power. The extent to which could reach the influence of the chancellors is shown by the careers of Ivan Gramotin[14] and the members of the Shchelkalov family who held that rank.[15]

As persons devoted to form and routine, who derived their advantage from a detailed knowledge of existing conditions, it goes without saying that the chancellors of the council could not be well disposed to the question of reform. They were regarded as experts in their field, and in virtue of this they enjoyed great respect and influence. Others consulted them as oracles. They resented being told that they did not know how to carry out their work and had no idea how to comport themselves properly. This makes understandable the enmity which the chancellors of the council nourished toward the daring innovator, Ordin-Nashchokin. After all, just whom did he have the gall to teach and admonish? The chancellors of the council! As though the leading functionaries of the state did not know their business! He took it upon himself to re-educate them in the way of foreigners. From him could only be heard that, in foreign countries, things were done differently.

THE COURTIERS' INTERESTS

As the boyars, lords-in-waiting, service gentry of the council, and chancellors of the council clustered together in the antechamber, what was it they discussed among themselves in expectation of the tsar's appearance? What matters particularly interested them? In the later period of Tsar Alexis' reign there was much to discuss concerning difficult wars and incessant campaigns. Earlier victories were turning into defeats. More than once talk centered on speculation that the tsar would abandon the capital, to which the enemy was getting close. The cossacks were changing their allegiance in Little Russia. The godless Stenka Razin was rousing the cossacks and peasants against the boyars. The patriarch harbored a desire to exercise control over everything and became angry when this was denied him. He had left Moscow but did not relinquish the patriarchate. Never had there been such a dilemma before. The most holy patriarchs of the Eastern church were convened in order to have done with Nikon.[16]

The chancellors of the council began to insinuate that there was no abiding Afanasy Ordin-Nashchokin. He quarreled with everyone and was always reproachful. In his opinion, everything was being handled badly. He talked about new ways of doing things, as they were done in foreign countries. But what kinds of ways were those? What had he introduced in Pskov? If a military governor received an appointment to that city, he found himself with nothing to do. The business of government was carried on by the muzhiks! Now, what kind of absurdity was this! Yet, the great sovereign certainly showed his favor to Ordin-Nashchokin. He sent official documents directly to him by way of the Privy Chancellery, and Ordin-Nashchokin forwarded his written communications to that same agency. Since the Privy Chancellery had been opened, it was possible for anybody to write whatever he wished to the great sovereign.[17] A person might lodge an accusation against anyone, and no one would know. But was all this really any wonder? If only Ordin-Nashchokin had sprung from an honorable old family! Just see—where did he come from? To be sure, he was a smart fellow! No one denied that he had a mind. But did that mean everyone else was stupid? Here went Matveev,[18] aiming to become a boyar—and succeeding. Why, he even managed to worm his way into the close circle surrounding the tsar. But at least Matveev was restrained and showed proper respect to honorable persons. Although he liked the new ways of doing things, he did not shout about them like Ordin-Nashchokin.

THE SYSTEM OF PRECEDENCE

Notwithstanding all the various concerns, what certainly most occupied the people gathered in the antechamber were matters pertaining to the system of precedence [*mestnichestvo*]. Muscovite Russia had retained many vestiges of the past. Among them was the strength of family relations, which were made stronger to the extent that other kinds of relations were weak. The idea of the unity of the family, regardless of its size or the number of its branches, still continued to exist. Should one member find himself in a position where he had to pay a sizable amount of money, the rest of the family were responsible for pooling their resources to settle the account. The senior members of a family, honored with the name "lord," had to look after the conduct of the younger members, even the adults, who were admitted into service, and punish them for misbehavior. The crown, sharing the general view concerning the strength of family relations, called upon the older members to answer for the deportment of the younger.

Under conditions in which family ties were so strong and in which the responsibility of different family members for one another was so important, the significance of the individual necessarily evaporated in the face of the preponderance of the family. A single person, as such, was quite inconceivable apart from his blood relations. It was impossible to envision a hypothetical Ivan existing by himself. He could only be thought of as Ivan in conjunction with his brothers and nephews. Consequently, by reason of this merging of the individual and the family, if any one person was honored, this elevated the prestige of the entire family; if one member was humiliated, so was the family. It becomes apparent why a person of high rank who occupied an important position would not wish to serve under the direction of, or as an associate with, a person who was lower than he either in rank or prior service. If we can use our imagination to visualize that an entire family constituted a single entity, that each member was combined with all the other members, it can be understood why the hypothetical Ivan would not wish to serve as an associate with Vasily if some member of Ivan's family stood higher in rank than some member of Vasily's family. It must not be forgotten that the independent individual, as he is thought of today, is able either in the name of a higher morality or some other consideration to rise above the motives of personal ambition. But it was impossible for the early Russian to surmount these motives because he had no right to dispose of the honor that belonged to the whole family. On the contrary, he had a sacred obligation to safeguard it, come what may.

It should occasion no surprise, then, to find a sharp inconsistency in conduct. On the one hand, the Russian of old was under ordinary circumstances unfailingly obedient to the great sovereign. Indeed he was usually referred to as the great sovereign's slave [*kholop*], and even his personal name on such occasions would reflect this status. For it was not his full name that was used in connection with the great sovereign, but a derogatory diminutive.[19] On the other hand, he became obstreperous when matters arose that touched on the system of precedence. When at dinner in the presence of the tsar he would climb under the table if compelled to sit below a person to whom he could not yield in accordance with genealogical calculations. He would undergo beatings with rods and whips, or suffer forfeiture of his landed holdings and possessions, but still he would not carry out the tsar's will. For, if he did, what would be the value of his life? How would he appear in the eyes of his family, as well as of all respectable people? As far as they were concerned, the disgrace to their family honor constituted an unforgivable crime. Thereafter everyone could taunt the relatives of such a scoundrel, saying: "Did you know that you may have less precedence than I do? For your relative Ivan was ranked lower than Vasily, but I am equal to Vasily, or even higher than he. My younger brother on such-and-such a military campaign was equal to, or even higher than, the eldest brother of Vasily . . . ." And so on.

The members of sixteen aristocratic families had the right to bypass the lower ranks of the nobility and ascend directly to the rank of boyar: Cherkassky, Vorotynsky, Trubetskoy, Golitsyn, Khovansky, Morozov, Sheremetev, Odoevsky, Pronsky, Shein, Saltykov, Repnin, Prozorovsky, Buinosov, Khilkov, and Urusov. The members of fifteen families first became lords-in-waiting, and then boyars: Kurakin, Dolgoruky, Buturlin, Romodanovsky, Pozharsky, Volkonsky, Lobanov, Streshnev, Bariatinsky, Miloslavsky, Sukin, Pushkin, Izmailov, Pleshcheev, and Lvov. Of these thirty-one names, twenty belonged to princely families.

Some princes added to their surnames the designations of their former patrimonial principalities,[20] as in the case of Romodanovsky-Starodubsky. By the end of Tsar Alexis' reign this convention came to be considered improper, and the Romodanovsky family was prohibited to sign their names as Starodubsky. But the famous military governor, Prince Grigory Grigorevich Romodanovsky, submitted this petition. "I am in receipt of your Great Sovereign's charter, in which I am ordered henceforth not to sign my name as Starodubsky. I shall not sign anything in that manner without your decree. Previously, I have used that form because: It is known to you, Great Sovereign, that we were once princelets of Starodub, that my ancestors, my father and uncle, used to sign their names Starodubsky-Romodanovsky, and that my uncle, Prince Ivan Petrovich, suffered on behalf of you, the Great Sovereigns, at the hands of the robber who was falsely called Tsarevich Augustus.[21] By your Sovereign's grace, all this has been registered in the records. My uncle's sufferings are publicly proclaimed in church when, on the Sunday of the first week of the Great Fast, he is commemorated as Starodubsky-Romodanovsky. Have mercy. Do not command that our trifling honor be taken from me." The sovereign did show his mercy, and did not command that the honor be withdrawn.

The tsar customarily took a young man from a noble family into the palace as a gentleman of the bedchamber. In this capacity he would join the other gentlemen of the bedchamber, who had the duty of sleeping at night, approximately four at a time, in the sovereign's room. Proceeding in a fixed routine of succession every twenty-four hours, they were entrusted with removing the sovereign's robes and footwear. From this post, members of foremost families moved ahead directly to the rank of boyar, while those with lesser names advanced to lord-in-waiting. Thereupon they became known as privy boyars or privy lords-in-waiting. They were also called boyars or lords-in-waiting of the throne room.

It became a cherished goal to reach the most prestigious prerogative by acquiring for oneself and other members of one's family the right to attain the rank of boyar without having to go through that of lord-in-waiting. There were ambitious persons who tried to do so without the recognized qualifications. Thus, for instance, a certain Golovin, who had been advanced from the class of service gentry to the rank of lord-in-waiting, submitted a petition stating that no other lord-in-waiting was as old as he, and that his father had been a boyar in the reign of Tsar Michael. For lodging that petition he was sent to prison, and his appointment as lord-in-waiting was rescinded. Instead, he was granted something quite different. "You, scoundrel, are not to be admitted to any honor. The boyars have sentenced you to be beaten with the whip and sent to Siberia, but the sovereign has decided to show you his mercy."

Family honor was such a sore spot among the old Russian nobility that, notwithstanding the obvious preeminence of one family over another, the members of a family who had to defer to another would resort to desperate measures in the hope of extricating themselves from their onerous subordination. In this respect there took place a remarkable encounter involving a dispute over precedence between two families of the highest rank. In 1663, at a solemn dinner in the sovereign's presence, Prince Yury Trubetskoy was assigned a place higher than Nikita Sheremetev. The Sheremetevs knew full well that the Trubetskoys ranked higher than they, but it was difficult for them to concede the point. They recalled that they, the Sheremetevs, were an old Muscovite noble family, while the Trubetskoys, even though of the nobility, were related to the Lithuanian princely line of Gedimin and, as such, were descended from princes who had migrated to Moscow.

Accordingly, the eldest of the Sheremetevs, the boyar Peter Vasilievich, submitted this petition. "My brother has been in service—and I through him—at the side of Prince Yury; and we are prepared to serve in the future with the Trubetskoys to the extent that this is compatible with the genealogy of his family. However, Prince Yury is a foreigner. In our generation and in relation to us, there has not been anyone in our family who has ranked lower than he. So if anyone, not knowing his worth, begins to discredit me, then there cannot be allowed to take place any dishonor to us or our parentage."

The sovereign was much incensed at this new claim, when the many existing quarrels on the basis of old claims for precedence had already become intolerable. He ordered Sheremetev to be told the following: "You have dishonored Prince Yury by saying that he is a foreigner. The Trubetskoys are not foreigners. They are an old and honorable family."

A fine was imposed on the Sheremetevs for the dishonor done to Prince Yury Trubetskoy, in an amount equivalent to half the proceeds of his uncle, the boyar prince Alexis Trubetskoy. The Sheremetevs had good reason to be concerned that someone, ignorant of his own worth, would dishonor them as a result of their concession to the Trubetskoys. Several times the Sheremetevs had to defend themselves against the claims of one family or another—the Trubetskoys, Pleshcheevs, Buturlins, and Godunovs.

If the government incessantly had to come to the defense of the oldest families, it can well be appreciated how difficult it was to uphold newly elevated people, kinsmen of the tsar who had emerged from obscurity to attain the rank of boyar and others, like Ordin-Nashchokin, who had risen to prominence with meteoric suddenness. In such instances it was necessary to cast about for various justifications.

On one occasion Prince Lvov submitted a petition with regard to the tsar's father-in-law, the boyar Ilia Miloslavsky. Lvov received a reply confirming that he was indeed eligible to be given a service assignment together with Miloslavsky. The reasons put forward were that he was a third brother in his own family and, second, no one had ever before lodged a petition involving the tsar's in-laws.

It was even harder to justify the high appointment given to Ordin-Nashchokin. The table attendant Matvei Pushkin once submitted a petition in which he complained about the subordinate position he had been given relative to Ordin-Nashchokin in the conduct of negotiations with envoys representing Poland. Pushkin declared that this assignment violated his standing in the system of precedence. Ordin-Nashchokin also then entered a petition, asserting that Pushkin's petition was improper. The sovereign answered Pushkin that the system of precedence had not been applied earlier in such cases, and that it was not applicable in the present case. Pushkin countered by insisting that theretofore it had been custom only for *honorable* persons to conduct negotiations with foreign envoys, and not persons so inferior as Ordin-Nashchokin. According to Pushkin, that was why no petitions had been lodged before in similar cases. As for his own genealogical standing in comparison with Nashchokin's, he maintained that the difference between them was well known to the great sovereign. In response, the sovereign merely reiterated his earlier statement that the system of precedence had not been applicable theretofore and that it was not applicable in the existing case.

Pursuant to this reply Pushkin made a concession initially and set off to attend the negotiations. Later, however, he repented of his weakness and ceased attending. The sovereign had him sent to prison. Moreover, Pushkin was ordered to be informed that it was quite appropriate for him to serve with Ordin-Nashchokin, and if he should choose not to do so, his landed property and holdings would be confiscated. Pushkin replied: "Happen what may, even if you, Sovereign, should command that I be punished by death, Ordin-Nashchokin nonetheless remains next to me an inferior person and without a registered genealogy." Standing fast on this position and claiming illness, Pushkin did not take any further part in the negotiations.

The system of precedence was used not only to ascertain relations among different families, but also to determine the relations among members of the same family. Its application led to disputes over family seniority, such as had distressing importance in early Russian history when arguments over this issue arose within the princely dynasty. In early Kievan Russia seniority of age took preeminence, and the nephews of a family, notwithstanding various favorable circumstances, generally had to yield to the rights of their uncles. Efforts by the nephews to rise up against the rights of their uncles were considered sinful. In northern Russia, in Vladimir and later in Moscow, the matter quickly took a turn in the opposite direction. The clan relations among the princes were destroyed. The son of the eldest brother began to inherit seniority at the expense of all his uncles. This revolution in the relations of the members of the ruling family could not remain without influence on the relations in other families. If such a revolution could take place in the ruling family, it is reasonable to believe that there also occurred concessions, compromises, and limitations in respect of the rights of the junior uncles as against their senior nephews. This would be especially true in view of the impact excited by the decisions of the great sovereign regarding disputes over precedence. The great sovereign, who himself ruled in consequence of the new conception of the superior right of an eldest brother's son over his uncles, could not but be favorably inclined to the limitation of uncles in favor of nephews. Hence it is not surprising to find that, in disputes involving the system of precedence, such limitations found expression in the sovereign's new Code of Laws.[22]

From the period in question one interesting instance of family strife can be cited by way of example. In 1652 Prince Grigory Romodanovsky submitted a petition in which he stated that it would be improper for him to receive an assignment at the side of, and hence below, his nephew Prince Yury, because "his genealogical position is equal to mine." Prince Yury then pressed a petition against his uncle: "Although he is genealogically my uncle, he is nevertheless eligible to hold an assignment at my side. For he is the eighth son of his father, while I am the first son of my father, and my grandfather was his father's elder brother." The sovereign told Prince Grigory: "I command you henceforth to become reconciled with your senior kinsmen." But Prince Grigory did not obey the sovereign, for which he was placed in fetters.

Chancellors also entered into disputes in exactly the same way over their official appointments to various state chancelleries. The chancellor Elizarov, who had been admitted to the rank of chancellor of the council while retaining his post in the Chancellery of Military Tenures, lodged a petition protesting that it was improper for him to be ranked below the chancellor of the council Gavrenev simply because the latter held office in the Chancellery of State Service and Appointments, which was considered superior to the Chancellery of Military Tenures.

It was with concerns and ambitions such as these that the nobility crowded together in the tsar's antechamber. Not all of them, however, remained there. The privy boyars drew nearer the doors of the tsar's throne room, where they were allowed admittance. After deliberating together and awaiting the proper moment, they entered. The throne room was a place forbidden to the others, who remained standing in the antechamber. How important it was to be able to enter the throne room is exemplified by the following incident. Tsar Michael appointed the boyar prince Yury Sitsky to greet Prince Valdemar at the border.[23] The boyar Michael Soltykov was commissioned to perform the same duty on the outskirts of Moscow. The orders containing these appointments specified that adherence to the system of precedence was to be dispensed with in this case, but only as a solitary exception to the rule. Nevertheless, unbeknown to the Saltykov family, Prince Sitsky made a personal appeal to the tsar in the throne room while no one else was present. As a result the sovereign commanded that a charter permanently suspending the system of precedence be granted to Sitsky, authorizing him thereafter to stand in a position higher than Saltykov and his relatives. The Saltykovs were later able to rectify this matter under Tsar Alexis.

SESSIONS IN COUNCIL AND SPECIAL ASSEMBLIES

At long last, the doors opened. The great sovereign entered, and everyone upon seeing him bowed to the ground. In the main corner opposite the entrance, the sovereign seated himself on a large throne and summoned to his side those for whom there was some assignment. If the tsar called for a boyar and he was not present, then immediately officials were sent to locate him. When he finally arrived, a stern reprimand lay in store: "Why were you late?" Justice was swift for those who made mistakes, failed to fulfill the tsar's commands, or carried out orders improperly. The sovereign forthwith ordered them removed from his chambers or sent to prison. Sometimes the sovereign carried on lengthy conversations with various boyars. When this happened, all the rest stood waiting. If they tired, they went into the courtyard to sit down, later returning upstairs. On occasions, one of those in attendance would himself approach the sovereign and bow to the ground before him. He might present a petition, perhaps that he be given permission to go to his village. Others might approach, requesting leave to be present elsewhere as guests, at a wedding, a christening, or someone's name-day celebration. It was necessary to request permission because everyone had to assemble once more at the palace in the evening. Among the petitioners some presented fancy loaves of white wheat bread to the sovereign. These were individuals who were observing their name days. The sovereign would inquire after their health and congratulate them, whereupon they went with loaves of bread to the tsaritsa, the tsareviches, and the tsarevnas.

Following the reception of the boyars, the sovereign usually went to attend the divine liturgy with the entire court. Afterwards he devoted himself to business either in the antechamber or the throne room. Particular days of the week were assigned for the submission of reports from each chancellery. On Mondays were received reports from the Chancellery of State Service and Appointments and from the Ambassadorial Chancellery; on Tuesdays, from the Chancellery of the Exchequer and the Chancellery of State Revenues; on Wednesdays, from the Chancellery for Kazan and the Chancellery of Military Tenures; on Thursdays, from the Chancellery of the Royal Household and the Chancellery for Siberia; and on Fridays, from the judicial chancelleries of Vladimir and Moscow. The directors of the various state chancelleries themselves approached the throne with the reports and read them before the sovereign.

If the sovereign had some important matter to resolve, he summoned into council either the privy boyars and lords-in-waiting of the throne room by themselves, or all the boyars, lords-in-waiting, and members of the service gentry. This was called a session of the great sovereign with the boyars on affairs of state. The boyars, lords-in-waiting, and service gentry of the council all seated themselves according to genealogical rank. Those of lower standing than others seated themselves on benches at a greater distance from the tsar, boyars with lower genealogical rank below boyars of higher rank, lords-in-waiting below the boyars, and the service gentry of the council below the lords-in-waiting, likewise according to genealogical rank rather than service. The chancellors of the council normally stood, but sometimes the sovereign invited them to be seated. Even here the course of affairs did not proceed without disputes and confusion, as when the Pushkins were sent to prison for getting into an altercation with the Dolgorukys while the sovereign was sitting with the boyars.

After everyone was seated the sovereign announced what he had in mind and ordered the boyars and members of the council, upon having considered the matter, to determine the means for its implementation. Then anyone who had an idea about how to carry out the task made known his advice, but others, "adjusting their beards, do not answer anything, because the tsar admits many into the rank of boyar not on account of their intelligence, but in virtue of their high genealogical standing, and many are not versed in reading or writing." When a decision was reached, the sovereign and the boyars ordered the chancellors of the council to make note of it for the record.

"The sovereign has commanded and the boyars have determined."[24] In that famous phrase is reflected the aforementioned course of deliberations. The tsar would order his advisers, "upon having considered the matter, to determine the means for its implementation." The councillors would then determine the means, and the decision would be reduced to writing. If anyone is inclined to find in this expression some sort of constitutional significance, then similar importance should be attached to another phrase employed in early times: "By the command of the great sovereign and by order of the chancellors, such-and-such is to be done."[25]

When after a meeting it was necessary to compose a document to a foreign government, this task devolved upon the chancellor of the council in charge of foreign affairs. The chancellor ordered a clerk to write it out, and then made any needed changes, striking out some items and adding others. When the document was ready, the boyars alone listened to it be read. Then they heard it again, this time with the tsar. The same procedure was followed with all other decisions. If the matter was not very important or if for some reason the sovereign was unable personally to attend a meeting where it was to be brought under discussion, he commanded the boyars to reach a decision without him. He would, in other words, direct them to sit in council about such a matter. The boyars met in the palace, and from this circumstance arose the expression "to raise matters up to the boyars."[26]

Besides the customary sessions of the great sovereign with the boyars there were also held extraordinary meetings, to which were invited the high clergy and elected representatives from other social classes. These extraordinary meetings, or assemblies,[27] were usually concerned with the question whether or not to begin a dangerous and difficult war. Such a war would impose a period of lengthy and burdensome service on persons constituting the army, and call for financial sacrifices from the taxpaying part of the population. Consequently it was necessary to summon elected representatives of all ranks from both parts of the population in order that they might express their opinions. If they should say that a war ought to be started, then they would have no further grounds for complaint in having laid this burden upon themselves. Tsar Alexis, when he let his military men proceed with a campaign in Lithuania, said to them: "Last year, several assemblies were held in which representatives elected by you participated. At those assemblies, we discussed the injustices of the Polish kings.[28] You heard about this from your elected representatives. Stand, therefore, against the unholy persecution of the Orthodox faith and against injury to the Muscovite state."

The elected representatives, or advisers,[29] arrived for the assembly from various parts of Moscow and from the outlying regions. They consisted of people from different ranks: for example, two persons each from among the table attendants, crown agents, service gentry of Moscow, and palace attendants; two persons each from the service gentry and junior boyars of large cities and one each from the small cities; three persons from among the foremost merchants; two persons each from the commercial and cloth guilds; and one person each from among the urban taxpaying communities, the tax-exempt suburbs, and the commercial and manufacturing districts of cities. There were no elected representatives from among the peasants. Sometimes, the townspeople from outlying regions were not called either. There would be summoned only the foremost merchants of Moscow, the senior members of the commercial and cloth guilds, and the chiefs of the urban taxpaying communities. The advisers had a consultative voice. Their opinions or declarations were taken under consideration. The declarations were submitted jointly by social class or region. But each adviser was permitted to submit his own opinion separately.

The advisers would unanimously recommend that it was necessary to begin a war. The military men then declared their readiness to shed blood for his most illustrious tsarist majesty. The merchants announced their willingness to pay a fifth or tenth part from their revenues and businesses. The great sovereign would then decide that it was impossible to postpone the war. The military men at court were given marching orders and messengers were dispatched to the military governors in the outlying regions with instructions to send forth the service people, the service gentry and junior boyars, from their landed holdings and possessions.

NEW SERVICE REQUIREMENTS AND SOCIAL CHANGE

Now it is time to become acquainted with this numerous class of service people, scattered throughout the central, western, and southern regions of the country. First of all, it is a good idea to pay attention to their name, which always can tell a great deal, especially when one traces the changes that it undergoes in the course of time. During Russia's earliest history there could be discerned an initial division of the people into military and non-military, the magnates and muzhiks. The military people bore in relations to their leader, the prince, the name "retinue" [*druzhina*]. This name, whatever its etymology, conveyed the meaning of a voluntary association or company. In Muscovy the name "retinue" disappeared because it ceased to have any meaning. With what was it gradually replaced? From the retinue there first emerged the "court" [*dvor*] and the "courtier" [*dvorianin*], who acquired ever greater power. At first the boyars and junior boyars[30] preserved in relation to the courtiers their preeminent and independent status, such as had been enjoyed formerly by members of the princely retinue. But later, with the growing importance of the sovereign and his court, the name "courtier" [or "member of the service gentry"][31] gained ascendancy over the name "junior boyar" and the latter came to designate the lower class of military men.

As the earlier meaning of voluntary association or companionship with a leader was lost, there appeared fully developed the meaning of service to the sovereign. Thus the name "service people" [*sluzhilye liudi*] became applied to men in military service. It was used in contrast to the rest of the people, who did not undergo any change in status, but who maintained as before, in relation to the military men, their significance as muzhiks. But the military men themselves were no longer magnates [*muzhi*]. They had become service people, slaves [*kholopi*] of the sovereign. The term "serviceman" [*sluzhilyi, sluzhashchii*] continues to the present day. There can still be heard among the people the characterization "This is a serviceman" [*eto sluzhashchii*] in drawing a distinction between him and a merchant or tradesman.

There existed, moreover, another name, "military tenant" [*pome-shchik*], which connoted reward for service. Whereas the name "service-man" signified an individual's relationship to the sovereign, the name "military tenant" indicated his relationship to the land and the people on it, who were obliged to provide for the support of the fighting man. The early period of Russian history saw the retinue receiving its subsistence from the prince in the form of money, whereas the later formation from the retinue of a service class in Muscovy was attended by the system of granting military tenures on tracts of land.

This can be attributed to the fact that the grand prince became a sovereign ruler. He settled in a single location and determined with precision his relations to the land, becoming its proprietor and manager. It is not difficult to appreciate what an impression was created in the country by the granting of land tenures to military men—an impression not unlike that which was evoked when the Germans obtained tracts of land within the provinces of the Roman Empire. Next to the comparatively few landed proprietors there appeared a numerous class of people who utilized the land and enjoyed the advantages of full proprietorship during the time granted for their use of it. Landed proprietors likewise began to acquire military tenures. The land became earmarked for distribution as grants to military men, so that the military tenants became the main landholders. It became impossible for the people to conceive of a serviceman without a grant of land, and the term "military tenant" for a landholder took firm root among the people, remaining even after the military tenures themselves had disappeared.

LAND, MEN, AND WAR

The transformation of the princely retainers into military tenants inevitably exerted a strong influence upon the change in the character of the Russian military class, independent of any differences in temperament between people in the south and north, or in the personalities of the princes and their activities. Darting about with their princes from one region to another and always ready to join the retinue of an opposing prince, the members of the mobile retinues naturally preserved the qualities of courage and bravery. They were persons who never laid down their arms in the perpetual war with the barbarians of the steppes and in the incessant internecine struggles between princes. Since the retinue was comparatively small, the actions of its members were always in plain view. The fortitude of each one was conspicuously evident in the minor skirmishing which constituted most of the military engagements of the time. Under such conditions it is only to be expected that the desire to excel was quickened. War was the main and constant activity. In a word, the military character of those people was preserved in full.

Besides the desire to maintain their honor everywhere, at home in Russia and in other countries as well, incentives of a different kind arose for displaying courage. The material well-being of the retinue depended on the wealth of the prince, and that wealth could only be accumulated and safeguarded by the sword of the prince's retainer. "With the retinue, I shall acquire silver and gold." Thus spoke St. Vladimir, and ordered that silver spoons be brought out for the retinue, which complained about the wooden ones that had been put on the table for them.[32]

But this characteristic of the retainers must inevitably have changed when the fighting man was given a military tenure, where he spent all his time while peace prevailed until summoned to war. In becoming a landholder and landlord, he lost his military significance as he developed other relations and interests. He became accustomed to his peacetime situation, which assumed for him a natural and permanent quality, while war became occasional, exceptional, and disruptive of his habitual way of life. This sort of disruption hardly could appeal to him. If possible, he preferred to locate the enemy quickly, fight him, and return home. But it was usually necessary to prepare for a long journey and bid an indefinite farewell to family and household. Things might take a bad turn for the family in the landlord's absence, and they might suffer. Life on a military tenure usually was based on a hand-to-mouth existence. There were no reserve supplies for a rainy day, while participation in a military campaign meant extraordinary expenses and indebtedness—ruin!

It was certainly advantageous were a man by nature brave and enjoyed fighting. But as time passed the service class became transformed into a caste. Upon receiving a military tenure the sons of a serviceman had to appear at the first call for military service, whether they were courageous or not. Otherwise they stood to lose their position and means of livelihood.

In this way the placement of service people upon the land as military tenants extinguished the character of the early retinue. Instead of a permanent military force, such as the retinue had been, with a martial spirit and an appreciation of its military obligations in conformity with the desire to maintain its honor, there was created a class of peaceable citizens, landlords who only occasionally and temporarily bore what had become for them the onerous duty of fighting. With every summons to war there took place in the families of the military tenants scenes similar to those which today occur in families before the departure of recruits into the army. How many sacrifices and deprivations he must endure!

Here he had lived the life of an independent man, complete master of his house, surrounded by an obedient family, slaves, and peasants, and now it was necessary to go into service under another's command. What sort of a military leader would he chance to get? Sometimes one encountered terribly harsh commanders! Those with good fortune would have connections. Relatives then could submit a petition and this might lead to an assignment on the staff of a commander. Otherwise, too bad!

And what about returning from war? Would one return uninjured? What if one should fall prisoner to the Tatars, Lithuanians, or the godless German Lutherans! It should be recalled that the wars of the seventeenth century, whose failures resulted from faulty organization of the Russian army, were incapable in their turn of raising morale or inspiring confidence in the service people. Nor should be forgotten the utter lack of preparedness on the part of the Russian serviceman for military duty and his inability to handle his weapons, which were anyway very poor in quality. This should dispel any surprise at the testimony of a contemporary Russian,[33] who likened a regiment of service people to a flock of sheep. "The weapons of the infantry are wretched, and they do not know how to use them. They fight only hand-to-hand with spears and halberds—dull ones at that. In battle, they lose three or four or more of their own men for each of the enemy. It is shameful to look upon the cavalry. The horses are useless, the swords, dull. The cavalrymen themselves are shabby and without proper uniforms. They do not know how to use their weapons. Some servicemen do not know how to shoot their firearms at a target, or even how to load them. Should they kill two or three Tatars, they become amazed at themselves, regarding it an enormous success; but if they lose a hundred of their own men—well, it's nothing! No consideration is given how the enemy can be killed, their sole concern being how to return home quicker. They pray in the following manner: 'Grant, O God, that we may incur a light wound, that it does not cause much pain, and that a reward may be forthcoming on account of it from the great sovereign.' When fighting takes place, they look to see where they might hide behind a bush. Sometimes entire companies conceal themselves in woods or valleys. They wait until those who have been in the fighting return, at which time they join them, as though also coming from battle back to camp. Many of them say, 'May God grant me the opportunity to serve the great sovereign, and not have to draw sword from scabbard!' "

From this it is understandable why there existed among the Russian servicemen in the seventeenth century a tendency to evade service, to be excused from a military campaign because of illness, to become involved in one way or another with civilian duties, to bribe military governors and crown investigators so as to be left alone, and to hide from them. During periods of service, military governors and company commanders again were offered bribes to release servicemen from duty. Finally, there was desertion from the ranks. The Code of 1649 stipulated punishment with the whip for the first such offense. A second was subject to whipping and a penalty based on monetary income and profits from land held in military tenure. A third offense called for the whip and confiscation of a military tenure. For desertion in battle the penalty was merciless whipping and confiscation of half of one's income in money and from land. Should a company commander release a serviceman without a decree from the sovereign and the commander's knowledge, he was to be beaten with rods and imprisoned. For the same offense a commander was subject to severe punishment—"whatsoever the sovereign shall decree." The warnings in the Code did not help. Reports from military governors continued to be filled with complaints about desertion by servicemen.

The system of granting land in military tenure weakened the fighting qualities of the service people. Moreover, servicemen failed to gain much by way of advantage in other respects as well. They were given land, on which they lived and from which they drew their subsistence, as compensation for their service. The quiet and idle life on a military tenure steered them away from experience with actual military service, which was their main assignment. Consequently, whenever the time came for them to perform such service, it took on the aspect of a dreadful, and for some unbearable, burden. Nothing could have been worse than these prolonged periods of rest on military tenures following the conclusion of military campaigns. For, in general, nothing is more harmful to a person than a brief expenditure of energy succeeded by a long duration of inactivity. Nothing so effectively will turn a man away from action and work, especially when he considers that he has the right to give himself over to idleness and when he knows that he has an important function and responsibility, recognized by everyone, which he will carry out if called upon, but which in the absence of such a summons invest him with the right to do nothing.

But, it might be asked, what about the responsibility of looking after one's household in the countryside? Under the stagnant conditions of that time, characterized by an arrested development at a primitive level, this economic activity was quite uncomplicated. The main problem was how to have an adequate amount of manpower at one's disposal. Since human resources were not abundant to begin with, the problem became one of getting the small number of laborers to produce as much as possible, while expending as little as possible on them. The shortage of workhands, the enticement by wealthy landlords of agricultural peasants away from poorer landowners, and the necessity felt by the government to provide a basis for the maintenance of the latter, that is, to furnish them with workers for their lands, combined to result in enserfment of the peasants. Yet, even after enserfment, the peasants continued to be attracted elsewhere and to leave. Accordingly, the lodging of complaints with the authorities over enticement of peasants and the pursuit after absconded peasants became the military tenants' most important activity. Mention was made earlier of measures undertaken by the government to prohibit the departure of servicemen from their regiments. It should be mentioned that there did exist an exception to this policy. Commanders were authorized to release servicemen to go home in the event of domestic calamity and the flight of their work force. The archives are full of records concerning absconded peasants, and the Code of 1649 devotes an entire chapter of thirty-four articles to this subject.

On the other hand, since he was a servant for whose needs the sovereign provided, the military tenant was not encouraged to exert himself in the direction of economic improvement. The sovereign gave him land, and the servant was content. The sovereign gave him permanent workers and took his side in the event they had to be retrieved after fleeing from their toil. As for the family's future, here again his needs were met. The wife and daughters of a military tenant were given lands for their support. The sons, after they had grown up, entered the sovereign's service, at which time their father's military tenure was transferred to them. Consequently there arose the inevitable habit of living day after day with no particular cares. When someone developed a desire to build his material prosperity, only one method was considered proper—to serve in the civil administration and draw compensation locally for the performance of official functions,[34] which meant enriching oneself at the expense of those for whom the administration of civil matters was a necessity.

NEW MILITARY UNITS

The inefficiency of Russian servicemen, or military tenants, in their encounters with the enemy had long become apparent. It inevitably led to thoughts of reform. Throughout Europe such reforms proceeded along the same path. In the West the members of the original military forces, the warrior bands, also were given tracts of land. They began to live in their own houses, on their own lands. Notwithstanding that they enjoyed a greater degree of independence than their Russian counterparts, notwithstanding that the absence of a centralized state organization and of security compelled each landholder, or noble, constantly to be armed and always on guard, which certainly contributed greatly to maintaining a fighting spirit and led to the development of knighthood as an institution stemming from the primitive necessity of protecting the weak against the strong—notwithstanding all this, the wars of the feudal period were distinguished by their small scale and brief duration. Vassals in the West were quite as reluctant to leave their homes for long periods as were military tenants in Russia. Under their condition of greater independence the vassals were able to reserve for themselves a definite time limit, beyond which they did not stay on with a military campaign.

West European governments could not go far with their feudal levies, and so they had to turn once more to the warrior band! The retinues in various countries, as for example the cossacks, did not cease to form distinctive groups. But in the West there were no steppes, no enormous plains where bogatyrs might freely lead a life on horseback or roam the prairies. In the West the retinues formed a mercenary military force. Such were the Landsknechte in Germany, the Brabantines in the Netherlands, the Swiss companies, and the Italian condottieri. In some countries with rather weak political unity the retinues led to the same consequences that were seen at the start of the Middle Ages, the time of greatest movement by warrior bands. The Italian condottieri themselves established states. The governments of other, stronger states utilized the retinues as mercenary troops or hired guards, that is, in the same way they had once been used by the western and eastern Roman emperors. From such hired bands, the next step was to create a permanent national army.

But it took a long time before Europe was finally cleared of wandering retinues, seeking service with different sovereigns and changing their service at the first opportunity. In Russia they appeared at the beginning of the seventeenth century, with the reign of Boris Godunov. They became especially numerous under Tsar Michael, when through bitter experience the deficiencies in Russian military organization became abundantly clear. At that same time, however, the training of Russian military personnel was undertaken with the aid of foreign officers in accordance with foreign organization and tactics. There appeared different types of military units with foreign designations, signifying the transition to a permanent military force.

Regiments of reiters, or cavalry soldiers, came into being, for service in which persons were selected from among palace attendants, the urban service gentry, young sons of the service gentry, junior boyars holding little or nothing in the way of military tenures, and freemen. They were given a salary of thirty rubles a year, weapons (carbines and pistols), powder, and lead. It was up to them, however, to furnish their own mounts and uniforms. Reiters also were conscripted from among the peasants, in the ratio of one from every hundred peasant households. The requirement for furnishing peasant recruits was extended to church lands, to lay landholders who were unable to render service themselves on account of age or illness, and to lands in possession of widows and unmarried girls. The regiments of reiters formed in this manner received training according to new military methods from their colonels, lieutenant colonels, majors, and captains, who were either foreigners or Russians (table attendants and members of the service gentry), who had mastered the new techniques.

In the northwest, near the Swedish border, there was established a settlement of infantry soldiers. It consisted of peasants who lived on their former tracts, cultivated the fields, and utilized the meadows and ponds, but who did not pay taxes or quitrent and who were trained in military discipline by foreigners. At first they were ordered to train for military duty on a daily basis; but in 1650 the sovereign decreed that they be granted a measure of relief, with military instruction to be administered only one or two days each week, so that they need not be absent from their fields and other work.

On the borderlands along the steppes, there were settled dragoons, "organized in permanent residence,"[35] whose duties were to serve both as cavalry and infantry.

The number of soldiers living in settlements was small during the exhausting and prolonged wars in the reign of Tsar Alexis. In 1653 messengers sent from the tsar began galloping from city to city. Arriving in town a messenger gathered the service gentry and junior boyars in a meeting and delivered to them the sovereign's gracious message. He encouraged them to have their children, brothers, and nephews who were not already in service and who were not busy on military tenures to enlist as soldiers. He assured them that, if they did, they would without fail receive the sovereign's salary and favor. The sovereign had ordered that they be enrolled in the service lists for duty with him and in Moscow. They would receive their maintenance, and money would be provided for their uniforms. If they should not enlist as soldiers, henceforth they were not to be called servicemen and should never be allowed to enter the sovereign's service. Instead, they would thereafter be agriculturists. It was at the same time ordered that, in the commercial and manufacturing districts of cities and in the tax-exempt suburbs, a census be taken of the nephews, sons-in-law, foster children, co-owners of property, and all the varieties of domestic workhands who were related to or associated with the musketeers, as well as their domestic servants who were not indentured slaves or field workers. The decree further stipulated that half of their children, brothers, and nephews were to be conscripted into military service, while the other half were to remain with them at home.

In this manner were constituted regiments of "soldiers," or *zheldaki*. Each regiment was designated after its commander's name, for example, the Agei Shepelev Regiment. As mentioned, each person who enlisted as a soldier was promised maintenance and money for a uniform. A sergeant [*serzhant*] received nine dengas daily for maintenance, a supply officer [*kaptenarmus*] and a subaltern [*podpraporshchik*], eight. A captain [*kapitan*] drew a salary of seven rubles a month, and a lieutenant [*poruchik*], five. Half a ruble as travel allowance and an equal amount for clothing were also provided. Soldiers' wives and mothers received a free allowance of salt.

But if the old servicemen sometimes had to endure hardships under military commanders, the soldiers of the new military units found that their colonels had even less occasion to stand on ceremony with them, who were persons of most inconsequential origins. The soldiers of the Agei Shepelev Regiment complained that their colonel beat them, maimed them, and cast them into prison without the sovereign's decree or inquiry for the sake of his own extortionate profit, and that he took from them sizable gifts. The soldiers sought to take vengeance on the civilian population for their injuries and losses.

COSSACKS AND MUSKETEERS

Next to these service people with new, foreign names—soldier [*soldat*], reiter [*reitar*], and dragoon [*dragun*]—there was preserved an old type of military organization consisting of the city garrison cossacks [*gorodovye kozaki*], who received a salary from the government during periods of active duty, and to whom in peacetime the government granted households, cultivable land, and exemption from quitrent and taxes. Also untouched were the musketeers [*streltsy*]. These regiments, dispatched on campaigns in wartime, constituted garrison forces in times of peace, acting as police and fire departments in the cities. The musketeers occupied separate neighborhoods in the cities, each one with his own house, crafts, and trade. Together, they carried out their duties in the sovereign's service. In Moscow alone there were more than twenty regiments of musketeers, with from 800 to 1000 men in each regiment. One of them was a select regiment,[36] always to be found near the tsar, as a guard for him and the tsaritsa in all their travels. The officers of the musketeers were regimental commanders [*golovy*], battalion commanders [*polugolovy*], company commanders [*sotniki*], platoon leaders [*piatidesiatniki*], and squad leaders [*desiatniki*]. Appointed to the top three ranks were persons from the service gentry and junior boyars, while musketeers provided personnel for the two lower grades. The musketeers were given a permanent monetary salary, cloth for uniforms, and salt.

SUMMARY OF EARLY MILITARY REFORMS

Such were the military forces of Muscovy prior to the reforms of Peter the Great. Preparatory moves for those reforms were already taking shape, not through abolition of what was old, but through the introduction of innovations. Yet, as usually happens, the first steps were uncertain. In the first place, the changes were inaugurated hesitantly and without any official recognition of their superiority. The old militia on horseback retained its predominance, so that no one from among the important gentry desired to serve as a reiter or soldier. The descendants of the old retainers regarded the new military units just as they regarded the musketeers—with scorn. As before, the only permanent military force was the musketeers. As soon as a war was over, all the military personnel dispersed to their homes. Also dismissed to go home were the service people of the new units, the reiters and soldiers.

MAINTENANCE OF THE MILITARY FORCES

In a variety of ways land had to provide for the maintenance and subsistence of the military personnel. In peacetime, one individual with military responsibilities might obtain his living from a military tenure, while another might derive his likewise from a hereditary landed estate. In both cases the burden of support was borne by the peasantry, which was attached to the military tenures and to the landed estates. When war came, a military man would have to be given assistance in the form of a monetary salary. The cost of this was assumed not only by the peasants, but also by the working people of the cities. Depending on the demands of war, they paid money in an amount equivalent to a twentieth, tenth, or a fifth of the amount derived from their accumulated wealth and income. These circumstances make evident that the poverty of the state and the absence of a permanent military force were the main conditions behind the summoning of assemblies, which were convened usually on the occasion of war. It was necessary to ascertain how prepared the military forces were for undertaking a campaign and how ready the commercial and industrial segments of the population were to provide money for this purpose. When a permanent military force appeared and stable sources of revenue were assured, the assemblies were terminated. Finally, a third type of maintenance for military personnel was that which derived from the performance of administrative functions.

CENTRAL AND PALACE ADMINISTRATION

The performance of administrative functions provided the means of support for persons of different classes, ranging from boyars to the very lowest service people. The boyars, lords-in-waiting, and members of the council established themselves in various crown chancelleries [prikazy]. The crown chancellery was one of the most prominent and characteristic features of Muscovy. Because of its very simplicity, it is impossible to determine the time of its origin. The sovereign would commission one of his close assistants to take permanent care of some matter or perhaps several matters, either related or unrelated to each other, and would assign one or two persons to aid him. For conducting correspondence and executing other written work, there inevitably appeared chancellors and clerks. Thus would be created a chancellery. Because such an agency had its own expenditures, there would be assigned to it the administration of certain cities or categories of taxpayers. From these it collected taxes. With the expansion of state activity, each new matter led to the formation of a new chancellery, and they thus proliferated ever more.

Not all the chancelleries can be dealt with here. There simply were too many of them. It is nonetheless possible to describe those which, better than the rest, exemplified the distinctive traits of early Russian organization.

Here, then, were the chancelleries[37] in which were concentrated the economic functions of the great sovereign and the management of the following palace offices and facilities [tsarskie dvory]: the royal treasure-house, beverage preparation facility, kitchen, bakery, granary, and the stables. The character of the great sovereign as lord and master, and his relations to his servitors are here clearly discernible. A treasurer and two chancellors presided over the Chancellery of the Royal Treasure-house, where were deposited the tsar's treasury, gold and silver vessels, and a vast variety of both expensive and inexpensive fabrics. This, then, was a household treasury, from which could be withdrawn items and money to meet the different needs of individuals in the tsar's household and also to pay the salaries of various people. The sovereign dispensed fine cloth to persons close to him and in general to those who served him personally. He presented high dignitaries with coats of velvet, gold, and satin on sable. When the great sovereign desired that a boyar be granted some article of apparel as a gift, he ordered that not only the cloth itself be given, but all the materials needed to trim it.

On one occasion, for instance, the sovereign wished to present a gift of the finest dark-red fabric to be purchased on market row, as well as a stipulated quantity of decorative trim: five arshins of cloth purchased for 2 rubles, 16 altyns, and 4 dengas per arshin; 15 arshins of gold lace at 10 altyns per arshin; 14 arshins of taffeta ribbon for trim at 3 dengas per arshin; 14 buttons with enamel and ruby spangles at 1 grivna per button; for edging, one and a half arshins of satin, for a total of 1 ruble, 16 altyns, 4 dengas; and 2 zolotniks of silk at 2 altyns—for a grand total of 20 rubles, 5 altyns, and 4 dengas. It was decreed that all these items were to be given as a present. The caftan itself, however, had to be sewn together at the boyar's house, where he had his own tailor as part of his domestic facilities just as the great sovereign had tailors and furriers, some 100 people in all, as part of the royal treasure-house. Clothes were sewn domestically, but stockings and gloves for the sovereign and the tsareviches were made in the Novodevichy convent, whose nuns excelled at this type of handwork.

It might happen that a person no less distinguished than the boyar Artamon Matveev[38] could be found on market row engaged in purchasing gold, silver, and gold lace trimmed with silver. Why was it that Matveev, a boyar, took charge of such an errand? Was he a treasurer or did he generally serve as manager of the tsar's palace facilities? No, his usual duties consisted of conducting foreign affairs and administering the Chancellery for Little Russia. But he was a person very close to the sovereign and his family, and because of this he went about placing orders for stockings and gloves.

Besides purveying to the leading dignitaries, the royal treasure house also provided annual quantities of cloth, silks, and taffeta to be made into clothing for the service gentry, crown agents, palace attendants, grooms, falconers, choristers, fire tenders, the tsaritsa's craftswomen, and seamstresses. Other items included velvet caps, sable hats, cloth for lining, and leather for boots. Every year the royal treasure-house also sent fabrics to the musketeers, and the Don Cossacks received an annual allotment of cloth, silks, and sables.

The great sovereign was gracious in not neglecting to remember the clergy. Indeed, from the cathedrals of Moscow and other cities, as well as from ordinary churches supported by the tsar, there came to the royal treasure-house a continuous stream of priests, deacons, sextons, and church servitors seeking to obtain the tsar's allowance of money and cloth. Some churchmen were given such contributions annually, while others received them once every several years, depending on different arrangements. More than 18,000 members of the clergy would call on the royal treasure-house after fabrics. Nor were disbursements limited only to the Russian clergy. It was always possible to find in Moscow monastics from Greece, whether bishops, archimandrites, or ordinary monks, who came for donations. They would have in their possession charters granting them the right to be in Moscow for a certain period of time in which to collect money for church development. The royal treasure-house provided them with vessels, brocades, and velvets.

Whence came the money for all these expenses? The Chancellery of the Royal Household held the answer. It was administered by a boyar and majordomo, as well as a lord-in-waiting, a member of the service gentry of the council, and two or three chancellors. With jurisdiction over more than 40 cities, it obtained revenues in the form of taxes from residents of commercial and manufacturing districts. It also collected duties from tollhouses, state franchises, and all sorts of profitable appurtenances to arable lands. Besides the 40 cities, it exercised supervision over eight Moscow suburbs inhabited by boilermakers, pewterers, blacksmiths, carpenters, fishermen, upholsterers and tentmakers, potters, stovemakers, and masons. The chancellery took in annual revenues of more than 120,000 rubles, which then were paid out for all kinds of palace expenses. Within the jurisdiction of the Chancellery of the Royal Household lay the following offices and facilities: a beverage preparation facility, kitchen, bakery, and granary. These had the same characteristics as those of the royal treasure-house. From the 30 cellars of the beverage preparation facility there were drawn each day some 325 gallons of wine, and from 1,300 to 1,625 gallons of beer and honey. There arrived from various countries envoys with numerous suites, and regardless how long they remained in Moscow, they were provided with food and drink at the tsar's expense. These were guests, and it was inconceivable for a host to have them pay for their own subsistence. Besides foreigners, certain designated Russians also were authorized by the great sovereign to be granted rations of food and drink.

The kitchen daily prepared many different kinds of dishes for the sovereign's table and for distribution elsewhere. From every dinner and supper of the tsar, fire tenders were dispatched with dishes as largesse to the boyars, members of the council, and gentlemen of the bedchamber. If one of them failed to receive his gift, there would arrive at the palace on the following day a complaint to the majordomo, full of invective for the stewards. What was the meaning of this oversight? Nothing had been done to provoke the anger or displeasure of the tsar. What sort of dishonor, then, was this? A petition might be sent to the tsar himself: "I fail to see that I am blameworthy in any respect, and yet I have been dishonored before my brothers in the distribution of the tsar's largesse." An investigation would begin. Since everything was recorded, it was possible to find in the registers the names of recipients, nonrecipients, and those entrusted with conveying the food. Should no entry be found in the registers, it meant that someone had forgotten to fulfill his assignment. Messengers offered apologies to the injured party, while the tsar visited his wrath on the majordomo and lord-in-waiting. The stewards would be held in confinement the whole day. Should there be an entry located in the registers indicating that a delivery had been dispatched with such-and-such a fire tender, he would be summoned for interrogation: What had he done with it? Perhaps he ate it himself, or dropped it in the dirt, or spilled it. In that case the fire tender would be beaten with rods in front of the palace.

Every day there were prepared for the sovereign's table and for distribution as largesse more than 3,000 dishes. The amount of fish alone exceeded 100,000 rubles in value annually. Many of the supplies came from rural districts assigned to the palace. They sent rye, oats, wheat, millet, hemp, live sheep, ham, chickens, eggs, cheese, butter, and hops. They were obliged also to furnish a specified number or quantity of flaxen reins, bast, mat bags, horse collars with tugs, hame straps and breech bands, shafts for sleds and wagons, shaft bows, firewood, and hay.

Connected with the granary were some 300 storehouses. Grain of all kinds, the produce of fields cultivated for the tsar, was brought there from villages assigned to the palace and cities in the grain-producing regions of the south and southeast. However, that grain was not intended only for the tsar's use, but was given as an allowance to the clergy, court servitors, and other classes of people, like the musketeers. The grain was taken from the granary and sent to the tsar's mills in Moscow and to various villages for grinding. It was then brought to the bakery, where, besides supplies for the palace, breads and fancy loaves were baked for distribution to a wide variety of people.

For the production of sour cream, milk, and cheese there was established near Moscow a dairy with 200 cows. Other dairies also were located in nearby villages. The cows were purchased from Archangel,

Kholmogory, and various districts, at a cost of from 2 rubles and 1 altyn to 6 rubles. Fresh fruits and vegetables for palace use came from the sovereign's gardens, of which there were more than 50 in Moscow and its environs, and in various cities. In the gardens of Moscow alone, there were 14,545 apple trees, 494 pear trees, 2,994 cherry trees, 72 beds of raspberries, 14 grapevines, 192 plum trees, 260 beds of red currants and 252 shrubs, and 74 beds of black currants.

Whenever supplies were not forthcoming from the rural districts assigned to the palace, arrangements were made with contractors to furnish them. Sometimes purchases were made directly in various places by the palace. If a large quantity of nuts was needed, three crown agents from the granary were sent to make purchases in Tula, Kaluga, Kashin, Yurev Polsky, and Pereiaslavl Zalessky. There and in the countryside round about these cities, they scoured markets large and small. Military governors were ordered to have local officials ready for the selection of nuts and their transportation to Moscow, to have clerks available for completing the necessary paperwork, to have musketeers and cannoneers standing by, to have barns prepared for storing the nuts before their delivery to Moscow, and to have guards on hand for protection. With similar ceremony was hempseed oil purchased in the city and county of Kaluga. From the townspeople of Mozhaisk and Viazma, as well as their environs, were purchased apples, pears, bergamots, plums, and cherries. They were packed in barrels and covered with syrup, or salted in the case of plums, and sent to Moscow. Grapes packed in syrup were brought from Astrakhan.

In Astrakhan were located the sovereign's own vineyards. There was an old vineyard planted by Russians in 1647, two vineyards begun by the Holsteiner Yakov Davydov, a vineyard started by the Frenchman Poskazaius (!) Podovin (Poitevin?), a vineyard purchased from Ushakov, and nine vineyards appropriated for the sovereign. The inhabitants of Astrakhan did not dare sell grapes from their vineyards without advance written permission from the tsar, and merchants were forbidden to buy any from them under penalty of severe punishment. In Astrakhan and along the Terek river much effort went into the manufacture of wine for the tsar's use. Foreigners were sent for, Poskazaius Podovin among them, who taught the art of winemaking to the Russians. In 1658 there were sent from Astrakhan to Moscow 3,920 gallons of wine for use by the great sovereign; in 1659 there were sent 3,250 gallons, pressed from grapes out of the tsar's vineyards.

The royal treasure-house had need of another expensive item of merchandise that could be procured in the south—silk. In 1658 there arrived some 35 pounds of raw silk, made by foreigners and Armenians who were masters of silk production in Astrakhan. Orders were issued for the Russians to sell it to the treasury, and for the treasury then to sell it to Persia. In 1673 the hetman Samoilovich,[39] in compliance with a directive from the tsar, sent to Moscow some Ukrainians who were supposed to tell what time of year and in what kind of soil to sow anise. Having done so, they were then dispatched to the vicinity of Nizhny Lomov and Shatsk, southeast of Moscow.

The Chancellery of the Horse originally was administered by a boyar of the horse, the foremost boyar in rank and honor. In the seventeenth century that title was abolished, and a master of the horse took over the function, assisted by a member of the service gentry and some chancellors. They had responsibility for more than 40,000 horses.

It is understandable that no boyar could be installed to head the Privy Chancellery, founded by Tsar Alexis to take care of correspondence about which he did not wish everyone to know. It consisted of a chancellor and several clerks. Besides its primary function, this chancellery also had jurisdiction over matters of special interest to the tsar. It administered the production of explosive ordnance and supervised those who were masters of this art. Also it was given charge of the tsar's favorite pastime—birds, gerfalcons, and hawks. The breeding of pigeons was undertaken to keep these predators fed, for which purpose a special facility was established that maintained more than 100,000 pigeon roosts. These innocent birds were also under the jurisdiction of the Privy Chancellery, which because of its name came to be viewed as something most sinister, in which some persons purported to see an institution comparable to a secret police.

The Ambassadorial Chancellery, which "supervised matters pertaining to all neighboring states," did not for a long time possess much importance, for problems concerning relations with foreign countries were settled in the palace by the sovereign with his boyars and members of the council. When negotiations were to be undertaken with foreign envoys, again the tsar would appoint certain of his boyars and members of the council for this purpose. Consequently the Ambassadorial Chancellery constituted merely an office of the boyar council for foreign affairs. As such, it was headed by a chancellor of the council. Only after the treaty of Andrusovo[40] was the conduct of diplomacy entrusted to a single boyar, Ordin-Nashchokin, who was given the splendid title "Lord High Protector of the Ambassadorial Affairs of State and of the State Seal," which is to say, lord chancellor. Afanasy Ordin-Nashchokin, by virtue of his Western outlook, entertained a high regard for the Ambassadorial Chancellery, referring to it as "Russia's eye" in the sense that foreigners used it as a standard for making judgments about the whole country and its people.[41] He strictly insisted that chancellors not mix their drinking and night life with diplomatic business, and that they exercise restraint in conversations with foreigners.

Yet it was quite difficult for them to fulfill their primary duty. For another administrative agency was attached to the Ambassadorial Chancellery and placed under the direction of the chancellor of the council in charge of foreign affairs. This was the Chancellery for Novgorod. It exercised administrative control over, and collected revenues from, the cities of Great Novgorod, Pskov, Nizhny Novgorod, Archangel, Vologda, and other cities along the coast and borders. Moreover, after 1667 there were attached also to the Ambassadorial Chancellery not only the Chancellery for Little Russia—which was appropriate enough—but also the chancelleries for Vladimir and Galicia.

The kinds of matters that fell under the authority of the Chancellery of Military Tenures are self-evident from the very name. Since no distinction existed between military and civil service, the Chancellery of State Service and Appointments had charge of administering assignments to both categories of duty. The same people were called upon to serve in the one or the other category. But because there later came into being special military units, new chancelleries were formed for the administration of musketeers, reiters, cannoneers, and foreigners in Muscovite service.

The Chancellery of the Exchequer administered the foremost merchants, the merchants of the commercial guild, the members of the cloth guild, the master silversmiths, the merchants of numerous cities other than Moscow, and the mint. The Chancellery of State Revenues collected customs duties and income in Moscow and other cities from shops, storehouses, cellars, and weights and measures. The Chancellery of Financial Control was in charge of receipts and expenditures for Muscovy as a whole.

The Chancellery for Criminal Affairs held jurisdiction in matters relating to criminal acitvity throughout Muscovy. There were two tribunals for the disposition of civil cases pertaining to the service class—the judicial chancelleries of Moscow and Vladimir. Agencies that administered particular regions were the Chancellery for Kazan, the Chancellery for Siberia, the Chancellery for the Principality of Smolensk, and the chancelleries for Novgorod, Vladimir, Ustiug, Kostroma, and Galicia.

The total number of crown chancelleries exceeded forty. The income they received from the entire realm was 1,300,000 rubles, excluding Siberian revenues. Alongside the sizable chancelleries dealing with matters of different kinds, there were also the Chancellery for the Commemoration of Souls, in charge of arranging memorial services for deceased tsars, and the Chancellery of the Apothecary, with jurisdiction over the pharmacy and some thirty foreign medical men, together with their twenty-odd Russian students. There existed a special Chancellery for the Collection of Provisions for the Musketeers. Besides a Chancellery for Stonework, there was also a Chancellery for State Storehouses.[42]

The chancelleries had numerous clerks. Divided into senior, intermediate, and junior clerks, their salaries ranged from 2 to 40 rubles in one chancellery, 4 to 65 in another, 5 to 50 in a third, and from 1 to 20 in still a fourth. Some clerks received grants of land from the state, ranging in size from 1,025 to 1,435 acres.[43] Apart from the clerks who were regularly enrolled in various service categories and were salaried, there were also unenrolled clerks, serving without regular pay. Divided into senior and junior clerks, they obtained remuneration solely from receipts. A particular chancellery might have a fairly large proportion of unsalaried clerks, indicating that it was possible to make a living, without depending on a government salary, from revenues received by clerks for registering documents. Thus for example, in the Chancellery of State Service and Appointments there were 74 salaried and 33 unsalaried clerks.

SERVICE POSTS OUTSIDE MOSCOW

As boyars, lords-in-waiting, service gentry of the council, and chancellors filled various posts in the chancelleries, there still remained service people of lower rank for whom no openings were available in any of them. They had to find one way or another of providing for their needs. Some petitioned to become military governors, and their requests sometimes were granted.

Happy was the member of the service gentry who prepared to go to some city where he had just been assigned as military governor. The prestige was great and the recompense, substantial. His wife also was pleased, since she was sure to reap certain benefits as well. The children and nephews were delighted, for after the elected chief of local administration [zemsky starosta] had paid his respects to their father and mother or uncle and aunt, he would do the same to them. All the members of the household staff, the stewards and servants, rejoiced. They now felt assured of being well provided for. The small children likewise leaped up and down with glee, since they would not be overlooked either. Much more grandiloquent now, because inspired by elation, were the nonsensical pronouncements of the household holy man, for he could also look forward to receiving gifts. This entire aggregation would then arise and betake itself off, fully confident of a prosperous future. Already in the distance could be seen the cathedral church of their new city.

THE RUSSIAN CITY

At first glance all Russian cities looked much alike. In the center stood the citadel, or fortress, constructed usually of wood and only rarely of stone. It might happen that a master city builder, some Dutchman perhaps, would have constructed a protective earthen rampart around it. Inside the citadel stood the cathedral church. Also located there was the provincial administrative office, from which the military governor administered provincial affairs and dispensed justice. In front of it were beaten debtors found in default of payments. Likewise within the citadel was the police and judicial district office for criminal affairs, as well as the state storehouse, or arsenal, in which were kept gunpowder and artillery ordnance. Finally, the citadel contained one or more prisons, the residences of the local bishop and the military governor, and the dwellings of nearby military tenants and landowners for use when the city was under enemy siege.

Beyond the wall lay the commercial and manufacturing district. It had an enormous square where on market days grain and all kinds of other merchandise were displayed. In the square stood the town hall, the center of civil administration, where sat the elected chiefs of local administration and where they met with the taxpaying townspeople to conduct official business. There was a large commercial hall, customshouse, liquor warehouse and drinking establishment, and a stable for horses. Farther along stood the residences of the taxpaying members of the urban community, comprising "a house (a warm habitation), a bathhouse with dressing room, an unheated storeroom and basement, and an outdoor storage cellar." Such a complex did not represent anything especially elegant by way of construction, amounting perhaps to some three rubles in overall value.

In winter the houses were warm inside, but summer in some cities could be quite cold. When spring came, and a few warm days had made themselves felt, official police criers appeared on the streets of the citadel and the commercial and manufacturing district. They would shout: "All persons are strictly forbidden to heat their houses and bathhouses! No one is to walk about or sit up late in the evening with a light! For baking bread and any kind of heating, stoves or ovens are to be lit in gardens and underground in empty spaces at some distance from the houses. The flames are to be shielded most carefully from the wind with bast screens!"

By order of the military governor, the city's houses and bathhouses were sealed, so that it was necessary for the residents to live in their unheated storerooms. Should low temperatures return, and in many places they returned with some frequency, the people shivered with cold. Some had nothing warm with which to allay their discomfort, for their stoves in the garden might have collapsed and they found themselves unable to build new ones. Not a single stone or brick could they locate for this purpose. All would have been taken to Moscow for urban construction projects there or for other building projects related to the tsar. Soup could not be prepared or bread baked anywhere. And thus, both because of frost and out of a need for bread, the people would leave their homes to live in rural districts and hamlets.

In the midst of these unpretentious neighborhoods, filled with small houses and annexes, there could be found churches. They also were generally of crude construction, some being of stone or brick, while most were made of wood. Next to the churches stood the houses of priests, deacons, and other church servitors. The parishioners elected their priest. When they did so, they obtained from him a written agreement: "They have elected me, the priest (so-and-so), in mutual agreement, and have submitted a petition bearing their signatures to the bishop concerning me, that I, a priest, am to serve on the basis of church revenues provided by contributions from the lay community, and that I, a priest, am to minister in cases of illness, childbirth, and all spiritual needs, and to serve God's church. I have not made a gift of any money for this church post, and neither have I purchased it. While serving in this church, I shall not call the church building or any sacred utensils my own, nor shall I have anything to do with the sale of church candles, the gathering of candle stubs, or the collection of church revenues. I, a priest, will not sell or pledge this ecclesiastical post, will not register it in my name, and will not certify any documents pertaining to the ownership of the land. Upon my death, in no manner shall my wife, children, near relatives, and kinsmen have any concern with this church post. I will neither appoint nor reject churchmen without the approval of the lay community. Should I in any way fail to fulfill the provisions of this agreement, the parishioners shall, with the bishop's permission, dismiss me from this church post." The existence of such written agreements is explained by complaints that priests gathered together churchmen under their own control and came to regard church holdings as their personal property.

In conjunction with the churches were to be found almshouses, or "houses of the beggarly brethren." Near each church was a cemetery, and at the edge of the city stood the charnel house, where were taken for burial in a common grave the bodies of criminals who had been executed, persons in disgrace with the tsar, and those who had died of drunkenness, suicide, or drowning.

REGIONAL AND LOCAL ADMINISTRATION

The time came for a new military governor to arrive in the city. The old governor would relinquish to him the fortifications, buildings, arms, supplies, money, and records. The new governor inspected everything to make sure it accorded with the lists, made an accounting over against the records of receipts and expenditures, and verified the registers of the servicemen, the taxpayers of the commercial and manufacturing district, and the county service people on call as the tsar's palace attendants, their children, brothers, and nephews who had reached maturity, their dependents and domestic workhands.

The governor brought with him a lengthy instruction written in the name of the tsar. It enumerated all his responsibilities and stipulated how he was to carry out the sovereign's business. He was to insure that everything belonging to the sovereign was maintained intact, and that guards were posted everywhere. He was to make certain with the greatest diligence that in neither the city nor the county should there exist any brigandage, theft, murder, fighting, robbery, illegal sale of liquor, or dissipation. Whoever should become known for these violations was to be seized and, upon investigation, punished. The governor was to dispense justice in all civil cases. He was to see that all the sovereign's revenues were obtained in full from the city and the county.

Standing in second place after the voivode was the chief of the local police and judicial district [gubnoi starosta], who had charge of criminal cases. He was elected by people of all ranks from among the service gentry or the junior boyars, though occasionally he was appointed without election by the crown.

The other main figure besides them was the chief of the city and county administration, there being but one head for both city and county because the peasants of the county were grouped together with the commercial and manufacturing taxpayers of the city by the same general economic obligations. Jointly they paid taxes and provided for the support of the governor, who in his turn governed the city and county together. In light of this connection between the taxpayers of the commercial and manufacturing district of a city and the county peasants, the latter sent to the town hall elected representatives to sit in the council.

Just as soon as an election of a chief of local administration was completed, a clerk would execute a written instrument to be signed by all the electors. It would state the following: "All the townspeople have elected and chosen for service in the community as chief of the city and county administration the following person (the name). He is to administer and take care of all kinds of matters in the community, while we, the people of the community, shall obey him. If we should not obey him, he shall oblige us, willingly or unwillingly, to attend to community affairs, but he shall not engage in any truculence toward the community. Whatever happens to the community on account of his truculence, he shall himself restore to good order." Besides the chief of local administration, certain cities also chose several administrators to serve as his associates.

The main item in the deliberations of the elected officials with the representatives of the townspeople and peasantry in the town hall was the apportionment of taxes. In this regard they were concerned with the election of tax assessors [okladchiki]. Chosen from among the higher, intermediate, and lower classes of people, the tax assessors were to be drawn from "qualified and knowledgeable persons, proficient in their work, who were known from their manner of life to be morally above reproach and dedicated to justice, and to whom the assignment of determining the standards of tax assessment for individual households was familiar." The townspeople also elected local officials [tselovalniki] to sit in the town hall and perform services for the central government.

The governor was forbidden to intervene in the collection of revenues, to deprive the community of its right to determine the rates of taxation for individual households, and to interfere in other matters pertaining to the community. He was not allowed to impose rates of taxation upon the townspeople and inhabitants of the county without an inquiry and decision by the members of the local community. Likewise he was not to meddle in local elections. With regard to the officials chosen to perform services for the crown, he could accept only the decision of the local electorate, certified by the signatures of the local administrators and members of the clergy. He might neither replace them nor put them in prison without cause, in his own self-interest. But if they were at fault he could both replace them and put them into prison, because as governor he was obliged to see to it that the local administrators, the officials chosen to perform the business of the crown, and the revenue collectors [denezhnye sborshchiki], who were wealthy men, did not abuse persons of less wealth and social standing, and that they did not collect excessive amounts of money from the local community.

A second item for discussion at the meetings in the town hall was the municipal economy. Here it was decided how to divide the cultivable land in all three municipal fields for a certain number of years until the next redistribution of the local community. At the same time, the townspeople would decide that no one was to transfer his land to a stranger for as long as one year or even a single summer. Should he do so, he would forfeit his landed property to the local community.

Finally, discussions were held in the town hall about the communal needs of the townspeople and the country dwellers, and about the cases that had to be brought to the attention of the local administrators or concerning which information was to be sent to Moscow. The chief of local administration stood foremost in this capacity, for as representative of the city and county population it was he who submitted petitions "on behalf of all the town and rural people."

TOWNSPEOPLE, TAXES, AND TROUBLES

Heavy were the civic obligations borne by the elected chief of local administration. For the local community comprised the taxpaying people, and the payment of taxes was an onerous burden in seventeenth-century Russia. A taxpayer was fixed to his city. If he should leave and stop paying his share, it was left to the local community to make up the amount for which he was responsible. During the Time of Troubles the taxpayers became scattered, and under Tsar Michael the government endeavored to return them to their former places of residence. For otherwise the deserted households were unable to pay anything, and no revenues were accruing to the treasury. The Code of 1649 permitted migrants who settled in a new location to remain where they were; but of course it could not allow them to move again from city to city, thereby avoiding taxation.

Since the burden of taxation lay heavily upon the settled population, it is understandable why there were many who desired to leave. In 1658 the death penalty was declared for migration from one town to another, as well as for marriage in another town without a written release. "They are fleeing!" wailed the communities in petitions to the tsar. "Their households are abandoned and empty. We cannot pay and are perishing under indebtedness!" The crown ordered that those who absconded be apprehended. But how was it possible to catch a fugitive in a country whose dominant features were a thick forest and a boundless plain? The enactment of the death penalty for unlawful flight demonstrates better than anything else the powerlessness of the measures undertaken by the government.

The fact that people were fleeing and leaving their households was one source of trouble for the local communities. But there was another. When newcomers arrived, they settled and built houses. Thus entire suburbs appeared next to the existing cities. The newcomers, however, were not subject to taxation. As such, they were spoilers, people who pledged themselves to dependence upon bishops and boyars, and engaged in trade and industry, but who paid no taxes to the crown and did nothing to help shoulder that burden. Again petitions went out from the local communities. At first they remained unanswered, because the wealthy did not wish to lose people who had become pledged to them. Only after an uprising in Moscow, when petitions were again submitted at a national assembly, was the Code of 1649 enacted, containing the following provision: "The suburbs belonging to bishops, boyars, and people of all ranks, which have been established in cities on urban lands, shall pass irrevocably to municipal status. Suburbs shall not be built on crown lands, and urban lands shall not be purchased for this purpose. Landed properties and land grants located in or near cities shall be appropriated in the sovereign's name and shall be joined to the cities with respect to taxes and crown service. In exchange, landowners and property holders shall be given land from the sovereign's villages. Those who dare pledge themselves in dependence upon private persons shall be punished with the whip and exiled to the Lena river in Siberia. Whoever accepts a person in pledged dependence shall suffer great disgrace. Lands on which live people who have pledged themselves shall be confiscated in the name of the sovereign." A loophole was foreseen and an attempt was made to close it: "Any person residing in a city who has houses and gardens outside the city limits shall keep there only a single caretaker. If he should begin to maintain numerous peasants and cotters, they shall pass into the category of taxpayers in the name of the sovereign."

Notwithstanding these measures there failed to materialize a rebellion of persons who had pledged themselves to dependence upon others. Nevertheless the government was not powerful enough to prosecute to a conclusion a struggle in its own interests and those of the local communities as opposed to the interests of private individuals. It threatened those who pledged themselves with the whip and Siberia, and those who accepted pledged dependents with some sort of ominous, but vague disgrace. In 1667 the crown was compelled to express itself more clearly. It issued a warning that it would confiscate the landed estates and land grants of those who accepted as pledged dependents persons who formerly had been pledged dependents but who since had become registered taxpayers, and also peasants who belonged to the taxpaying population.

The urban taxpayers occasionally had to suffer retaliation when their petitions successfully brought about the return of fugitives from the estates of wealthy neighboring landlords. Fugitive taxpayers from the city of Lukh[44] were accepted in the village of Myt, which belonged to Prince Repnin. In accordance with the Code of 1649, they were taken back to Lukh. Thereafter, Prince Repnin's overseer in Myt, Shibaev, together with two local peasant brothers named Strelov, never overlooked an opportunity to take vengeance upon the inhabitants of Lukh for the way in which the crown had resolved the question. On one occasion, at a fair in Tikhonova Pustyn,[45] located southwest of Moscow, three persons from Lukh were working at a stall displaying cakes, soap, and berries. Seemingly from out of nowhere sprang Shibaev with his peasants. Down to the ground toppled the cakes, soap, and berries, while the sellers themselves were barely able to flee to safety, closely pursued by the peasants from Myt with drawn knives. Another time, Shibaev appeared once more at the fair in Tikhonova Pustyn with a large armed crowd. He called for the townspeople from Lukh to be seized and brought before him. Upon hearing his orders, the townspeople dropped their goods and fled. Nonetheless, two were stabbed and the goods lost. On yet a third occasion, still during the fair, when all the townspeople had gathered at Tikhonova Pustyn for the festivities, leaving behind only the very old and very young, Shibaev suddenly appeared in Lukh, accompanied by seventy armed peasants. At the provincial administrative office, he shouted that he was going to kill the governor. From the office he went to the tavern, where he broke into the storeroom, demanding free wine. After that he rode through the town, crying, "Strike! Stab the townspeople to death!" From fear, women broke into headlong flight to the forest, while some of those who were pregnant gave birth. The people of Lukh did not dare venture close to the village of Myt. Yet it was near there that passed the highroad between Nizhny Novgorod and Balakhna. Consequently Lukh grew isolated, its inhabitants unable to go anywhere to trade.

Sometimes the urban taxpayers were visited by misfortune that originated with their own confreres, the wealthy merchants of Moscow. During the reign of Tsar Michael the commercial guild appealed to the government that its numbers be increased, and the sovereign decreed that such augmentation take place through the enlistment of the best people of the suburbs. In 1647, at the beginning of Tsar Alexis' reign, the commercial guild again submitted a petition, declaring that many of its people had died while others had become impoverished because of their services to the crown. There remained no one left to serve. The sovereign decreed that the membership of the guild should be increased with the best people from the small traders, artisans, hired workers, and others in the lower categories of townspeople in Moscow and other cities. But in 1648, taking advantage of the rebellion,[46] local city officials petitioned that their confreres who had been enrolled in the commercial guild be returned to them. The sovereign agreed to this, and the commercial guild openly admitted that it did not dare, through fear of the possible consequences, to lodge a counter-petition during that troubled time. The next year, however, when things had calmed down and apprehension had dissipated, the commercial guild once more submitted a petition requesting an increase in its enrollment.

Official tax records attest to the fact that the foremost rank of merchants then included merely 13 members, while the commercial guild totaled 158 in the highest, intermediate, and lowest categories. This stood in sharp contrast to the 350 families prior to the destruction of Moscow. In the cloth guild, there remained 116 persons. This information furnishes the best indication of the consequences that the Time of Troubles, with the havoc that it wrought in Moscow, had for the Russian merchant class, who were unable to recover throughout the seventeenth century.

As a result of the war with Poland [starting in 1654], there appeared in Moscow many prisoners who were White Russians. They were known as "burghers" [meshchane],[47] a name theretofore unknown in Great Russia. In accordance with the treaty of Andrusovo [in 1667], they received their freedom but desired to remain in Moscow. At first they were registered as taxpayers in the lower categories of townspeople and in the suburbs. But in 1671 a decree commanded that a new suburb be constructed for them beyond the Presentation [Sretensky] gate. This neighborhood received the name "Burghers' Suburb" [Meshchanskaia sloboda], and the burghers were placed under the jurisdiction of the Chancellery for Little Russia.

Numerous obstacles stood in the way of anyone who wished to leave his town and the status of taxpayer in exchange for the freedom of a person exempt from the payment of taxes. But did not there exist the possibility of entering the category of service people, whom the government also needed? Evidently the need for taxpayers was, from the very beginnings of the Muscovite state, just as great as the need for service people. Even then the princes in their treaties with one another constantly reiterated the provision that they would together regulate the taxpaying population, and that they would not accept any taxpayers into their own service. After the devastations of the seventeenth century, the need for service people was not in any way diminished. Yet the crown did not allow taxpayers to be transferred into the category of service people. It prescribed that free persons, who wished to do so, could be admitted into that category, but only if they were not taxpayers. One legal case involved a taxpayer who had enrolled of his own free will into the musketeers. It was decreed that he be returned to his former status as a taxpayer with two of his sons, while only a third son was allowed to remain in the musketeers. A single exception to the general rule prohibiting any change in the status of taxpayers applied in the case of people who had entered the ranks of the cossacks prior to the Smolensk campaign at the beginning of the war with Poland in the reign of Tsar Alexis.

If the government did not allow taxpayers to enter military service, it was even more reluctant to have them enter the civil service as clerks. To be sure, it was quite willing to afford them an opportunity "to earn a living with the pen," but only under condition that they did not leave the status of taxpayers. In 1668 two townsmen from Vologda submitted the following petition: "We have become impoverished because of fires and because of the introduction of copper money.[48] There remains nothing with which we can trade, engage in manufacture, or support ourselves. In Vologda there are to be found impoverished townspeople who earn their living in the notarial office by performing duties as notaries public. Grant us, Sovereign, permission to earn our living as notaries public and to divide equally with the present notaries the fees charged for the preparation of documents, lest in the future we become unable to pay your taxes and perform your services, and also lest we ourselves perish." Permission for this was granted, "provided that the other impoverished people have indeed taken to working as notaries public, and provided also that they shall continue to pay their taxes together with the other townspeople."

In their notarial office the notaries public drafted various kinds of legal documents and letters for others. Over the notaries public stood a supervisor, who was responsible for seeing that those documents and letters were formulated with his approval. He was to insure that the notaries entered into the documents the names of the parties concerned and otherwise completed them properly. He was to watch that merchants did not give advance payment for the documents before they had been recorded, but made payment at the time the records were completed and submitted to the provincial administrative office. The supervisor had to make certain that none of the notaries surreptitiously entered fraudulent eyewitness testimony in legal depositions, or prepared documents pertaining to guaranteed loans without the required certification, which would have meant the loss of registration fees. The supervisor also had the duty of submitting to the provincial administrative office reports, signed by witnesses, concerning those who defaulted and were subsequently excluded from the market place. Supervisors were appointed typically in the following manner. The notaries public submitted a petition attesting that their supervisor had become old and requesting the great sovereign to give his permission for a person whom they nominated to become their new supervisor. The great sovereign thereupon would grant the necessary permission. In small towns and suburbs the duties of notary public were farmed out to some single individual.

The same conditions of bondage that existed in Russia until just recently[49] with regard to peasants and household servants applied also in early times to taxpaying townspeople, who were fixed to their cities. Thus, when a free man married a widow who was classified as a taxpayer and he went to live in her house, or if a free man married a town girl and went to live in the home of his father-in-law, the one and the other became attached to the city as taxpayers.

TAXES AND EXTRAORDINARY IMPOSTS

It was the duty of the fighting men to serve; it was the obligation of the taxpayers[50] to pay for their support. This original relationship between the two parts of the population continued for centuries and shaped the fundamental view they held of one another. A man in military service regarded a townsman or peasant as an individual whose labor, and the custody of that labor, had for their immediate purpose the maintenance of himself, the warrior. The seventh chapter of the Code of 1649 begins as follows with respect to service by all military men in Muscovy: "The Sovereign Tsar and Grand Prince Alexis Mikhailovich of all Russia has established eternal peace and a peace treaty with the Polish, Lithuanian, German, and other neighboring states. If war breaks out for any reason between the Muscovite state and some other country, or if at any time the Sovereign commands that hostility on the part of some enemy of his is to be avenged, and if he then orders his boyars and military governors, together with military men of various ranks, to be sent against them, for that service the Sovereign orders that his Sovereign's salary shall be given to his Sovereign's military men of the entire Muscovite state, and that for the Sovereign's salary for the military men, money shall be collected from the entire Muscovite state."

Five years after the enactment of this statute, which merely gave articulation to ancient custom, a series of wars began that continued to the end of Tsar Alexis' reign, and carried over into the reign of his successor. Hostilities erupted with the Poles[51] and Swedes,[52] with the Ukrainian cossacks, Tatars, and Turks,[53] with Razin[54] and the rebels at Solovetsky Monastery.[55] It is easy to understand the plight of the taxpaying population.

Situations arose which saw the elected representatives of the townspeople returning to their cities after attending an assembly in Moscow. With them they would bring news that a decision had been made to go to war. Already stipulated in the Code of 1649 were the immediate consequences of such a decision. Money had to be collected. To this end a decree would not be long in forthcoming. It would direct the collection of "a fifth, tenth, or twentieth part of money." Thereupon the taxpaying population would come forth and, "in accordance with the holy and undefiled commandment in the Gospel of Christ," declare the truth concerning the amount that each one was called upon to pay out of his wealth and income. It was impossible to conceal anything. One's fellow merchants, who were well versed in the business of trade and knew everyone's income, would declare and assign the amounts to be paid. At the beginning of the Polish war under Tsar Alexis, the amount initially collected was a twentieth part of one's wealth and income. Then for several years this was increased to a tenth. In 1662 and for three years thereafter, a fifth was exacted.[56]

To support the fighting men, demands were made not only for money, but also for agricultural commodities, such as rye flour, biscuits, groats, and oat flour. Carts were requisitioned for military use. Sixty households were responsible for furnishing one horse with driver, a wagon with complete harness, and all the supplies needed for travel. These constituted extraordinary imposts, prescribed in case of war.

On a regular basis the taxpaying people paid direct taxes and also charges on the use of crown lands, pastures, forests, hunting and fishing places, shops, mills, etc. They regularly furnished money to pay the ransom for prisoners of war (eight dengas from each household and two dengas from each household of the service people). They paid to support the musketeers, the postal service, and the military governors, and to help maintain the clerks, guards, executioners, prison warders, and local judicial and police officials. They provided funds for the construction of the governors' buildings, the local police and judicial offices, and jails. They supplied money to the provincial administrative office for candles, paper, ink, and firewood, and paid a so-called "ice-hole money" for permission in winter to draw water, wash clothes, and water livestock in ice holes. The taxpaying population was also responsible for the erection and repair of fortresses within cities and the construction of bridges.

In 1658, when the war intensified, new means were sought out everywhere to increase the state's revenues and compel those to pay who had not yet made any contribution. Charters were sent to the cities. A census was ordered of all cotters, itinerants, and domestic workhands who performed no crown services or paid any taxes, and who lived free of exactions. A hue and cry arose among the cotters, and they submitted a petition: "It is not true that we, your orphans, are free from taxation! Since the year 1624 we have been paying annually to the treasury scheduled payments from households and unoccupied estates in the amount of 2 rubles and 10 altyns. For the Smolensk campaign we paid 2 rubles per household and are now paying 8 altyns and 2 dengas per household for grain supplies. From those same households we pay 6 altyns and 4 dengas on the number of household gates, 8 dengas per household for the ransom of war prisoners, and a ruble annually per household for the requisitioning of carts. In past years we have paid, together with the townspeople, a sum equivalent to the tenth part of our chattels and wages."

An idea of the money forthcoming from a city of moderate wealth can be gained from the example of Great Ustiug.[57] In 1670 the city paid "taxes and duties; support in kind to the governor and other local authorities; court fees to judges; dues of all kinds to agents of the local authorities; taxes on arable land; payments of black sable; post taxes for the maintenance of transportation and communication; street-cleaning taxes; payments for the construction of city defenses, frontier fortifications, and saltpeter works; a direct tax on tilled land; a tax on falcons; duties and fees to treasurers, secretaries, and clerks; and payments to bailiffs on the basis of the number of gates in a household. All these taxes and duties, amounting to 321 rubles, 13 altyns, and 5 dengas, were leveled on the urban taxpaying district, whose number of households in various economic categories made it subject to a tax liability computed on an assessment level of 11 1/12 taxpaying units.[58] Moreover, a total of 81 rubles, 12 altyns, and 5 dengas was derived from shops and storehouses, from places where goods were sold and stored, from bread shelves, cookshops, smithies, boats, bridges, meadows, glades, vacant households, the village of Piatnitskoe in the vicinity of Ustiug, and from hamlets with newly-ploughed fields on which grain was subject to taxation. Customs duties generated 4,910 rubles; bathhouses, 44 rubles; and drinking establishments, 4,530 rubles." Part of these revenues were spent directly for permanent municipal requirements or for extraordinary expenses in accordance with instructions from Moscow.

In some cities, revenues proved insufficient to meet municipal requirements. The following information was sent from the city of Great Novgorod: "From Novgorod, its suburbs, its commercial and manufacturing districts, and its surrounding county, there is collected the assessed sum of 11,318 rubles in the form of direct taxes, payments for crown lands and facilities, customs duties, and alcohol taxes. In Great Novgorod the sum of scheduled expenditures for monetary salaries to the musketeers, cossacks of the city garrison, and individuals serving under contract to the government, and of unscheduled expenditures of all kinds amounts to 7,656 rubles. Allowances in grain for the support of musketeers, cossacks of the garrison, and persons under contract to the government amount to 57,156 bushels of rye, 43,344 bushels of oats, and 1,836 bushels of barley.[59] It will be necessary to provide 4,705 rubles in money at the lowest market price for grain. The total amount necessary to disburse for all kinds of scheduled and unscheduled expenses and for grain is 12,362 rubles, not counting the additional costs of new expenditures."[60]

The drain on resources had to be cut. Salaries were taken away from the regimental and company commanders of the musketeers and from the commander of the city garrison (because all of them were military tenants who held lands furnished by the government). The platoon and squad leaders of the musketeers had their salaries reduced, as did also the civilian clerks. Moreover, it was decreed that this reduced salary should be paid only to those who did not have lands furnished to them by the crown. Cannoneers were ordered to take the place of police officers in the provincial administrative office and throughout the surrounding counties, for which they would be compensated by a monetary salary and grain allotment. Blacksmiths and carpenters in the employ of the crown were not to be given a monetary salary or grain allotment; instead, they were to be furnished daily subsistence as the need for government work arose. Guards at the provincial administrative office and gatekeepers were deprived of their grain allotment. Nevertheless, despite these reductions, revenues still fell short of expenditures by 1,044 rubles. From Pskov and its suburbs the sum of 13,329 rubles was collected, but salaries had to be provided in the amount of 15,387 rubles, creating a deficit of 2,058 rubles. In response to a report describing this state of affairs, a decree was issued. It provided that the personnel of military garrisons in Novgorod and Ladoga were to be provided support in the form of land, for many areas in the region of Novgorod lay empty; the salary of the clerk in Ladoga was to be cut in half, etc.

An estimate would be made establishing a goal for some particular amount to be collected as revenue. But what if it could not be collected?

What if some townspeople declared that they were unable to pay? Then would follow torture for the collection of money. Still, some people were strong. Bearing up under the blows, they would persist in not paying. In that event the bailiffs were provided with an instruction: "Should the townspeople against whom have been instituted procedures for collecting arrears under torture offer resistance and fail to pay the monetary revenues, they shall forfeit their households, shops, and property to the great sovereign."

DUTIES OF THE TOWNSPEOPLE

It was not only taxes and extraordinary imposts that weighed heavily on the townspeople. They were required also to perform certain services for the crown. This obligation took time from their own work, but failure to comply carried the risk of punishment. One such duty in particular imposed exceedingly heavy burdens because of the responsibility entailed. This was service as an elected chief of a liquor warehouse and drinking establishment, or his assistant. Individuals holding such posts were involved in the sale of wine as an item of accountability to the state treasury.

In 1652 the sovereign, in session with the clergy and members of the council, decreed: "In all cities where taverns have been located heretofore, there shall be established a single liquor warehouse and drinking establishment.[61] Wine shall be sold in buckets[62] and mugs.[63] One cup[64] of wine shall be diluted to make three cups, and not more than one such reconstituted cup of wine is to be sold to each customer. Drunkards shall not be allowed to sit and drink in or near the drinking establishment. Admission to the drinking establishments also shall be barred to vagrants, revelers, and players of dice. Wine is not to be sold, even on Sundays, during the Great Fast preceding Easter or the fast before the Feast of the Dormition. During the fasts prior to Christmas and the Feast of St. Peter, wine shall not be sold on Wednesdays and Fridays. Members of the white and black clergy are not to be permitted on the premises, and wine shall not be sold to them. Only large villages are to have drinking establishments. The administration of the liquor warehouses and drinking establishments is to be entrusted to locally-elected officials, who shall undertake their duties under oath."

The extent of the treasury's profit from the sale of wine can be determined from the fact that in 1674 one bucket of wine cost the treasury 20 altyns, which it then sold for one ruble. When dispensed in mugs, the price of a bucket of wine at the drinking establishment was 1 ruble, 16 altyns, and 4 dengas; when dispensed in cups, the price went up to 2 rubles. To brew a bucket of beer cost the treasury seven dengas, but it sold for two altyns per bucket. Thirty-six pounds[65] of honey was purchased for a ruble. This yielded seven buckets of mead, each of which was then sold for 6 altyns and 4 dengas.

Distillers sometimes were brought in from the Ukraine. Townspeople of the highest rank were allowed to prepare wine in small quantities of up to two buckets in their own homes on the occasion of important holidays and special family celebrations—marriages, births, christenings, or wakes. The preparation of wine was not permitted to persons of intermediate and low social standing, though they were permitted on festive occasions to brew a little beer or mead, after first giving due notice about their intentions to the liquor administration and paying an alcoholic beverage tax.

It sometimes happened that permits were requested for preparing small amounts of wine or beer, whereas the actual quantity produced was considerably greater. This meant a loss to the treasury. Occasionally, illegal sales were made in secret. When news of this got out, it became necessary to apprehend the culprit in the act unawares and to confiscate the forbidden products. A considerable commotion might ensue, but nothing could be done to avoid it. A liquor administrator had to remain always on the alert, keeping a vigilant eye. For if, by the end of the year, profits should prove to be meager, a stern query would be forthcoming as to why receipts were so poor in comparison with previous years. A dutiful administrator and his assistants would have to reimburse the state with their own money, or face the prospect of flogging for failure to meet the expected revenues.

An additional difficulty for the liquor administrator lay in the fact that it was not always possible to sell alcoholic beverages for cash. Many people did not have any money on hand. With them it was necessary to accept credit. The debts they accumulated had to be collected at the end of the year, since the treasury would not wait for any reason. To collect the debts from customers for past consumption, an alcoholic beverage administrator had to remain on the best of terms with the local governor. This meant that he did not dare stint on gifts to the governor on holidays connected with members of the tsar's family, a practice known as "honoring His Tsarist Majesty." Nor could he hold back on the cost of items presented to the governor at dinners given by the latter, for custom required an invited guest to gift the host on such occasions. Even the sending of money to Moscow could not be accomplished with empty hands. The irksome importunities of crown chancellors and clerks for compensation had to be satisfied. One alcoholic beverage administrator related the following: "As regards the revenues of the drinking establishment, we paid the governors in kind and money several times by way of honoring His Tsarist Majesty, as well as for the delivery of revenues to Moscow, for the collection of debts, and for dinners. Upon our arrival in Moscow, we had to favor the chancellor several times with gifts in honor of His Tsarist Majesty. Likewise we had to present gifts to the clerk and junior clerks. Upon submitting the collected revenues, it was necessary to obtain receipts by providing on several occasions compensation in kind and money to the chancellor and clerk. We furnished the money that was paid in honor of His Tsarist Majesty out of our own pockets, except for what we acquired in the form of aid from our colleagues. We did not take anything from the collected state revenues, and we made the contributions voluntarily, without any coercion."

Besides compensating the governors and paying for the delivery of revenues to Moscow, the administrators of drinking establishments also had to contend with soldiers. The absence of discipline and the indulgence of their superiors, reflecting a society where the strong can do as they like with the unarmed and the weak, created a climate in which soldiers could with impunity give themselves over to violent behavior. Mention has been made of the brute force that a civilian overseer of a village might allow himself to use in a neighboring city. This was even more true of soldiers. On fast days, when it was prohibited to sell wine in the drinking establishments, soldiers nonetheless would appear there and begin to sell their own wine, pouring it from flasks into cups for persons who had no intention of observing the fast. At their quarters, where they stood on sentry duty, they sold all kinds of home-brewed spirits. A chief of the alcoholic beverage administration did not dare approach them to collect any revenues, for they boasted how they would do him to death. Notwithstanding the prohibition against it, they would gather at the drinking establishment to play at dice and cards. They did not allow drunkards into the drinking establishment, but sold wine to them outside on their own. Sometimes they beat the barkeeps half to death. The harm to the drinking establishment from all this was enormous, and yet it was the administrator and his assistants who had to answer for everything.

Townspeople also were called upon to serve in many other capacities: as chief administrators and assistants for collecting customs duties and grain for support of the musketeers, as collectors of duties and monetary revenues in the provincial administrative offices, as collectors of money for the branding of horses at the livestock market, as collectors of duties on bathhouses and on the passage of goods across bridges, as captains, lieutenants, and sergeants in the local police forces, and as investigators responsible for lodging charges in all cases involving theft.

Should there arrive in a city a decree from the tsar directing that an election be held to choose an administrator and assistants for the collection of customs duties, the elected chief of local administration would summon the townspeople to the town hall. Invariably the question arose whom to elect. It was desirable to choose people of means, who would be able to reimburse the state for any deficiencies in collection. But such were nowhere to be found. The wealthiest usually had been selected to administer the liquor warehouse and drinking establishment. In such an eventuality the community would decide to forward a petition to Moscow, pointing out that there was no one available locally to be elected, and asking the great sovereign to send an administrator from Moscow. Moscow, which had its own pressing needs for administrators, could not spare anyone. Instead, another decree would be dispatched to the petitioning city, ordering that the duty of customs collection should devolve upon the same persons who already had been chosen to supervise the alcoholic beverage facility. Thus the same group of people would find themselves weighed down with two heavy responsibilities at the same time.

SUPPORT OF LOCAL OFFICIALS

As mentioned earlier, the taxpaying inhabitants of cities and towns, together with their surrounding counties, gave money to support the governors and crown clerks. The funds furnished by a community were disbursed by the elected chief of local administration, who kept a daily written record of expenditures. Typically such records contained entries reflecting payments of the following sort: On 1 September [New Year's Day according to the old Russian calendar] the local governor was given a pie worth 5 altyns and some burbot, a type of fish, worth 26 altyns; one of the clerks, a pie worth 4 altyns and 2 dengas; another clerk, a pie worth 3 altyns and 4 dengas; and a third clerk, a pie worth 3 altyns and 2 dengas. On the same day, the first of the new year, the governor extended an invitation to dinner, an honor that called for reciprocation. The elected chief of local administration thereupon brought the governor an envelope containing 4 altyns, as well as 3 altyns and 2 dengas for his wife, 8 dengas for his son, 8 dengas for his daughters, and 6 dengas for the most important residents of his household. On 2 September the elected chief of local administration again paid a visit to the governor, this time bringing a quarter of beef, valued at 12 altyns and 4 dengas, and a fish—a pike—worth 6 altyns. One of the clerks received a quarter of beef worth 9 altyns and 4 dengas. On 3 September the elected chief presented the governor with more pike, worth 19 altyns. While at the governor's courtyard, he purchased a shovel for 2 dengas and a hundred tallow candles for 8 altyns and 2 dengas. He also bought five quires of paper for the town hall at a cost of 11 altyns and 4 dengas.

On 5 September the governor was sent a quarter of beef worth 12 altyns and 4 dengas, while two clerks each received a quarter of beef at a cost of 9 altyns and 4 dengas per quarter. On 6 September another quarter of beef was presented to the governor. On 7 September the elected chief and representatives of the peasant communities attended a dinner at the house of a clerk, bringing with them an envelope containing 16 altyns and 4 dengas for their host, 8 altyns and 2 dengas for his wife, and 3 altyns and 2 dengas for his mother. On 8 September there was sent to the governor 12 altyns' worth of pike; on the 9th, a quarter each of beef to the governor and a clerk, and on the 10th, more pike to the governor. The 11th saw another dinner held at a clerk's house, to which was brought an envelope with 13 altyns and 2 dengas for him, 6 altyns for his wife, 3 altyns for his mother, and 10 dengas for his daughter. This was followed on the 12th by a day-after feast, at which 12 altyns were presented to the clerk. That same day a quarter of beef was sent to the governor. On the 14th the governor received three-quarters of a bushel[66] of turnips, worth 3 altyns and 4 dengas. On the 16th the governor was given fish, both pike and burbot, worth 11 altyns; one of the clerks received some fish at a cost of 3 altyns. Moreover an honorarium of wine and beer, in the amount of 6 altyns and 4 dengas, was awarded to the clerks in the town hall. On the 17th, the name day of the tsarevna Sophia,[67] a pie worth 5 altyns was presented to the governor, and other pies were given to the clerks. A quantity of fish was likewise sent to the voivode and the clerks. A quarter of beef was delivered to the governor on the 19th, etc., etc.

Such were the kinds of entries to be found in the expense records maintained by an elected chief of local administration. This would be an appropriate time to take a look at the kinds of expenditures that were recorded in the ledgers of the elected representatives of peasant communities, who were sent to the city from their counties for the payment of money.

"I went to the governor, bringing with me grain and loaves of bread worth 2 altyns, together with an envelope containing 3 altyns. I also gave his people 2 dengas. When I again went to the governor, I brought him grain and a loaf of bread worth 2 altyns, a hindquarter of beef worth 26 altyns and 4 dengas, a carcass of pork valued at 1 ruble, a carcass of mutton worth 13 altyns, and 3 rubles in money. To one of his nephews I gave a ruble; to another, 10 altyns; to his wife, 1 ruble; to his majordomo, 21 altyns; to all the people of his household, 21 altyns; to his steward, 10 dengas; to the young children, 2 altyns; to the overseer, 2 altyns; and to the servants, 3 altyns. Upon going to the clerk, I presented him with grain, a loaf of bread, and two and a half rubles in money. To his wife I gave 1 ruble; to his two nephews, 1 ruble; to all the people of his household, 10 altyns; to his steward, 3 altyns; to his overseer, 2 altyns; to the gatekeeper, 1 altyn; to the young children, 8 dengas; and to the domestic holy man, 4 dengas. To the entire police force together I gave 6 dengas, besides 2 dengas to the officers stationed where delinquent debtors are punished. Also, while paying out the money, I put 2 dengas in the watchman's bag. For making official entries in the records the city officials charged 2 dengas, and the chief of local administration took 4 grivnas for hay that was promised the governor."

CONFLICTS BETWEEN COMMUNITIES AND LOCAL OFFICIALS

These payments by peasant communities to the governors and clerks were considered quite normal. Consequently they elicited no protests or complaints. But when some governor cultivated a taste for high living, stormy remonstrances reverberated through the town hall. The point would be reached when the clerk of the town hall sat down to compose a petition from "the humble elected administrator of the city and entire county" on behalf of the townspeople and rural population: "A new governor has assumed his duties in our community. Upon his arrival he exacted from us a sum of money in the amount of 120 rubles. Since then he has taken from us a monthly allotment of 12 rubles for grain, as well as 6 bushels of rye, 6 bushels of oats, and 6 bushels of barley from each taxable land unit,[68] for an annual total of 594 bushels. Furthermore he makes us provide him with up to five or six barrels of beer, each of which requires approximately 18 bushels of grain. At Christmas and Easter the governor demands from us a side of meat, bringing the toal to 126 sides annually. On the Feast of St. Peter, we have to provide him with a mutton for each taxable land unit, and 2000 eggs. On other days we have to furnish him with ordinary supplies—meat, fish, and loaves of bread. From the post drivers he collects 30 rubles annually, and on a daily basis procures tallow candles in the amount of a quarter of a ruble. Finally, he acquires hay for horses at 50 rubles annually. He does not allow us to elect our own officials—administrators of collections from the community, their assistants, police officers, or other local officials. Instead, he appoints those who give him more in money and goods."

At the same time that the clerk in the town hall would be thus engaged drafting a petition, another clerk in the provincial administrative office would be composing a petition from the governor against the local community: "The representatives of the rural districts pay their monetary revenues negligently. From the place of punishment for indebtedness they insolently recriminate against me, demanding that I not exercise my authority over them. On one occasion, during the punishment of debtors, they began to shout at me with outrageous impudence, after which they proceeded to organize a rebellion. Bolting from the place of punishment and the provincial administrative office, they forcibly resisted the police officers, whom they then assaulted. They made their way to my house with insulting rudeness and boasted about taking all kinds of pernicious actions against me. Meanwhile, the elected chief of local administration started to bark at me . . . and call me a thief in the presence of many people. He does not carry out his duty of administering the state revenues."

In cities near Moscow where petitioners from local communities enjoyed readier access to the tsar than in outlying areas, the governors and clerks exercised greater moderation in drawing their subsistence. On the other hand, the situation existing in cities located at some distance from Moscow was conveyed in the proverb "God dwells aloft in heaven serene; the tsar, far distant, is never seen." In more remote cities, the appointed crown officials easily became unscrupulous. They aroused the antagonism of the local communities, for whom the full implication of the proverb seemed to possess distressing relevance.

It is unnecessary here to recount the rebellions that occurred in the time of Tsar Michael and the beginning of Tsar Alexis' reign among peasant communities which were administratively tied to distant cities. In 1673, when the reign of Tsar Alexis neared its end, the inhabitants of Kaigorodok,[69] led by Aniky Toshkinov and Dmitry Berkutov, refused to deliver state revenues to the governor. Instead, they mounted a rebellion against the governor and intended to kill him. They ejected him from office and drove the police officers and local officials out of town. The government dispatched a company of musketeers to quell the uprising, which was brought to a halt with the imposition of torture and by use of the gallows. It was, incidentally, not only from the townspeople that difficulties arose to haunt the governors. Indeed, sometimes it was the townspeople who had come to the aid of a governor. Once, in the town of Shuia,[70] there erupted a loud commotion. When the townspeople came out to see what was the matter, they found their governor, Borkov, lying on the ground, scarcely alive. He had been on a visit and was returning in the company of a neighboring landholder, the crown agent Kashintsev, a man of frightful temper. When the two of them got into an argument, a fight ensued in which Kashintsev tore out the governor's entire beard by the roots.

It was the locally elected chief of city and county administration who represented a community before the crown. Should problems emerge from any quarter, whether the governor or some other, the chief of local administration would submit petitions in the name of all the taxpaying town and rural people. He furnished money and supplies for the maintenance of the governor and the clerks. When such provisioning became burdensome and disquieted a community, the chief was expected to remonstrate with the governor on behalf of the local populace. However, the chief did not always possess sufficient courage to carry this out. Sometimes the elected chief entered into collusion with a governor against those in his own community who had elected him. In such a case the members of a community would themselves petition the crown against their chief: "He has created a state of appalling disorder in our community affairs, displaying deceitful cunning in financial transactions, which has resulted in unconscionable profit to himself. He has conspired with the governor and the local holder of the crown franchise for customs collections. He eats and drinks with them constantly, spending entire nights with them. He incites the governor and customs collector against us, and they in turn fraudulently cheat and impoverish us. We beg you, Sovereign. Command that he be made to take his leave of us." No other recourse existed for a community which had elected a corrupt chief of local administration than to request the crown that he be expelled from the city. For should a chief who had been replaced by someone else remain in the place of his former residence, the community was sure to suffer. He was, after all, usually a powerful man of considerable wealth.

The weakness of society, and especially of local communities, was evident is still another respect. If a local resident should in some way misbehave, the community could anticipate that unfortunate repercussions would follow for themselves. Perhaps one of their number might become intoxicated and do something stupid, get into a fight or kill someone—the community had to answer for his actions. Next to the governor clustered the clerks, who only awaited such an occurrence so that they might aggrandize themselves at the expense of the community. Immediately they would attempt to implicate as many people as possible in the incident. Thereupon, the community would lodge a petition: "We should like to express a grievance against a member of our community named Korob. He drinks and carouses disgracefully, gambles, plays cards, beats his wife, and tortures her unlawfully! We beg you to command that he, his wife, and his children be driven out of town so that we may no longer be subject to penalties and disgrace."

The members of a family would take exactly the same course of action, notifying the sovereign in a petition that a relative of theirs was behaving badly and failed to calm down despite correction by elder members of the family. The family would then take the opportunity of giving notice to the sovereign lest they fall into disgrace in the future.

The weakness of the local community was felt most acutely whenever dissension or conflict broke out between rich and poor townspeople—a phenomenon which was not peculiar to any single city, such as Pskov. The following petition from Pskov was typical of others drafted at this time: "We, the townspeople of intermediate rank and the lowliest poor people of all the city districts, do submit this petition. Our grievance is against the townspeople of the commercial and manufacturing districts, the former elected chiefs of local administration, the present chief, and the wealthy people. They have bound us to assessments and taxes that lie outside our ability to pay. At the same time they have eased their own burden. Yet, even on the basis of less exacting assessments for themselves, they have not paid their taxes fully for many years. Instead they leave large notes of indebtedness. These debts they do not calculate in the records of the elected local chiefs. Rather, conniving with each other, they fail properly to credit the accounts of the intermediate and lowliest townspeople."

All these matters were referred to the government in petitions addressed to the great sovereign. For its part, the crown did not remain indifferent to such appeals. A certain community might request that an elected official take the place of an appointed one, and the government would readily accede. Another petition might ask that a commander of the city garrison (later known in Russia as komendant), be relieved and that the community be permitted to elect a new one. To this, the sovereign would consent. On one occasion an elected chief of local administration submitted a petition in the name of all the town and rural population, in which he related that a stranger of imposing appearance had arrived from Moscow with written authorization allowing him to take the place of the single clerk in the town hall. The original clerk, the petition stated, was a man of proven ability, never having incurred any losses or notes of indebtedness, while the newcomer was inexperienced and unsuited to the post. The original clerk had been relegated nevertheless to caring solely for communications and transportation. In this case the great sovereign commanded that the clerk from Moscow be expelled from his new post, notwithstanding his written authorization.

MEASURES AGAINST ABUSES

Measures were taken against abuses in the dispensation of justice. It was ordered that governors and administrative officials desist from rendering judgment in cases where they themselves might be implicated in wrongdoing. Such cases were to be judged by governors in neighboring cities, not farther than 100 miles distant.[71] Another order prohibited appointing as governors any member of the service gentry whose landed holdings and estates were near the cities in which he was to serve.

Toward the end of Tsar Alexis' reign, it was decreed that certain requisitions for the support of governors be eliminated. These consisted of payments in money and kind to a new governor upon his first arrival, monthly compensation, contributions on holidays, and whatever else the elected chiefs of local administration spent out of community funds for the benefit of the governors. Certainly the governors could not be expected to cut off themselves abruptly from these requisitions and contributions. Hence the elected chiefs still contrived to bring pies and fish in the customary manner. Evidence for this exists in the fact that Tsar Fedor[72] found it necessary to repeat his father's decree. In addition to enactments concerning requisitions, an important attempt was made to reform the relations between the townspeople and the governors, but it could not be carried through to success.

ORDIN-NASHCHOKIN'S REFORM EFFORTS

The governor of Pskov in 1665 was Tsar Alexis' renowned close friend, Afansy Lavrentievich Ordin-Nashchokin. Upon assuming his new post, he discovered that conditions in the region entrusted to him were utterly deplorable. Commercial trade constituted a source of wealth for Pskov, which was situated near the borders with Poland and Sweden. But trade had declined as a result of wars with both those countries. There also prevailed in Pskov another evil, one which was common to all cities in early Russia. This was the dominance of the so-called "loud-mouthed big shots."[73] They were rich merchants who, having seized all power in their hands, strove to promote only their own interests, forgetting about the welfare of the majority of townspeople. This evil had become deeply rooted in Pskov, where the memory of the bloody struggle between the rich and poor during the Time of Troubles was still fresh in mind, and where an even more recent riot had renewed the unrest.[74]

Upon becoming governor of Pskov, Ordin-Nashchokin had no intention of merely deriving his livelihood from the post. He began to consider ways to improve the welfare of the city which was his birthplace. In this instance, as with other problems, he looked to the West. Acting in accordance with examples drawn from foreign countries, he proposed to the elected chiefs and the city council that the following measures be taken. Pskov would conduct trade with foreigners free of any duties for certain specified periods of time. Some would enjoy this privilege for two weeks starting the 6th of January; others, for two weeks starting the 9th of May. Furthermore, residents of Pskov who were not members of the taxpaying community would be prohibited from trading with foreigners. Said the governor. "In all countries, those commercial enterprises prosper which are conducted without the imposition of customs duties."

Much earlier there had been heard in Russia, and especially in the leading cities, bitter complaints from Russian merchants about foreign traders. The latter, operating in concert and having access to large amounts of capital, were capturing commerce for themselves. In order to make themselves independent of the foremost Russian merchants in the pricing of goods, the foreigners usually entered into relations with the poor people and offered to advance money to them. The poor people, being satisfied with a small return for their effort, then bought up various goods for the foreigners at a low price. "Through lack of restraint, Russians have engaged in trade for the benefit of foreigners in exchange for a small return. In so doing, they have fallen into the direst financial straits. Those residents of Pskov who once had their own means of livelihood likewise have become impoverished through the activity of those who cooperated with foreigners in lowering the price of goods."

In order to forestall such clandestine contractual arrangements with the foreigners and deter Russian petty traders from accepting advance payments of money on contract with them, thereby lowering the price on Russian commodities, Ordin-Nashchokin proposed to the wealthy merchants of Pskov that they prepare a written register of the petty traders in that city and its suburbs according to their degrees of kinship and personal acquaintance. The wealthy merchants would then supervise the trade and activity of the petty traders, and provide them with loans (from municipal funds, that is) in the amounts that the petty traders theretofore had obtained as advance money payments from foreigners

when working for them. In December, after having made various purchases with the money thus lent them, the petty traders were to bring the merchandise to Pskov, where it would be recorded in the town hall. Each wealthy merchant would then be required to accept the goods from the petty traders whom he had registered and to price the items in such a way as to include an additional amount for the support of the petty traders and for the purchase of another stock of goods by the following May. After the fair, at which they were to dispose of the merchandise at prices that undercut the foreigners, the wealthy merchants were to pay the petty traders the amount for which they had sold it.

The governor then devoted his attention to the sale of alcohol, a matter of some importance in that it constituted one of the main sources of income for the treasury. As Pskov was a border city, persons entering from abroad were readily able to smuggle in distilled spirits and foreign beverages, which cut deeply into profits from the domestic sales outlet. The municipal liquor administration faced a deficit in its anticipated revenues. Called upon to make up the difference, it sought to recover its losses from the local residents and to confiscate the contraband. Such action failed in its purpose of enriching the treasury and only served to bring about the ruin of those upon whom the imposts were leveled. Consequently Ordin-Nashchokin proposed to establish the private retail sale of alcohol, with the treasury being reimbursed at the rate of two dengas per ruble of alcohol sold. Should someone's transactions in alcohol exceed sales in other commodities, the proportion paid to the treasury was to increase to one grivna per ruble of alcohol sold.

Finally, the governor proposed a new organization for the municipal administration. It was to consist of fifteen persons elected for three years, five of whom would sit in the town hall each year. The five elected administrators were to be charged with the responsibility of rendering judgment in all commercial and personal injury cases, transferring to the governor only cases involving treason, robbery, and murder. Should a dispute erupt between a member of the service gentry and a townsman, the decision was to be made by a member of the service gentry (acting as judge) together with elected townsmen. The judicial fees collected from cases decided by the five townsmen were to be deposited in the town hall for civil expenses. The suburbs of Pskov were supposed to have a similar organization.

Ordin-Nashchokin's proposals created a deep disquiet among the people of Pskov, who became divided into two factions, one favoring

AFANASY LAVRENTIEVICH ORDIN-NASHCHOKIN

the reforms and the other opposed. The lower classes, or "inferior people," supported the innovations, while the upper classes, or "better people," threw their weight behind the status quo. Because of these quarrels the matter was prolonged from April to August. Only on 13 August did the townspeople draft a set of petitions which incorporated the governor's proposals. After being borne to the cathedral of the Holy Trinity, where the townspeople received the blessing of Archbishop Arsenius, the petitions were sent to Moscow. Thus a new administrative organization was introduced in Pskov.

Ordin-Nashchokin, despite his successes, could not long remain in Pskov. He was summoned to carry out a vital assignment, the conduct of peace negotiations with Polish representatives. Consequently a new governor appeared in Pskov, Prince Ivan Khovansky, who resisted innovations and was especially opposed to newcomers like Ordin-Nashchokin. As mentioned earlier he had experienced a confrontation with Ordin-Nashchokin, whom he regarded as a court favorite who was being given advancement by the tsar to the dishonor of older families.

Arriving in Pskov, Khovansky perceived that Ordin-Nashchokin, having divested the governor of his judicial functions, had contrived some sort of dubious scheme in placing lower-class muzhiks to act as judges and administrators, and that he had founded private taverns to take the place of state drinking establishments. These new arrangements, as indicated earlier, had failed to appeal to some segments of the lower-class muzhiks and certainly had never satisfied any of the wealthy merchants. They told Khovansky that Ordin-Nashchokin had instituted the reforms quite arbitrarily, imposing them forcibly upon the townspeople. As for the petition, Khovansky was told that an altered version had been fabricated in the town hall one night. After being signed that same night, it had been sent off by Ordin-Nashchokin to the tsar in Moscow.

"In Pskov there have been established newly-founded privately operated taverns, in which drinking goes on constantly, leading to all manner of delinquency. A body of elected officials has been organized, who sit in judgment over the townspeople independently of the provincial administrative office (that is, the governor). In court cases they bring members of the service gentry to the town hall under police escort, causing the service gentry much personal distress. On their own authority those same elected officials issue passes for Russians to cross the border where they, through inexperience and lack of due caution in writing, will be victimized by the foreigners. The elected chiefs of local administration and the better citizens have informed me that an altered version of the petition had been drafted one night and signed that same night. Who drafted it should be made a matter of official investigation. There were a mere fifty signatures on it, and only a few of those belonged to the better citizens. The petition was composed in a correct and grammatical style, indicating that a person of intelligence had done the work, since muzhiks would have been incapable of it."

Khovansky's communication elicited the following response from Moscow: "You are directed to administer justice and mete out punishment to persons of all ranks, and to abolish the recently founded tribunal. The privately operated taverns shall be abolished. The former crown franchised drinking establishments shall be reestablished in their previous locations and shall be farmed out to franchise holders. Should no one be forthcoming to purchase a franchise, the drinking establishments are to be given over to the custody of better citizens who shall bo bound by the appropriate oath."

Khovansky's stay in Pskov was not of long duration. His successor, Prince Danila Velikogo-Gagin, was a man without the same degree of influence as his predecessors enjoyed in either Pskov or Moscow. Consequently, during his tenure as governor, the former disputes could once again be raised and decided without interference from the governor. It so happened that Ordin-Nashchokin was then in Moscow, serving as director of the Ambassadorial Chancellery, the very agency which exercised jurisdiction over Pskov. He obviously could not remain unconcerned over the dismantling by the hostile Khovansky of the arrangement he had established in Pskov. Upon Khovansky's departure from Pskov, a certain secretary there by the name of Mina Grobov, who had retained his loyalty to Ordin-Nashchokin, began to arouse the partisans of the latter's organizational measures.

Through Khovansky's efforts, as mentioned earlier, the sale of alcohol through private outlets was abolished and a system of distribution through crown franchises was supposed to take its place, provided someone could be induced to bid for the franchises. Such a bidder was found in the person of one Kuzma Andreev. He made a month's payment of more than twice the amount that the treasury had received from independent sales. But, with Velikogo-Gagin as governor, the independent alcoholic beverage retailers, Davyd Bakharev and his associates, dispatched a petition to Moscow: "The elected city officials, Semen Menshikov and his colleagues, seeing the success of our enterprise and realizing that it was going to produce a substantial yield to the state treasury, have conspired with each other and have given the franchise for alcoholic beverage collections to their associate, the elected city official Kuzma Andreev. In so doing they have forgotten the fear of God and their solemn oath. To justify their action they have labeled our taxpaying drinking establishments disreputable private taverns."

This was followed by another petition to Moscow, this time not just from the independent tavern keepers: "We, your poor orphans, the people of intermediate and lowliest status, have a grievance against certain wealthy townspeople of Pskov: Nikita Ievlev, Mokei Sigov, and their associates. These wealthy people conduct all kinds of municipal and community business, and they select petitioners and dispatch them to you, Great Sovereign, in Moscow, without municipal or community consultation with the intermediate and lowliest people and without signed decisions. Consequently there exists enormous distress, resulting from the imposition of ruinous and frequent taxes."

A report was submitted to Moscow concerning Kuzma Andreev and his associates, who had arranged for him to obtain the franchise. It was charged that the sum he had to pay for the franchise was very small. Even so, the holder of the franchise and his associates, the wealthy citizens, were oppressing the weak. They refused them the right, guaranteed by law, to prepare alcoholic beverages at home on special occasions. They sought to enrich themselves from the operation of the drinking establishments, and they engaged in various kinds of smuggling. In consequence of these complaints, there arrived from Moscow a decree. It stipulated that, because Semen Menshikov, Kuzma Andreev, and their associates failed to do their part on behalf of the poor and powerless citizens of Pskov, they jointly were to pay the sum of 9,366 rubles annually for the drinking establishments. To be added among those required to make the aforementioned payments were Nikita Ievlev and Sergei Pogankin because they had fled from service on the city council and failed to take the appropriate oath.

Finally, in autumn of 1668, a petition arrived in Moscow from the elected chief of local administration, Stepan Kotianikov, and all the people of Pskov. It asked the sovereign to restore everything that had been instituted by Ordin-Nashchokin and eliminated by Khovansky, so that freedom might prevail in the area of alcoholic beverage sales, as was the case in Smolensk. But nine people did not affix their signatures to the petition: Semen Menshikov, Sergei Poganskin, Kuzma Solodovnik, Ivan Chirev, Nikita Mikhalev, Peter Zarubin, Yury Beloborodov, Mokei Sigov, and Afanasy Samoilov. These nine people also had powerful patrons in Moscow—the chancellors of the Ambassadorial Chancellery, Gerasim Dokhturov and Lukian Golosov. Ordin-Nashchokin constantly warred with them. He remonstrated with them that they sullied the reputation of the Ambassadorial Chancellery, by which foreigners made judgments concerning all of Russia. It was the one chancellery that had to be less susceptible to censure than any of the others, and yet its chancellors were combining an interest in alcoholic beverage sales with diplomatic affairs.

The chancellors retaliated against Ordin-Nashchokin by always acting against him. So it was with the petition from Pskov. They drafted their summary report of it in such a way that it was rejected. It is understandable that Ordin-Nashchokin could not just stand back and calmly brook this sort of intransigent opposition.

The sovereign found himself in a perplexing quandary. On the one hand, he was being told that the people of Pskov were restive and that a minority was oppressing the majority of citizens, who might easily turn to violence. At the same time, reports reached him with warnings about the considerable loss to the treasury that would result from the introduction of private alcoholic beverage sales in Pskov at a time when the country, beset by an expensive war, stood in desperate need of money. Tsar Alexis turned first to Ordin-Nashchokin for his opinion as to "how revenues from the sale of alcoholic beverages could be put in good order, and from what individual or group of individuals could be collected, without rousing the people to defiance, any shortfall in expected collections, so that returns from the sale of alcohol should not be lost unnecessarily."

Ordin-Nashchokin replied: "In 1666 I organized the administration of Pskov after the manner of foreign countries. This resulted in great profit to your state treasury and brought an increased amount of plentiful revenue to the local authorities in Pskov. I took this action without any ulterior motive, for the sake only of fulfilling my duty in the realization of your magnanimous and majestic grace, and in the hope of obtaining forgiveness for my sins in the life hereafter. In spite of this, Sovereign, my efforts maliciously were labeled as self-aggrandizement by bigoted enemies, and accordingly Stenka Kotiatnikov was forbidden to collect the duties on alcoholic beverage sales.[1b] The chancellors of the council for some reason chose to forget my real intentions. The reorganization that I put into effect in Pskov was also carried out in Smolensk. But Pskov is more important than Smolensk, for it lies along the border with two foreign countries. The inhabitants of the city and county have fallen into direst poverty, and without such reorganization as I have suggested, there is nothing with which they can be aided. I am trying in every way possible, Sovereign, to bring your subjects, God's people, into agreement. I have held conversations and have sent written communications to Pskov. The secretary Mina Grobov has replied to me by letter, expressing his earnest desire to find a way by which the divisions that have arisen among the residents of Pskov may be terminated. He also mentions that they have decided already upon the name of the person who is to make up any deficits in the collection of revenues. A decision also has been arrived at as regards that which will bring about a lasting improvement in Pskov. Placing my trust in your sovereign grace, I carried out the same reorganization in Smolensk by the authority of your decree. My colleagues, the chancellors of the council, are very well aware of this. Since Smolensk has suffered no detrimental effects in the collection of beverage duties, and since conditions in Pskov are well known in the Ambassadorial Chancellery, it is safe to say, Sovereign, that revenues from Pskov should far exceed those from Smolensk."

Ordin-Nashchokin was quite forthright in stating that he had intervened in Pskov through the secretary Grobov to bring about a reconciliation among the factions. His own words furnish evidence that the last petition from Pskov was evidence of such reconciliation, that is, of his intervention. It was easy for Ordin-Nashchokin's enemies to suggest that the supposed reconciliation had been attained by force and that persons of upper class had failed to sign the petition, which sought reinstatement of Ordin-Nashchokin's organizational innovations. In order to resolve the problem, there remained only one recourse—to have the highest level of government itself approach all the inhabitants of the city and region of Pskov, and inquire of them directly what they wanted.

On 11 March 1669 the governor of Pskov, Prince Velikogo-Gagin, received the following directive from the tsar: "You are commanded to promulgate our sovereign decree to our people of all ranks: If the former manner of collecting alcoholic beverage revenues should be reestablished for all the residents of Pskov, will a profit accrue to our treasury, and will this impose any undue hardship upon the citizens of Pskov, the inhabitants of the countryside, and people of all ranks?"

The governor sent the answers to Moscow.

Archbishop Arsenius solemnly attested in his episcopal capacity that the people of the city and county would not be benefited by the existence of privately operated taverns. On the contrary, if they had to make up a deficit in excess of 9,000 rubles to provide crown revenues from the operation of taverns, they would be utterly ruined.

A large number of other clergymen and church people, 101 in all, consisting of archimandrites, hegumens, priors, abbotesses, mothers superior, the protopope of Holy Trinity cathedral, the priestly elders of crown-supported and parish churches, the entire clerical order, and the overseers of peasants on monasterial and ecclesiastical landed estates, issued a statement to the effect that on no account should privately operated taverns be permitted, for the reason that vulnerable persons among the citizens of Pskov, the clergy, and the peasants of the country-side might fall into extreme poverty and disgrace through intemperate indulgence and other weaknesses associated with inebriation.

The service gentry and junior boyars, numbering sixty persons, declared themselves unable to issue an answer on account of their ignorance of the matter. Eighty-nine persons belonging to these groups did not even make an appearance in the city to be queried about the issue.

Two hundred thirty-eight of the wealthy, intermediate, and lowest categories of townspeople stated that it was impossible to have taverns. They maintained that taverns would bring about a tremendous decrease in revenues to the crown treasury because they would lead to the certain ruin of townspeople who were too weak and unable to control their drinking. Instead, they insisted that drinking establishments should be operated in the future as crown franchises.

The cossacks, musketeers, cannoneers, and gatekeepers, a total of 2,115 persons, said that they, like the service gentry, did not know what recommendation to make.

Of the peasants in the county of Pskov, 241 declared that the collection of revenues from the sale of alcoholic beverages should devolve as before upon all the inhabitants of Pskov, with due precautions and contractual agreements, through the issuance of crown franchises. If this were done, profits would accrue to the treasury. On the other hand, they maintained that it would be inappropriate to have privately operated taverns in the city and county. Should a deficit occur in the revenues of the franchised operations, they assured the central government that they, the peasants of the rural district, were prepared to assume the payment of it themselves. Another 670 peasants stated that they had no opinion one way or another.

In Moscow a final decision was reached. The drinking establishments were to be operated as franchises Prospective purchasers were to be sought, but If no one came forward with an offer, then elected persons were to assume supervisorial duties under oath. As it turned out, no purchasers of the franchises could be found.

THE NEW COMMERCIAL STATUTE

Ordin-Nashchokin's innovative proposals failed to take hold. Nevertheless, in 1667 he was able to express his pet ideas in the New Commercial Statute.[76] Here he made his frequently repeated reference to the West and the example offered by foreign governments: "In all neighboring

countries, free and profitable trade is regarded as one of the major concerns of state administration. They look after trade with the greatest
diligence and maintain the principle of private enterprise as a means for
promoting the collection of duties and furthering the material prosperity
of the commonwealth."

The Statute provided that merchants in need of investment capital be
given assistance by the customshouse in Moscow and the town halls in
cities elsewhere. It prohibited persons who were exempt from the payment of taxes to engage in trade with foreigners, other than through
Russian merchants, or to sign contracts directly with foreigners. Instead,
they were to consign their goods to Russian merchants. The Statute
obligated the wealthy merchants to protect those who were poor by
providing them with the opportunity of acquiring goods and a sufficient-
ly large inventory from the Russians so that the poor merchants would
not lower prices for the foreigners or accept money from them under
contract.

There existed a custom of long duration whereby a merchant of the
highest rank from Moscow would be appointed with a group of associates to supervise the conduct of the trade fair in Archangel at the time
of the arrival there of foreigners and collect the customs duties. The
Commercial Statute stipulated that this leading merchant and his colleagues be selected on the basis of investigation into their qualifications,
and not out of friendship or enmity. They were to be chosen from capable and upright candidates, not on account of wealth, but because of
their demonstrated capacity for efficient work. The local governor was
to exercise no jurisdiction over the appointed merchant or his associates
in any matter pertaining to the commercial customs duties. All legal disputes arising out of the commercial activities between Russians and
foreigners were to be settled by the appointed merchant and his colleagues in the customshouse.

The Commercial Statute increased the amount of duty on foreign
spirits because of the great losses and deficits that plagued the government drinking establishments as a result of the widespread importation
of alcohol. Foreigners were required to deal only with the merchants of
the city where they came to trade. They were forbidden to establish
commercial contacts, enter into contractual agreements, or negotiate
loans with Russian merchants from other cities who happened to be
passing through. Merchants from Moscow were permitted to traffic in
all kinds of goods freely with foreigners in all border cities and at trade
fairs. A foreigner was not to trade with other foreigners under penalty
of confiscation of all his goods in favor of the sovereign. The duty on

the sale or exchange of foreign merchandise was set at two altyns per ruble, and of Russian goods for delivery in foreign countries, at one grivna per ruble. However, if a foreigner brought with him certain kinds of coins, either zolotoys or efimoks,[77] he did not need to pay any duty, and whatever he purchased with zolotoys or efimoks could be taken abroad duty-free. Foreigners engaging in trade in the border cities were supposed to present all such zolotoys and efimoks to the treasury office where they would be issued Russian currency of small denomination in exchange: one ruble for a zolotoy and half a ruble for each efimok from Lübeck. If merchants from the East—Persians, Indians, Bukharans, Armenians, Kumyks, Cherkesses, and foreign residents of Astrakhan—should go for purposes of trade to Moscow and other cities, they were to have collected from them in Astrakhan transit duties on their merchandise in the amount of one grivna per ruble ad valorem. Should they remain in Astrakhan to trade, the customs duty would be ten dengas per ruble. The export duties on Russian goods that they took with them out of the country were set at one grivna per ruble. The same amount, one grivna per ruble, was to apply to Greeks, Moldavians, and Wallachians. If they went to trade in Putivl the sum to be collected was set at ten dengas per ruble. No foreigner was allowed to sell his goods at retail or take them to trade fairs. Admittance to Moscow and other cities of the interior was allowed solely to those foreigners who were granted a written pass bearing the official red seal.

During Tsar Alexis' reign, Jews were able to obtain such passes and have them authenticated with the required seal. They would arrive in Moscow with cloth, gems, and other merchandise, upon which they received a commission from the court. Thus in 1672 Samuil Yakovlev and his associates, all of whom were Jews from Shklov,[78] were sent abroad from Moscow for the purchase of Hungarian wine. Greeks, on account of the identity of their religious faith with that of the Russians, were permitted freedom of access in the reign of Tsar Michael and the beginning of the reign of Tsar Alexis. But in 1647 they were restricted in the conduct of trade solely to the border city of Putivl.

In a broadly sweeping manner, the Commercial Statute of 1667 fulfilled the wishes of the Russian merchants when it excluded foreigners from the interior cities of Muscovy. In 1669 a foreigner named Peter Marselis, who had settled in Russia, submitted a set of articles to the Ambassadorial Chancellery in which he offered arguments in favor of altering the Commercial Statute. The case he made consisted of four points. First, considerable harm resulted from the policy of conducting trade in Archangel after 1 September, since many ships faced dangers and perished owing to the lateness of the season, while Russian vessels returning upstream from Archangel along the Northern Dvina were unable to make their way in time to the Volkhov river. Second, foreigners should be permitted to pay their customs duties in efimoks and not zolotoys. Furthermore, they should be allowed to introduce zolotoys into Muscovy in order to sell them or give them in payment to anyone whomsoever. This would induce them to bring many zolotoys and efimoks into the country. Third, under existing procedures the customs duties paid by foreigners were being reduced so that Muscovy could acquire zolotoys and efimoks. If they were allowed to purchase goods in Moscow and other cities, Marselis said he confidently expected a large sum in zolotoys and efimoks to be accumulated, a sum exceeding that of the revenues from customs duties, because all those efimoks would be exchanged at the monetary bank, where a profit of 14 kopecks would be realized from each efimok. Permission to purchase goods in Moscow and other cities needed be given only to those foreigners who brought in efimoks and not zolotoys. Fourth, there existed at one time in Moscow and at the trade fair in Archangel the practice of issuing many small coins to various people so that they would deposit efimoks in the treasury to obtain them. In this way many efimoks were brought to Moscow. If a decree were to be issued authorizing the issuance to foreigners of small coins in exchange for the deposit of efimoks at the rate of 16 altyns per efimok, then as before a substantial number of efimoks would be introduced.

In accordance with custom, there were summoned to the Ambassadorial Chancellery the foremost merchants and other persons engaged in trade, before whom Marselis' proposals were read. The leading merchants quickly realized that the crafty outlander, whom they greatly despised, desired to see his fellow foreigners regain access to the cities of the interior, tempting the government with the prospect of a vast infusion of efimoks. Accordingly they submitted a reply: "The foreigners have violated already the first point made by Marselis. Last year many of their ships entered the port of Archangel after St. Simeon's Day (1 September). Moreover, those who arrived before that day engaged only in petty trade prior to St. Simeon's Day. They always deliberately waited to conduct major trade until the final days so as to obtain Russian merchandise at a cheap price, raise the price of their own goods, and prevent the Russians from closely inspecting defective imported items during the last hectic period of commercial transactions."

As for the second point: "The number of zolotoys in Moscow has not undergone any increase as of the present time. In writing that foreigners should be able to bring zolotoys and efimoks anywhere, Marselis cherishes a desire to acquire control over all Russian trade. They will sell their zolotoys and efimoks to the Persians, Armenians, Kumyks, and Tatars at a high price, and those coins then will be taken out of Muscovy. But if Russian merchants in Moscow and other cities should take in a small number of zolotoys and efimoks in exchange for merchandise, then that money, collected at retail, will not accrue in quantities sufficient to benefit the treasury. What will happen is that foreigners will begin to sell zolotoys to other foreigners at 40 altyns and efimoks at 20 altyns. At that rate they will be able to purchase Russian goods at a cheap price, as low as half the price at Archangel. For example, a foreigner would be able to sell 4 zolotoys at a rate of 40 altyns, thereby obtaining a total of 4 rubles, 26 altyns, and 4 dengas. Using that money he could purchase 360 pounds[79] of potash for 5 rubles. While Russians would be selling potash for 9 or 10 rubles in Archangel, the price of potash to foreigners in Moscow would drop to 4 zolotoys for each 360 pounds. Thus the foreigners will be able to manipulate the price of all kinds of goods sold by Russians, lowering it to half the amount prevailing in Archangel."

The Commercial Statute abolished a multitude of minor duty payments—duties on carts and the storage of goods, ad valorem and toll charges, imposts on the use of inns, etc.—and converted them into an excise tax levied on the sale of merchandise.

The first part of the Statute points to the example of foreign countries, where commerce was regarded as one of the most important concerns of the state. Towards the end there are included provisions, patterned after those of foreign countries, which were intended to forestall extravangance: "In cities along the frontier, locally-elected chiefs of municipal administration and their assistants are to question foreigners and most diligently inspect their trunks, chests, and boxes for undeclared pearls and precious stones lest any such items of great value be secreted among ordinary goods. It is essential to guard against the domestic purchase of such items in the same way that foreign countries, seeking to protect their stockpiles of silver, prohibit any excessive purchases of such items and forbid them, together with silks and broadcloth, to be worn by common people of no rank so that they may not become impoverished thereby. It is imperative to restrain the common people from purchasing such items by imposing heavy duties and stern regulations. All foreign states take such precautions to shield their people from needless destitution."

Having established that the governor of Archangel was to refrain from supervising the wealthy merchant who was supposed to dispense justice to persons engaged in trade, Ordin-Nashchokin added an important stipulation at the end of the Statute, paving the way for Peter the Great's project to "put the house in order." Specifically, he proposed the establishment of a special chancellery for merchants. "Because of numerous delays that are encountered in having commercial matters administered by a variety of chancelleries, it is fitting that the supervision of merchants be entrusted to a single appropriate chancellery, to which the sovereign shall appoint one of his boyars. This chancellery is to serve as a defense against other countries for persons engaged in trade in all the frontier cities, and as a protection and source of justice for them against the imposition of taxes by governors. This single chancellery shall dispense justice and mete out punishment whenever merchants lodge legal charges against persons of other ranks." Thus there came into being the Chancellery of Commercial Affairs.

TENSIONS BETWEEN URBAN TAXPAYERS AND SERVICE PEOPLE

As is evident from the foregoing, the life of cities prior to the reforming activity of Peter the Great creates the impression of a conflict that pitted the Russian townspeople against foreigners on one hand and their own countrymen on the other. The rivalry with foreign commerical competitors ended in a victory for the Russian merchants. Of greater importance, however, was the other struggle, against their own people.

That struggle, as indicated earlier, stemmed from the manifestly predominant position enjoyed in primitive, undeveloped societies by the armed element of the population as opposed to the rest of the people, who served as workers and directly supported the former. In such instances it was a sign of strength and maturity that the productive segment of the population desired to extricate itself from this obligation of furnishing direct support by separating itself and striving to attain a position of independence. In Western Europe this movement was characterized by the formation of urban communities and their struggle with the lords, followed later by the liberation of the village population. For both these results to occur there had to arise a substantial level of activity in the areas of manufacture and commerce, an accumulation of wealth, and a rivalry between liquid capital, money, and immovable property, land.

In Russia during the period under consideration there was evidenced a stagnation in industry and trade, with impoverishment as the consequence. The seventeenth century witnessed circumstances that were even more unfavorable than before for fostering an increase in national wealth. The cities and commercial guilds were unable to cope with the dislocations associated with the Time of Troubles, while subsequent wars did not cease to deplete them. News arrived from even the wealthiest cities that monetary revenues were insufficient to cover expenditures for the salaries of the people in military and civil service. Moscow replied that monetary salaries were either to be cut or eliminated altogether and replaced by grants of land, of which there existed an abundant supply.

In a country where lands are distributed in place of monetary salaries and where the availability of land exceeds that of money, in such a country no thought is given to the emancipation of peasants. Quite the contrary, consideration is given to their enserfment. For if it is land that comes to be distributed in return for service, it is necessary to have upon that land a permanent work force. Otherwise the salary becomes no kind of salary at all. One condition explains the other.

At the very time when the peasants were being enserfed in the villages, there was nothing much to be expected from the cities. For the peasants were being enserfed precisely because of the poverty of the cities. In the cities the townspeople were attached also to their places of residence and occupations. They could not leave under pain of death, but had to remain where they were, labor, furnish salaries to military men, and support the governors. Their interests remained constantly in conflict with those of the armed portion of the population. The townspeople submitted petitions regarding pledged dependents and peasants who, though working on a par with them, did not lend any help with the payment of taxes.

In petitioning against the pledged dependents and peasants, and in demanding the return of their brethren who had left the city for the village, the townspeople were asserting themselves against the interests of those people to whom the pledged dependents had commended themselves, to whom the peasants belonged, and to whom had gone the departed townspeople, their brethren, when they sought to avoid the payment of taxes. Only the undiscerning could fail to understand whose interests were served when a decree ordered that suburbs and villages belonging to private parties were to pass to the sovereign, while the names of their inhabitants were to be entered in the rolls of taxpayers. It is known what sort of revenge was taken against the townspeople for their petitions.

Under such conditions of conflicting interests any step forward required that the urban population be separated from the rest, so that they might govern and judge themselves apart from the jurisdiction of the local governor. It was essential to divorce them from the service people, for in such a conflict of interests, buttressed by centuries of tradition fostering the belief among the service people that they deserved to be supported by the labor of the working classes as a matter of natural right, there was no hope for any cohesion or cooperation. Whenever two persons are found locked in a fight with one another, it is necessary first of all to break them apart. Only later, when their mutual hostility has cooled with a gradual change in relations, can the time come to think about reconciliation, unification, and cooperation. Elections by themselves would be of no help where the townspeople were compelled to choose someone from among the service people as administrator. Consequently the separation of the working taxpayers and their release from subordination to the service people, carried out during the period of reform [under Peter the Great], was a natural and necessary development.

Yet the initial steps in this direction were taken at a time prior to the reform by a predecessor of the great reformer. For as soon as the Russian people, through the leadership of Ordin-Nashchokin, began to direct their attention to the West, they immediately perceived why it was that Russia had not developed in one particular area, namely, wealth. They began to understand that wealth derives from strenuously pursued commercial and manufacturing endeavors, and from the growth of cities. It was in this regard that Ordin-Nashchokin declared trade to be one of the most vital concerns of the state. During the period of [Peter the Great's] reform this view was adopted fully by the government and upper classes. Accordingly there appeared a succession of measures for improving trade and manufacture. Before all else, a separation of the commercial and manufacturing people into a distinct social class began to take place, whereupon began the process of putting the house in order.

CONDITIONS IN TOWN AND COUNTRY

The condition of the city serves as a barometer indicating the state of the villages and vice versa. If the cities happen to be impoverished, this is a sign that the villages will also be found in most unsatisfactory straits. If the agricultural population shows evidence of undergoing attachment to the land, this is a sign that the city is destitute. The enserfment of the peasantry was the outgrowth of early Russian history. This phenomenon displayed in the sharpest and most distressing manner the bankruptcy of a poor country unable to satisfy the requirements of its political situation with the resources available to it. A bankruptcy of this sort, affecting a historical, vigorous, and young nation, was bound to bring about a turning point in national life. It would lead to a search for a way out of a desperate situation and encourage the tendency to do away with a ruinous imbalance by establishing cities in a land of villages, thereby improving the economic condition of the country. Such a turning point is signaled by activity in the direction of reform. It is with such reform that modern Russian history begins.

Because of the inadequacy of native resources, it became necessary to borrow elsewhere. Regardless how great or burdensome it was for the people, the necessity and advantage connected with such borrowing were obvious. If the enserfment of the peasants was a natural outgrowth of early Russian history, their emancipation was the result of Russian historical progress throughout a century and a half along a new path. The quarrel between ancient and modern Russia was indeed brought to a conclusion, as is evident in the outcome.

RELATIONS BETWEEN PEASANTS AND TOWNSPEOPLE

The enserfment of the peasants and its effects constituted the most momentous and important phenomenon in the life of the village during the period under consideration. As concerns the component elements of rural organization and activity, the village inhabitants can be divided into three different categories: the peasant, cotter, and workhand.[80] They were distinguished from each other by the extent of their economic resources. The conditions of life differed from place to place in consequence of various factors, depending on whether the village was a crown village, a crown village attached to the tsar's palace by payments and work obligations, a village under the control of a monastery, or one belonging to a wealthy lay landowner or a minor lay landholder.

Attention has been given to the relations between the taxpaying peasants and the city in whose county they resided, or in other words, between the rural inhabitants and the taxable townspeople, who jointly were held responsible for the performance of labor and the payment of taxes. If there existed antagonisms among the townspeople themselves, based on a division between the wealthy and poor, in which the latter complained to Moscow concerning their oppression at the hands of the former, it ought to come as no surprise that similar antagonisms arose between the townspeople and the county peasants. This impelled the peasants to sever their ties with the townspeople and organize themselves in rural district communities.

Towards the end of Tsar Alexis' reign the county peasants of Ustiug began to lodge complaints against the townspeople: "The town inhabitants meet with great frequency in the town hall to discuss their own municipal affairs. From the taxable manufacturing and commercial district of Ustiug they collect many different kinds of revenues, as well as money for the postal service. They elect local administrators from among their own number. The officials thus elected show no concern for the county peasants and give no consideration to matters affecting the county as a whole. Moreover, it is impossible for the county peasants to assemble in the town hall for consultation on countywide issues, since the local officials in Ustiug do not permit it. Consequently the peasants of the rural district are made to suffer lengthy administrative delays, economic loss, and lack of representation.

"All manner of injustice results from the lack of representation. The peasants find themselves enslaved by the townspeople in everything. In their pride the local officials tyrannize us peasants and treat us as though we were their slaves. By virtue of their power and great wealth they have been able to purchase for themselves from our brothers, poor peasants like ourselves, the very best hamlets in the county and thus have become proprietors of numerous rural districts. But as soon as they began to exercise control of the hamlets, they forcibly sloughed off the payment of all kinds of duties from their own shoulders onto us, the distressed peasantry.

"Through their coercion, we have grown impoverished and destitute. We had to put up our last small villages as collateral to obtain short-term loans from them in which, because of need, we had to borrow up to twice and three times the value of those villages. With such large amounts of money lent out on contract, they have taken over proprietorship of our hamlets and have kept many peasants for themselves as sharecroppers. Others were not permitted even to become sharecroppers. Consequently, because of the burdens imposed upon them by the new proprietors, those peasants one by one have taken leave into parts unknown.

"Finally, as regards military conscription, the local officials have been issuing calls for selections to be made by their own townspeople, but they have not called for any selections by people in the county. This is done to avoid taking as soldiers anyone from their hamlets. Only independent peasants are to be conscripted. Consequently the peasants have been fleeing one by one."

In 1675 there assembled in Ustiug elected county representatives from all the rural districts. They drafted a petition requesting that there be established especially for the taxpaying population a county-wide administrative office and an all-county public administrator. The sovereign agreed to this proposal, and the peasants moved their elected representatives, together with the records of revenues and expenditures, out of old town hall and into the new rural district office.

The collisions did not end with this. It was pointed out earlier that the townspeople had gained control of peasant hamlets in the county. The peasants submitted a new petition, stating that the townspeople in the hamlets were failing to carry out their district and military obligations, and that they desired to foreclose on their hamlets, about which a petition had already been sent to Moscow. In Moscow no one could untangle this complicated problem, whereupon, according to custom, it was commanded that written depositions be submitted on the spot by the various social classes.

The clergy forwarded the following statement: "The governor Matvei Naryshkin has caused the county of Ustiug to be organized in accordance with the arrangement proposed in the petition of the former head of the customshouse and drinking establishment, Grigory Mylnikov, and his advisers, the peasants of the rural district Petrushka Khomiakov and his associates. At the time this was done, they were assembled together in the city of Ustiug upon Grigory's request, which he had issued ostensibly for the purpose of considering matters pertaining to transportation, communication, and the obligation of the local population to provide horses, carts, and guides. While the new arrangement is supposed to rectify past organizational shortcomings that gave unfair advantage to the urban population, we are not aware of any charges brought by the rural district peasants against the townspeople. It is our conclusion that in the future there is needed for us and the townspeople only the single, original town hall, as existed earlier. For the rural district peasants in the newly-established rural district office have begun to assess and collect much excess money. They do this on the pretext of meeting the needs of the entire locality. Yet it remains unclear to us why they decided to take seven rubles in addition to the usual two rubles from each taxable unit of arable land.[81] Moreover, their rural district office has now decided to assess and levy five rubles on each taxable unit of land prior to the collection of state revenues. In carrying through with their policy they have obliged the townspeople and us to incur a loss, while yet they refuse to divulge their financial records or give an accounting of such large sums of money."

The new elected chief of county administration, Kopylov, and his associates, the elected rural district officials, issued a declaration in which they stated that the peasants had seceded from the city administration because of oppression by the townspeople. The peasants put forward a proposal that, if there was to be but one town hall as earlier had been the case, there should continue to be retained an elected countywide public administrator. Such an official, they maintained, was

needed to sit together with the elected municipal administrators of Ustiug so that the latter would not keep revenues collected from the entire
county for their own city expenses.

LOCAL PEASANT ELECTIONS

Besides matters of common interest with the townspeople, the county
peasants also had their own community concerns, such as the election
of a local head. When such an election took place, the peasants would
execute a written statement: "We have chosen from our midst a good
man. In virtue of this, our election of him, he is to serve as head of the
peasants, in which capacity he is to see to the fulfillment of minor tasks
and small projects, being authorized to use our community revenues in
the hiring of persons suitable for these purposes. He is absolutely forbidden to steal in any manner whatsoever. Should he engage in theft, the
punishment of the great sovereign shall descend upon us all."

The peasants also elected individuals to act as their community representatives. This was a difficult responsibility because they had to come
into direct contact with the face of stern authority, the governor and
the crown clerks, whose provisioning took precedence over any other
matter.

Elections likewise were held for a local bailiff, at which time it was
customary to issue a written statement: "All the peasants have elected
so-and-so to the post of bailiff. He is to acquire in our rural district
information pertaining to official government business and the collection of revenues. He is initially to relay that information throughout the
entire rural district without receiving any payment for making his
rounds. Later he is to repeat the information for the benefit of those
who did not hear it the first time or who failed to abide by it. On that
occasion he shall collect from those concerned two dengas. He is to
make himself available to the local judge in cases involving government
matters. In a trial before the judge he is to certify who it is that lodges a
petition to the tsar against someone, and he is to confirm it again after
the trial. In compensation for his travels, he shall collect one denga from
the taxpaying peasants and one kopeck from cotters and landless peasants. His provisioning by the peasants shall consist of whatever is available, as much rye and oats as they will give."

Priests were chosen likewise by the peasant communities. When such
an election was completed, the community would issue a written announcement: "We, the peasants, have voted and elected so-and-so to be
the spiritual father of our parish. As soon as God permits and the bishop
ordains him into the priesthood, he shall commence his priestly functions

in our parish, celebrating the divine services, devoting himself to the needs of God's church, and attending to the sick and to women in childbirth with Holy Communion, prayers, and all other necessary ministrations. He is a good man. He is not a carouser or an alcoholic. He does not make a habit of consuming fermented beverages. It is because he is a worthy candidate that we, the local elders and members of the peasant community, have let our choice fall upon him."

All the aforementioned decisions of the peasant communities had to be set forth in written form. This was accomplished by a specially elected individual, about whom a statement similar to the following would be prepared: "So-and-so is to be the church secretary. He shall devote conscientious attention to the church. He shall be obedient and duly submissive to those in charge. He shall always be ready to execute in writing documents that pertain to all our community affairs. In payment for his services, he shall collect from us approximately two-fifths of a bushel of cultivated rye in the summer and fall."

Ever since the time of Ivan the Terrible there existed rural districts that were able to obtain charters authorizing them to select their own judges and court assistants. At the election of such persons the peasants submitted declarations of the following type: "We voted and elected so-and-so to serve in an official capacity as local judge. We voted and elected so-and-so to be a court assistant with him. As local constable, we elected so-and-so to serve with him, the judge, from such-and-such a date until such-and-such a date. The judge shall dispense justice to us peasants in matters involving petitions, contracts, wills, and all written instruments relating to land ownership or tenure. Furthermore he shall investigate crimes of theft, robbery, and murder. In all local matters and in the arrest of thieves, robbers, and murderers, the court assistant and local constable shall cooperate fully with the judge in the investigation and apprehension procedures. It shall be the obligation of us, the peasants, to go with the judge in pursuit of all criminals and to apprehend them together with him. The judge shall render his decisions and carry out decrees without delay. He shall accept neither bribes nor gifts. He shall not show favoritism to his friends or wreak vengeance upon his enemies."

SOURCES OF SOCIAL UPHEAVAL

All these instances of the electoral process in operation, which today tend to be regarded as indicating the existence of important rights and a strongly developed degree of social participation, did not in fact afford the peasants an opportunity to bolster their productivity or increase the results of their labor, so that they might satisfy the demands of the treasury without hardship. These rights did not protect a peasant from the governor, the crown clerk, the townsman, or from his fellow peasant who, having expended his worldly wealth on drink, undertook to follow the comparatively easy calling of a robber. The presence of the governor, crown clerk, local administrator, and the robber, coupled with the burden of heavy taxation, made life intolerable for the peasant, driving him from his home to beyond the Urals into Siberia.

Information reached Moscow that the county of Ustiug was becoming depopulated. When petitioners from the peasant communities appeared in the capital, they were asked about the reasons for the flight of the peasants. "The peasants," they answered, "hasten to get away from the heavy taxes, the exactions and graft of the governor, and from conscription into military service. For in addition to all the taxes, the governors Prince Gavrila Myshetsky and Yakov Zmeev have collected from us monetary duties based on 240 taxable land units[82] at a rate in excess of 2 rubles annually, besides rye and oats in the amount of 1,728 pounds each. Moreover, Yakov Zmeev had two nephews who were given 2 grivna per taxable land unit, while their majordomos received 1 grivna per taxable land unit. We paid 3 rubles per taxable land unit to the town hall. Some years we paid 3½ rubles to provide maintenance, beer, and clothing for the governor, while at the same time the governors levied duties in money and grain for their own subsistence before collecting any state taxes. While forwarding to Moscow payments based on revenues collected from us in the amount of 30,000 rubles, for which they gave us a receipt, those same governors also have been collecting 2 dengas per ruble for certifying documents with the official seal and 1 grivna for written authorization to transport each 288 pounds from a total of 653,760 pounds of grain from the Siberian reserve supply.[83] In addition to all that, on Easter, Christmas, and St. Peter's Day, we presented the governors with supplies for the table from the same taxable areas of land that had already been subjected to the payment of taxes.

"Prince Gavrila Myshetsky was commissioned to carry out among us the task of selecting and sending soldiers. In carrying out that assignment he chose to ignore those who hired themselves out in perpetuity to serve in a military capacity, for the assumption of which obligation they obtained sizable payments from the peasants while providing written guarantees with regard to their own part in the transaction. He proceeded to induct instead the householders themselves, the very persons who had hired the others to take their place. For his own personal profit he confiscated the written guarantees that had been given to many of the householders and returned them to those who had been hired. These latter individuals eventually came to control considerable sums of money belonging to the householders, who finally suffered ruin, with many of their homes falling into decay.

"Yakov Zmeev dispatched into our district musketeers and bailiffs who were in his pay in order to collect past debts by means of torture. Those musketeers and bailiffs were successful, through lethal torture, in extracting from the local officials and revenue collectors a total of 1,732 rubles. In like manner, Prince Myshetsky also has made use of such mercenaries, who then divided the spoils with him.

"Zmeev has gone on travels to the Cherevkovskaia district, a distance of over 66 miles, accompanied by his dogs and a suite of more than 50 persons. Along the way he requisitioned for himself, his dogs, and his suite boats for travel over water and carts with drivers for the overland journey. As they proceeded, he accepted expensive gifts and invitations to dine, and procured various provisions. The burden of paying for all this falls upon us, the urban and rural taxpayers of Ustiug, in the amount of 5,000 rubles and more annually."

Still, it was not only because of the governors, crown clerks, and exactions by treasury officials that the people of taxpaying communities suffered grievously and the county became depopulated. It was not only from under the bailiffs that they had to buy their way out. They also had to provide for and pay off their own brethren in the local community who were attracted to the easy life afforded by the robber's trade.

Several factors combined to render one's calling as a robber both safe and free from trouble: a sparse population, the dark forests, the unfamiliarity of people in a community with concerted social action for common defense, and the absence of a well-organized police force. Those same petitioners from Ustiug furnished testimony about the following conditions: "Numerous drinking establishments have been constructed throughout the rural districts, where many peasants squander their money on alcohol. Gathering together in a gang of 20 persons or more, they arrive in the summer, intent on brigandage. Torturing a great number of peasants, they burn them with fire and extort by force sums of about 100 rubles. The peasants resort to the expedient of pawning their paltry possessions and obtaining loans on their hamlets. After paying off the robbers, the peasants themselves scatter for parts unknown."

In response to such depredations, government military contingents were sent as a protective measure. This, however, often simply created different hardships: "Detachments of crown clerks and musketeers have been dispatched after the robbers. But the clerks impose upon us the assessment of a ruble for carts and drivers, and the musketeers, half a ruble. They furthermore put on official duty as many as 30 peasants for guides."

In 1670 a count was made of persons subject to the payment of taxes who were on the road near the city of Verkhoturie.[84] The number was 2,051. Accompanied by their wives and children, they came from various cities and counties: Totma, Ustiug, Vaga, Mezen, Solvychegodsk, Yarensk, Sysola, and Kaigorodok. To discourage such further uncontrolled travel, the government ordered that strong barriers be erected.

The crown diligently fostered settlement and establishment of peasant communities in the area near the Ural mountains and in Siberia, but it required that peasants who were admitted to become tillers of the soil come only from among unobligated vagrants and not from the taxpayers, children of taxpaying peasant families, cotters, or workhands. Exiled criminals were settled also as agriculturists in Siberia. This made life quite difficult for the established peasant farmers, for the crown ordered the latter to give their daughters and nieces in marriage to the bachelor exiles in order to dissuade them from moving and strengthen their ties to the locality.

In the north and northeast, the taxpaying peasants fled beyond the Urals; in the south, the peasants residing on military tenures absconded beyond the boundaries of Great Russia. There, a rather distinctive type of internal war was being waged. In 1672 this is the sort of petition the tsar would receive: "We, your slaves, the military tenants and landowners beyond the river Oka, do hereby lodge a petition. Our people and peasants, turning to banditry, have assaulted many of their military tenants, while others have resorted to fire. They have fled from us beyond the border into the cities of Little Russia, where they live under the protection of bishops and cossacks in the cities, suburbs, villages, and hamlets. Carrying with us your decree, and also chargers and travel permits from the governors, we have made expeditions to the cities of Little Russia in search of them, our fugitive people and peasants. However, the bishops, the local chief, and the cossacks do not release the fugitive and peasants to us. Instead, they assault and rob us. Many have been beaten to death; others have been plunged into water. Meanwhile those bandits, our fugitives and peasants, placing their reliance on the unwillingness of the local authorities to surrender them to us, descend upon our villages and hamlets, creating havoc. They reduce us to utter ruin, incite our last remaining people and peasants against us, steal our horses and other livestock, set fire to our buildings and threshing floors covered with grain, beat many of us to death, and burn others with their wives and children after trapping them in their homes. In the counties of Novgorod Seversky and Chernigov,[85] the number of deserters from the dragoons and of our fugitives and peasants who have settled under the protection of Bishop Lazarus runs to over 5,000 persons. Not a single one of them has been released, even if he has only just escaped the gallows."

It is apparent that life for the peasants was easier under large landowners than small military tenants. Yet, the big landowners customarily maintained continual residence in Moscow, which meant that their estates were left in the hands of stewards from whose cruelties the peasants likewise fled to the cossacks. In this connection a certain Bogdan Khitrovo wrote a somewhat naive letter to Prince Vasily Golitsyn: "You have graciously vouchsafed to write me that, from my hamlet in Kursk, six peasant families have taken to flight. May I entreat that you have an investigation launched to determine the possibility that their departure was occasioned by the brutality of my overseer, Savva Tancheev. In my small hamlet in Epifan, he drove away a lot of people by his harshness. I know that this happened not on account of drinking or personal profit, but because of his immeasurable brutality." What a striking example of administrative deftness! The man given charge of affairs in the hamlet in Epifan chased the peasants off by his brutal treatment, and of course no better man than he could be found to send to Kursk! At least he was not a drunkard or a thief.

As far as the peasants were concerned, the best situation they could hope to obtain was on landed estates belonging to monasteries. Yet even there strong grounds for dissatisfaction arose. In 1678 the peasants of the Tolvuiskaia rural district rose up in rebellion, declaring they did not desire to be connected with the Viazhitsky monastery. The leaders of the uprising were severely punished.

III

HARBINGERS OF REFORM

THE NEW TEACHERS

The awareness of economic deficiency, leading inevitably to a turning point in history, was coupled closely to a consciousness of moral inadequacy. The Russian people could not remain shackled by a Chinese-type attitude toward their own high degree of perfection and a Chinese-type assurance that they stood above all other people in the world because of the geographical location of their country. No oceans separated them from the people of Western Europe. Pressed by the force of circumstance, the Russians at first had to move from west to east. As soon as they had consolidated themselves there and founded a state, there inexorably arose the likelihood of a collision with their western neighbors. That collision proved to be immensely instructive.

At the very time, in fact during the very reign, when Russia's neighbors to the east showed themselves to be utterly powerless before Muscovy, when three Tatar khanates were conquered and the Russians began an unimpeded movement across Northern Asia to the shores of the Pacific Ocean—in that same reign there occurred frightful misfortunes in the West, where the end of the struggle saw the Russians compelled to cede their own territories to the enemy.[1] The meaning of this was inescapable. To the degree that the eastern neighbors were weaker than the Russians, to that degree were the western neighbors stronger.

This conclusion, shattering a Chinese-type view of one's own superiority, naturally and necessarily aroused in a vital people the tendency to develop closer contacts with those nations that had demonstrated their own predominance and to borrow from them in those areas where they held undisputed mastery. Because the Westerners appeared strongest in their knowledge and technology, it was in those fields that the Russians had to learn. Thus it was—starting with the reign of Ivan IV, when final victory was attained over the East but when disastrous calamities befell the powerful tsar, conqueror of Kazan and Astrakhan, after he turned his arms against the West—that the idea of developing closer relations with the West, of gaining access to the sea, and of learning from the maritime countries became the guiding principle of the government and of leading Russians.

As though on purpose, there ensued a succession of new misfortunes and humiliations brought on by the West. The adverse consequences of the wars with Poland and Sweden after the Time of Troubles nourished the idea even more. It became impossible to avoid following one of two alternatives, reform or revolution. In any event, the issue could not be resolved without struggle. Sensitive questions of vast importance had to be confronted squarely. Who were to serve as teachers? Were they to be strangers, foreigners, and most important, heterodox religious believers? If such as these were to be freely admitted and granted the high status of teachers, would this not constitute open recognition of their superiority and of unmistakable subordination to them? What would those people say, once they had gathered in their hands exclusive competence as teachers?

When Tsar Boris Godunov raised the question of the need for summoning new teachers from abroad, the country's old teachers, the clergy, replied that it could not be done because it represented a danger to the faith. It was better to send young Russians abroad, so they might study there and return home to instruct their own countrymen. The fate of the Russian young men sent to other lands by Godunov is well known. None came back.

The continuance of prolonged stagnation and backwardness could not lend the Russians the strnegth and ability they needed to come into peaceful and positive contact with civilization in order to master it. Quite the contrary, stagnation and backwardness had produced a spiritual weakness, which manifested itself in two ways. Either a person averted his eyes with terrible stubbornness from whatever was foreign and novel precisely because he did not have the strength or manly courage to gaze upon it directly and come to terms with it, shaking with superstitious fear like a child whom neither rewards nor punishments can induce to draw near his new governess, or else, should his fear be dissipated, he fell completely under the thrall of the innovations, being unable to withstand the magical spells of the sorceress Civilization. The second manifestation reinforced the first one.

Following Godunov's unfortunate endeavor, no new attempt was made. Yet the need to learn made itself felt ever more keenly. Then a means arose for satisfying that need without having to experience fear of the foreigner. Located next to Great Russia was Little Russia, or the Ukraine, and in a series of well-known historical developments, both of them were brought together through unification in a single political body. Beacuse of its conflict with Latinism,[2] Little Russia earlier had recognized its need for enlightenment and had passed through the preliminary stages of establishing the necessary schools. Thus it became possible for Great Russians to study without danger under the tutelage of Little Russians, who arrived in the garb of Orthodox monks. Similarly, it was also possible to learn from the Orthodox Greeks. Consequently there can be seen during the seventeenth century, before the era of reform, a comparatively brief period of time in which efforts were made to acquire education from the Little Russians, or West Russians generally, and the Greeks.

THE SCHISM

Even this advance toward accommodation, however, could not entirely resolve the problem. For the new teachers, regardless of their origin whether from Orthodox Greece or Orthodox Little Russia, inevitably came into collision with the old teachers. From this circumstance arose a struggle that was to lead to exceptionally important consequences. Great Russian youths, having studied Latin and Greek under the direction of Little Russian monks, grew more knowledgeable than their former teachers and spiritual fathers. They protested against what they had been taught of old and took exception with many of the interpretations of their spiritual fathers.

It is not difficult to imagine how the spiritual fathers reacted to this. What was the world coming to? Youngsters presuming to instruct their elders! What good could be expected from this? It was clear that the Kievan monks, steeped in Latinism, were indoctrinating their pupils in various heresies. And it was not enough that the Russians, learning only heaven knows what from the Little Russian monks in Moscow, developed a desire to go to Kiev and study there, in the very nest of Latinism. In what fine condition they could be expected to return! Such were the anxieties that were rife in Moscow at the beginning of the reign of Tsar Alexis.

The ingredients for a schism were already present, emerging out of an inevitable collision between the old teachers and the new. There was prevalent a growing realization of the need to make corrections in church books before having them reproduced on the printing press. This task was assigned to the most knowledgeable of the old teachers, the foremost protopopes,[3] who undertook to make such corrections as they saw fit. Thereupon the revised books were printed. Their appearance elicited from the new teachers, the Greek and Little Russian monks, an adversely critical response. The work of revision had been done improperly, with the result that additional errors rather than corrections had been made. The patriarch then commissioned the new teachers to carry out a revision all over again.

What did this mean for the old teachers? Until then they had possessed unquestioned authority and a reputation as experts. Now, humiliated before the whole world, they were declared to be ignorant. And who had done this to them? The monks who but recently had arrived from Kiev and Greece. But what did those monks know and what was it they taught, purportedly under the guise of Orthodoxy? Thus the schism, having germinated already, began to sink strong roots.

It is easy to understand the impression that was created among the many who remained faithful to the traditional ways by the protestations of the old teachers, who charged that the newcomers, the Greek and Little Russian monks, had brought with them innovations fraught with Latin heresies. After all, they insisted, the West Russians long ago had joined with the Latins, and the Greeks also had fallen away from the Orthodox faith, going so far as to have their books published by Roman Catholic presses.[4] The majority of people remained loyal to the authority of the church and the secular government, which had taken the side of the new teachers. But a certain part of the population declared itself to be on the other side. Consequently it had to reject the authority of the church and also that of the state as well. The "schismatics and ecclesiastical rebels" became at the same time civil rebels, refusing to acknowledge an authority which, in their eyes, persecuted the true faith and represented the power of Antichrist.

That which by a well-defined law always happens in consequence of a sudden liberation from authority of any kind occurred now in Russia with relation to the schism. Having once refused to accept the authority of the ecclesiastical administration, with its unitary set of doctrines and regulations compulsorily binding on all, the schism did not have the opportunity to create for itself a new church with a single governing body. It had to break up into numerous interpretations propounded by many different teachers who were unsupported in their preaching by any authority. Not long after the rejection of a particular authority there appears a strong tendency to break away from all authority, from all social and moral ties. The Hussite liberation from the authority of the Roman church in Bohemia led rapidly to the communism of the Taborites. The Lutheran liberation from the authority of that same church in Germany led to a similar phenomenon in the form of Anabaptism. Closely akin to these tendencies in the direction of unrestricted freedom were several of the manifestations associated with different interpretive trends in the Russian schism.

At this point it is possible that certain questions might be raised. Why was it necessary to push the schismatics to such extremes? Why was it found necessary to hunt them down for differences of ritual, for mere words, for matters of no essential consequence? Why could they not be allowed to use the old books and observe their traditional rituals? Questions such as these demonstrate an inability to separate oneself from the present time and indicate the habit of transposing the imperatives of the present into the past. This seriously hampers the study of history and places an obstacle in the way of a correct understanding of the past, and with it also of the present, as well as of the connection between them. In the first place, if a schismatic were told that he could make the sign of the cross whatever way he wanted, this would not have dissuaded him from referring to the followers of official Orthodoxy, with their use of three fingers, as servants of Antichrist. In the second place, the very fact of the suggestion having been made at all would only confirm for the schismatic the truth of his conclusion.

If in the seventeenth century there appeared people who, confusing essential issues with those lacking any real substance, were willing to lay down their lives for making the sign of the cross with two fingers and so on, then by what right can one hold that the other side, with their use of three fingers, suddenly had risen to such a great height that they could distinguish substantial from unsubstantial matters and gaze condescendingly on the errors of their lesser brethren? The persons whose authority the Orthodox recognized told them that forming the sign of the cross with three fingers conformed more closely to the true practice. They accepted this as the more correct practice and in this way drew apart from those who continued to bear witness to the faith of their fathers by bringing together two fingers. But in their sentiments concerning the importance of the matter, the two sides stood in perfect agreement with respect to one another. Just as the adherents of the two-fingered sign of the cross were firmly of the opinion that this was an essential precondition for salvation, regarding those using three fingers as enemies of God and servants of Antichrist, with whom no form of interaction was permissible, so likewise did their opponents regard them in turn, especially since no circumstances arose which could have been expected to alter their outlook.

Rebels against the church! Rebels against God Himself! What could be worse? What degree of contempt was strong enough to display toward such persons? The same people who persecuted the schismatics for their way of making the sign of the cross were the same ones who insisted that shaving off the beard meant distorting God's image in oneself and acquiring the likeness of a dog or cat. This was a clear indication that the attitude was everywhere one and the same, so that there could ensue

only a sharpening of the conflict without hope of concession or compromise. A change of outlook fostering an ability to discriminate between the essential and unessential could appear only a century or so
later, under the influence of new conditions. For the time being there
existed prospects only for condescension, concession, or compromise.

A church dignitary like Metropolitan Platon of Moscow[5] could only
have appeared on the scene in the second half of the eighteenth century,
but not in the second half of the preceding century, when it was possible for the following kind of incident to occur. In 1655 some White
Russians were sent to Vologda, whereupon the local priests inquired of
their bishop whether they should allow the newcomers to come to
church and minister to their spiritual needs. The bishop wrote the patriarch, who replied: "If anyone is not baptized properly, but has received
baptism by sprinkling with water instead of immersion, then he is to be
baptized again. The dead are permitted to be buried."

The collision between old and new teachers led to the schism, to
rebellion within the church. The clergy were unable to settle with this
challenge to their authority and teaching as quickly as the secular power
had disposed of, for example, the uprising of Stenka Razin. The rebellion against the church became permanent. The clergy acquired an un-
relenting and angry set of enemies who showed no inclination to spare
their adversaries in their complaints and accusations.

To be sure, accusations poured forth not only from the schismatics.
Society as a whole apparently also was affected, producing agitation
and disturbance that prevented the maintenance of peace. Leading Russians still harbored the dismal perception of their country's inadequacies
and backwardness. They realized that others had progressed further and
they appreciated the necessity for learning and adopting advanced developments. From this arose the tendency to listen attentively to the
comments of foreigners and heed critical remarks from different sources
concerning the existence of deficiencies in a wide range of matters.

A historical period of this kind is usually filled with aspersions and
imperious dictates. Efforts are made to eliminate whatever has been perceived as an alleged evil. But since those efforts are carried out with
superficial means, they usually miss the mark.

One such lamentable, scandalous evil, observed both by foreigners
and Russians, was the universality of rampant drunkenness. Foreigners
were given to making comments of the following variety: "There is no
country in the world where drunkenness is such a widespread vice as in
Muscovy. Everyone, whatever his calling, sex, or age, whether clergy or
layman, man or woman, young or old, drinks vodka at all hours, before,
after, and during meals."

A bishop issued a circular letter to the clergy of his diocese: "You should diligently provide God's people with instruction every day. Whenever you teach from Holy Scripture, let one person read and another follow with an interpretation, or let the same person carry out both the reading and explanation. But let there be something for the common people to learn from you. We have observed that among the common people, especially clergymen, there has become implanted the satanic evil of immoderate alcoholic consumption. This satanic artifice separates many persons from God." It posed no great problem to send a written communication with instructions "to read and interpret"; but it was a somewhat different matter to carry them out when there existed no proficiency for the task and none to be found. Admonitions about drink being the contrivance of Satan long had been forthcoming throughout the centuries, all to no avail.

Internally weak societies, such as Russia's in the seventeenth century, typically place their greatest reliance on outward power. It is the crown that sees to everything and is able to do everything. Thus, the hegumen of a monastery found it necessary to write to the great sovereign that, without a decree from the tsar, he was unable to cope with his brethren: "A considerable amount of animosity and agitation results from drunkenness. Some priests, attendants at the altar, choristers, and ordinary monks have become addicted to that habit. Because of this disorder, frequent shuffling has taken place in the office of hegumen. Long periods of time have elapsed in the monastery when there has been no hegumen, during which occasions the monks have become accustomed to live as they please." The tsar responded by sending a written order that alcoholic beverages were not to be kept in the monastery because the prevalence of drunkenness threatened the monastic order with utter ruin.

Nevertheless, several years later, decrees from the tsar were again issued to the monasteries. They contained new imputations of wrongdoing, implicitly recognizing that the previous directives from the sovereign had remained without effect: "In the monasteries of Moscow, in those near and distant, and in those that are registered and unregistered, the archimandrites, hegumens, cellarers and priors, treasurers and priests, and ordinary monks keep alcoholic beverages, spirits, beer, and mead, in their cells. Because of the consumption of these alcoholic beverages, participation in church services suffers. Archimandrites, hegumens, cellarers, treasurers, and cathedral canons in all monasteries are accustomed to keeping children, brothers, nephews, and grandchildren, to whom they give bread and other supplies from the monasterial stores and money from the monasterial treasuries. Those same monastic authorities permit servants working in monasteries to go to monasterial landed estates where they occupy salaried positions. When those servants return to their monastery with the salary they have earned, the authorities, their children, nephews, and grandchildren take from them bribes and gifts in money, spirits, honey, marten skins, and all manner of sweetmeats. On those who fail to oblige them, they take vengeance by way of beatings and severe banishments. They also take bribes and gifts from peasants on monasterial landed estates, both in the performance of duty and not. Moreover, the authorities go on visits to the homes of laymen for feasts and parties, compensating them with loans of monasterial grain and money from the treasuries."

Twenty years after these orders were dispatched, the metropolitan of Novgorod again struck a familiar refrain: "Hegumens, as well as married and unmarried priests and deacons, consume alcoholic beverages to the point of intoxication, exercising no concern for God's church or their spiritual children. All manner of disorder is evidenced by persons of every rank. A firm order is to be given that hegumens, married and unmarried priests and deacons, monks, and nuns are not to go to the tavern to drink, consume alcoholic beverages to the point of intoxication in public, or lie drunk in the streets."

CHURCH COUNCILS

Church councils likewise did not mince words in casting reproach. The council of 1667 decreed that priests were to educate their children, thereby preparing the children to take their place and preventing them from becoming slaves of Mammon. The clergy were to avoid profiting commercially from Christ's church or permitting candidates for the priesthood to be selected from among illiterate village incompetents, some of whom lacked the capacity to function as shepherds of livestock, much less of people. From disregard of such precautions arose rebellion and schism in God's church.

There was no shortage of criticism in the seventeenth century, a condition that was normal and necessary in a transitional period. Indignant protests and strong statements were made regarding drunkenness and ignorance. Yet they came from a most insignificant minority or, what was even more important, they originated with foreigners sojourning in the country. The Russians then picked up the comments and repeated them under the influence and direction of the foreigners. But criticism and advice cannot be of assistance in leading to any sort of improvement unless conditions favorable to such change, preceded by a lengthy period of preparation, have been created. When such conditions are absent, criticism can lead only to a search for the means whereby they can be established. If a society is young and vigorous, if it knows how to grapple with life, those conditions will begin to have their effect in preparing it for advancement. But how much time is needed for this? And should the criticism originate suddenly from without, when no preliminary groundwork for it has been laid, the results can be quite unfortunate.

Prior to the observations expressed in the second half of the seventeenth century by Greek and West Russian clergymen, the regulations and decisions of the Council of the Hundred Chapters, convened in 1551, held for everyone the force of undisputed authority. Then, suddenly, the church council of 1666 made the following declaration: "The articles contained in the proceedings of the Council of the Hundred Chapters were formulated illogically, ingenuously, and ignorantly; and the oath solemnized therein was devised erroneously, without proper judgment. We, the Orthodox patriarchs and the entire Sacred Council, do hereby dissolve and annul that false and invalid oath. We hereby ordain that council to be nullified and that oath to be void. Wherefore it possesses no binding force whatsoever, as though it never existed. This we do because Metropolitan Macarius[6] and the others who participated with him deliberated unsoundly in their ignorance and willfulness, in contradiction with ancient Greek and Slavic manuscripts, and without consulting or soliciting information from the holy ecumenical patriarchs."

The impact was powerful and devastating. These new pronouncements were themselves the product of unenlightened men, and the whole of society in its ignorance once more took its cue from determinations founded on faulty judgment. On the one hand, injured feelings led to an unyielding obstinacy, as might be expected in the face of insulting remarks that cast doubt upon the intellectual attainments of an individual and his forebears. "We are all ignorant, and our ancestors were ignorant." Such a categorical statement was bound to elicit a rejoinder: "Is that so?" Of necessity, the question had to be answered in the negative. On the other hand, the mere recognition of their own and their ancestors' lack of knowledge did not instantly endow those who accepted the authority of the critics with the means of liberation from ignorance. They continued to give the same regard as before to those pronouncements made by the Council of the Hundred Chapters that had not been refuted by the Greek patriarchs; they persisted in sanctifying that which did not deserve to be sanctified. While engaging in pursuit of those who made the sign of the cross with two fingers, they also cast an accusing eye on those who shaved their beards, cut their hair, or fell into similar "vile and immoral Greek customs." Those who indulged in such practices, and even those who associated with them, were excommunicated from the church.

THE CLERGY IN CONFLICT

Mention has been made that Patriarch Nikon in 1655 composed a reply to the clergy of Vologda, in which he stated that Orthodox White Russians, if they had been baptized by sprinkling, were to be rebaptized. This view could not be expected to change in only eleven years. But the question was raised anew by an outside source. At the council of 1667 the patriarchs of Alexandria and Antioch concluded that Roman Catholics should not be rebaptized. They were presented with a contradictory decision arrived at by a church council in 1621 under Patriarch Philaret.[7] The two patriarchs could not use the same phraseology in answering the tsar's grandfather as they did with Metropolitan Macarius. Hence, they offered the following explanation: "Should anyone take exception to the fact that the decisions of a council held under Patriarch Philaret have been abrogated, let him not be tempted, but recall that in early times one council would correct the decisions of another."

Nonetheless, for some the temptation was irresistible. In a short space of time the decisions of earlier councils had been overturned, and one of them, the oldest, was declared to be wanting because of ignorance and lack of proper judgment. Authority was given a severe blow as the ground of tradition began to slip away. Anxious to keep from falling, some tried to grasp with both hands at the former foundations of authority, while others, willing to make some concession to change, went partway, coming to a halt at a dangerous midpoint between two fires and associating Orthodoxy with beards and long hair. The secular government, endeavoring to contend against ancient piety, extended to the latter its helping hand. Patriarch Joachim[8] later used to assert that the vile custom of shaving the beard had been completely eradicated in the reign of Tsar Alexis. In fact, such was not the case. It is known from the roster of palace attendants, for example, that Prince Koltsov-Mosalsky was demoted from the rank of crown agent for having trimmed his hair. But could such outward measures prove helpful at a time when new teachers—the new authorities who insisted on recognition and deference to themselves—began to arrive not merely in the form of Orthodox Greek and West Russian monks? The pressing needs of the state revolved about such knowledge, techniques, and crafts as monks were unable to provide. Willingly or not, it became necessary to turn to foreign and heterodox teachers, who as might be expected swept into the country demanding acknowledgment of their superiority. This was done.

Important persons at the top typically accepted the notion that, not only were things done differently in other countries, but they were done better. As soon as the superiority of the foreigner was accepted, as soon as Russians assumed the status of pupils in relation to the foreigners, inevitably there sprang into being the process of imitation. This process, in the natural course of events, commenced with superficial appearances. The Russian shaved off his beard and trimmed his hair, on account of which he would be dismissed from the rank of crown agent. For his part, he would yield to force. But the use of force could no longer be justified in his eyes, and this disturbed him all the more. He understood very well which authority it was the crown sought to appease when it demoted him from crown agent to an ordinary palace attendant.

Yet, had not that authority been shaken? Did not the growing swell of criticism make clear that earlier ages had been limited in their efforts to a blind groping in the dark? Now, there appeared on the scene a whole chorus of new critics, making loud use of the epithet "ignorance" and becoming ever more deeply committed to their criticism because of the ensuing collision between the old and the new teachers, and the attendant jealousies that it provoked. The foreigner did not keep silent before the individual who refused to recognize in him the image of God and who urged that it was essential to drive out the harmful visitor. Nor did the foreigner limit himself merely to criticism and ridicule. There exists today a curious petition lodged by the residents of Kolomna against a certain Major Tsei[9] and his associates, who are described as "causing great injury and hardship for us, stealing all kinds of merchandise from out stores, and beating and robbing people on the streets. At night, after the sounding of the military tattoo, they wander the streets with the soldiers. They seize priests, whom they beat and maim, taking them afterwards to the major's quarters, where they lock them in a cellar and torture them for their own idle amusement. The residents of the city cannot go to church on Sunday."

PATRIARCH NIKON: BOGATYR OF REFORM

In the second half of the seventeenth century, at the time of national reorientation along a new historical path, the Russian clergy were plunged into a difficult set of circumstances. In those circumstances, instead of encountering support, it was beset by blows. Thus, the affair of Patriarch Nikon[10] struck heavily at it. It would appear almost as though

History, prior to the advent of a trying period of time, had wanted to give the clergy a powerful leader who could aid them through the vicissitudes of a troubled situation and emerge victorious from the strife. Indeed, since the time of Metropolitan Alexis, the Russian church had never found itself in so advantageous a position with regard to the importance of its leading prelate as it did with Nikon. The tsar—young, tractable by nature, and most pious in fact as well as in his official title—fell completely under the influence of the energetic patriarch. It was this very circumstance, however, this abundance of worldly material resources, which embodied the reason for Nikon's downfall. As a man of flesh and blood, he was unable to withstand the temptation presented by the offer of temporal dominion, and he fell.

Nikon allowed himself to assume the exalted title of "great sovereign," that is, the chief master or supreme ruler of a country. It was a title that bore no relation to the meaning of a patriarch, pointing rather to the existence of a dyarchy, to the condition that two masters occupied a single house. It entailed the prospect of an inevitable collision between them, the more especially so since Nikon's personality did not permit him to remain a great sovereign in name only. The high ecclesiastical significance of the patriarchate became for Nikon a secondary consideration. Wishing to become in reality a great sovereign, he flung himself in pursuit of worldly power. Of necessity he was bound to come into confrontation with the other great sovereign, the true and legitimate tsar. In the event, Nikon lost the contest because the absence of any basis for his unwarranted claims became quite clear to everyone.

Nikon's actions from the moment that he abjured his post in Moscow gave rise to a series of scandals that cast ever-increasing discredit upon the former patriarch. He completely lost sight of the church and the patriarchate, endeavoring only to regain for himself, Nikon, at least a fraction of his former importance and material advantage, if restoring them in entirety should prove to be unfeasible. But any society, no matter how deplorable its condition may be, could not but renounce an individual who had transformed a public function of enormous consequence into a private venture. Nikon lost his side of the case because he entered into battle against Tsar Alexis, whose piety and reverent respect for the church hierarchs was well known to all. This cast into even bolder relief the contrast between the mildness of the representative of secular authority and the truculence of the representative of spiritual authority, a monk and bishop, who was given to making his authority and power felt with more intensity than any provincial governor.

Thus the second half of the seventeenth century witnessed a development that was completely the opposite of the one which occurred in the second half of the preceding century. At that time there also took place a contest between representatives of the secular and the spiritual authority; and it seemed that victory had been gained by the former. However, this was only an illusion. The actions of St. Philip,[11] leading to his martyrdom for upholding the most sacred right within the purview of a church pastor, the right of restraining political power and not permitting it to degenerate into mere violence, constituted a great victory for the Russian church and its supreme pastor. For the greatest dignity to which the spiritual authority by its very nature can attain is holiness and martyrdom by way of sacrificing its life for its flock; the lowest degree to which a representative of the secular authority can stoop is to cause the martyrdom of a righteous man.

Nikon's character was not of a type that could take into proper account this inspiring example, for he did not look upon it with the eyes of a spiritual man. Instead, he was struck and upset by its surface appearance, which revealed to him nothing more than the deposition of an ecclesiastical hierarch by a representative of the secular authority. He failed to comprehend that, in this instance, the one who had conquered was the one who saved his soul by sacrificing his life. It was this lack of understanding about the matter that induced Nikon to try to make amends, as he saw it, by compelling Tsar Alexis to send a propitiatory charter to the coffin of St. Philip, seeking forgiveness on behalf of the person responsible for his assassination, Ivan the Terrible. In transferring the relics of St. Philip from Solovetsky monastery, Nikon intended to make use of them as a measure for insuring his own protection. But in what struggle, and with whom? He did not see that his personality caused him to resemble Ivan the Terrible instead of Philip, the persecutor rather than the martyr, and that the most serene Tsar Alexis bore not the slightest similarity to Ivan the Terrible.

Nikon's unspiritual proclivities proved to be especially harmful at a time when, in view of a profound reorientation, it was essential to gather together all the moral capacities of the clergy and provide them with a sufficient arsenal for various dangerous encounters. In order to preserve the importance of the clergy it was imperative to assume a position at the head of the movement, regardless of who may have instigated it, and to undertake a reform of the church. The reforms could not be limited to a demand for a greater degree of order in outward ritualistic practices and the promulgation of some well-meaning decrees, such as those insisting on the rebaptism of Orthodox White Russians. The church needed to have reforms of quite a different kind.

It was necessary to bring together in harmony the two main categories of churchmen, who were at that time divided into the black clergy, consisting of monastic administrators, and the white clergy, made up of married subordinates. They had to be united by kind and loving relations between those who govern and those who are governed. It was necessary by all possible means to oppose the system by which the church administration received support through mandatory exactions in money and kind at the local level. This would have prevented the subordinate clergy from being looked upon as a taxpaying resource obligated to pay for the support of the administrators, who otherwise were given to developing an imperious attitude, like that of the provincial governors, while their clerks bore a disagreeable resemblance to provincial crown clerks. Unfortunately, neither the inconsequential Joseph[12] nor his successor, Nikon, possessed personalities enabling them to conduct relations with their subordinates in a gentle and kind manner or respect them for their high pastoral dignity, thereby elevating them through this selfsame respect.

Vehement complaints started to be heard against both Joseph and Nikon, that they no longer held the same sympathetic attitude which earlier patriarchs had shown toward priests, that they ceased paying attention to their problems, and that they had handed them over as a sacrifice to the insatiable patriarchal chancellor Kokoshilov, who at that time developed a notorious reputation in Moscow. A priest wishing to present a request had to bring gifts not only to Kokoshilov and his wife, but even to his servants, or else he was kept from entering the chancellor's offices. The same situation obtained in outlying regions. On important feast days subordinate churchmen found themselves compelled to lavish gifts on more than 40 different persons close to the local bishop— the treasurer, the director of the episcopal administrative office, two secretaries, six clerks, the episcopal agent, majordomo, supervisor of the granary, steward, sacristan, cupbearer, cellarmen in charge of drink, the priest and deacon attached to the episcopal staff, the bishop's servants and treasurer, the altar attendants and bell ringers, the guards stationed at the episcopal administrative offices and the gates of the episcopal courtyard, the protopope and his associates, the subdeacons, hieromonks, and hierodeacons. It is impossible today to explain why there should have been included in this list two women, one of them with two sons, who were all to be the recipients of gifts. Contemporaries knew the reason, but it has since been buried with them.

The doors of the patriarchal administrative offices were closed to priests. They dared not approach the patriarch to speak with him about urgent matters or ask for the resolution of perplexing questions. Yet for laymen, including women, the doors stood open. These charges cannot be dismissed on grounds that they emanated from partisans of Patriarch Joseph's book revisions, for the complainants drew a connection between Nikon and Joseph, and reprimanded the former for his imitation of Joseph.[13]

After Nikon's departure from office there followed a lengthy vacancy in the patriarchal see, which likewise was bound to have harmful consequences for the clergy in that most critical time. The notorious Kokoshilov retained his former position, and complaints against him did not stop. In 1661 the patriarchal junior boyars lodged a petition against him: "Having gained enormous wealth for himself from the patriarchal household treasury, he now brings his kinsmen into the patriarchal household and enriches them while expelling and ruining us. He has taken a kinsman into the patriarchal household and has put him out on the best five and a half acres of land.[14] Prior to this time, that acreage had been allotted to two or three of us as remuneration. Moreover, Kokoshilov has taken for himself other of the more lucrative acreage that generates church revenues. He has purchased many landed estates for himself, as well as large houses in Moscow. All this he does by virtue of the power he enjoys through sitting in the patriarchal chancelleries, surrounding himself with his relatives and friends."

Finally, the example of the Nikon affair had a detrimental effect upon the Orthodox in its struggle with the schismatics, who were afterwards able to say: "If Nikon, your teacher, showed you the true way, then why did you depose him? Since when do people war against their teacher? But if Nikon is an enemy of God, of the Mother of God, of the saints, and of you, then why do you adhere to his various rules?"

IN NIKON'S FOOTSTEPS

The Nikon affair was over, but the distressing impression it created was revived in a case that involved Archbishop Joseph of Kolomna. This hierarch allowed himself to become upset over the fact that, at a time when the entire country was being placed under a heavy strain by the conduct of protracted wars, the crown had imposed the payment of taxes on landed estates belonging to the church. After having duly fortified himself by imbibing a bit of courage, he did not spare anyone—the tsar, the patriarch, or the boyars—in his speech. He observed that the great sovereign "has no idea how to govern; other people exert control over him. Previous sovereigns provided support for the holy places, but now they despoil them by exacting all manner of excessive duties. As for the boyars, the progeny of Ham, the sovereign has no inkling of what they do. And Patriarch Joachim is scarcely literate. At a church council only two hierarchs make any statements, the metropolitan of Nizhny Novgorod and me, while the patriarch just sits, thrusting out his beard. He is an irresolute coward, preaching first one thing and then another. When he starts to deliver a sermon, he whines and nothing comes out."

Joseph was affected by the temper of the new times, scoffing at the patriarch for his ignorance and his inability to speak up at a council or give a sermon. Yet, this demanding intellectual failed to appreciate one thing, that the higher wisdom for a bishop consisted precisely in his being able to cultivate a Christian attitude towards his neighbors and induce others to follow in suit, to persuade a worthless governor to temper his treatment of subordinates, and not surpass the worthless governor in the severity of his approach toward them. Joseph's notion of promoting conciliation was to shout "Which of you is able to grab anything away from me? I'm not afraid of anyone! Neither the tsar nor the patriarch can take anything of mine."

Upon those adjudged guilty of what the bishop regarded as infractions, severe penalties were imposed. They were slapped and whipped, put in chains, or deprived of food for up to three days at a time. Cathedral priests and choristers were cooled off at matins with a mixture of snow and ice water, and snow was forced down their breasts. During a prayer service a certain Peter Kirillov was beaten by the archbishop himself until he bled. While naked priests were being whipped with the lash, Joseph shouted "Strike harder, you lifeless relics!"

When he was summoned to appear before a church council, Joseph refused to volunteer a statement about anything. When witnesses with accusations were brought forward to give damaging testimony, he did not make any rebuttal. The council thereupon pronounced his deposition. The patriarchal charter enumerating his faults contained the following observation: "In an egregiously bestial manner and with outrageous intent, he has pounced upon the sheep of his flock as food to satisfy animal appetite, that is, his boundless capacity for corruption and falsity. He has not offered any justification to us for his enormities. Of all that his accusers bore witness against him, he stands convicted, and he has not offered a single word in his own defense." Joseph was sent to one of the monasteries of Novgorod, but with the right of acting as its administrator.

THE PATRIARCH AND THE TSAR'S CONFESSOR

In November 1674 the sovereign was in residence at the village of Preobrazhenskoe, when there suddenly arrived the table attendant Postnikov, son of his confessor, with a petition from his father. The confessor wrote that Patriarch Joachim had ordered him, even though innocent, to be placed in chains as a penance, and he requested the tsar's return to Moscow in order that he might be freed from the penance. It would be safe to assume that even the most disastrous defeats sustained by Russian military forces, as at Konotop and Chudnov,[15] could not have made a more startling impression on the pious tsar. He commanded his confessor be informed that he, the tsar, was arranging to come to Moscow early the following morning. Upon arriving he summoned his closest advisers—Dolgoruky, Khitrovo, and Matveev—and then sent for the patriarch.. The patriarch made his appearance "and told about the protopope's appalling violence, ignorance, and corruption, that he kept a young woman for a considerable period of time, that he did not allow the patriarch's confessor into his presence, and that he cast dishonor upon the patriarch."

The patriarch was angry and the evidence was irrefutable, being in the form of a written deposition that Joachim already had obtained from the young woman. Tsar Alexis made an appeal to the patriarch, who was mollified and agreed to leave the protopope deprived of the right to perform his priestly functions until a church council could be convened to render judgment. Not long afterwards, on 21 December, there was to be celebrated the patriarchal feast day in commemoration of Metropolitan Peter. In accordance with custom, Patriarch Joachim approached the tsar with an invitation to dine at his quarters. Alexis took advantage of the occasion to obtain from the patriarch his agreement to forgive the confessor and not bring the matter up at all before a council.

If events such as these took place in Moscow and Kolomna, what sorts of things were possible farther away where, according to the old proverb, "God dwells aloft in heaven serene; the tsar, far distant, is never seen"? From the county of Totma, for instance, word came that robbers had appeared. Participating in their brigandage and concealing the stolen loot was the prior of Taftenskaia hermitage, the monk Ferapont.

ECCLESIASTICAL PROPERTIES

Nikon and Joseph of Kolomna complained of the desolation being visited upon ecclesiastical holdings, but society could not sympathize with their disapproval. For one thing, the pressures they had to bear fell upon everyone as part of a war on behalf of the Orthodox faith; for another, everyone knew full well that the bishops were not being ruined.

In 1653[16] members of the sovereign's service gentry were dispatched to the patriarchal reserve[17] to take a count of the parish churches in the cities and counties, to make a survey of church lands and appurtenances held by churchmen as their own households, and to conduct a census of parishioners by name. When the tally was completed they were to arrange for the assessment of taxes in accordance with the following schedule: 4 dengas from each household of a priest, 2 from that of a deacon, and 1 from those of a church servitor, a woman in charge of baking altar breads, or a cotter; 6 dengas from the households of boyars, princes, service gentry, junior boyars, and court servitors or administrators; 4 dengas from the households of the taxable urban residents or peasants; 2 dengas from the households of cossacks, cannoneers, or musketeers; 1 denga from workers employed by cotters or boyars; 3 altyns and 1 denga from apiaries, fisheries, and designated beaver lodges; 3 dengas from each four acres[18] of church land under cultivation; 2 dengas from meadows for each haycock; and in addition to this schedule, 3 altyns and 2 dengas from each church for the ecclesiastical tribunal with jurisdiction over secular matters and for the travel expenses of its personnel; and 3 altyns and 3 dengas from each church for duty payments to the treasury.

Other hierarchs likewise imposed their own schedules of tax payments on the eparchics under their control. Moreover, duties on weddings and funerals were collected for the benefit of the bishops. Finally, there also existed other perquisites, such as the kind referred to by Jonas, Metropolitan of Rostov, in a letter to a priest in Yaroslavl: "May God grant you His protection for the support you have given us in the form of fresh fish from the Volga. You are the most generous of your fellow priests in Yaroslavl."

In the second half of the sixteenth century, during the reign of Ivan the Terrible, it was forbidden at a council of the church to engage in any further expansion of monasterial landed holdings. This prohibition failed to be observed. When the Code of 1649 was being drawn up, laymen of all ranks petitioned the sovereign to take back as his own all landed estates that had been granted to the church since 1580 in violation of Ivan the Terrible's directive, and then to distribute them to persons in service to the state. An order was issued to conduct a cadastral survey of such landed holdings, but this was as far as the matter was pursued. Tsar Alexis was unable, especially while Nikon remained active as patriarch, to carry out such a program. Instead, the tsar himself contributed to the continuing disregard of Tsar Ivan's prohibition. Thus, for example, in 1654 he donated to the Iversky monastery, then being constructed by Nikon, the entire suburb of Kholm.

CHILDREN OF THE WHITE CLERGY AND CROWN SERVICE

Tsar Alexis also retreated from taking any measure concerning children of the white clergy. Not all the sons of clergymen or church people were able to obtain ecclesiastical posts because there were too many of them for the number available. Moreover, there existed one mandatory prerequisite before installation could take place—a candidate had to demonstrate that he was literate. Not everyone could meet this requirement. Nor could one hope, without this skill, to become a clerk. What was such a person left to do? The crown was given to know that the illiterate offspring of the white clergy "live as vagabonds, engaging in disreputable business and brigandage." Thought was given to finding a better occupation for them.

At the end of 1660, when a protracted period of war required an increase in the size of the military forces, a decree was issued ordering the conscription of superfluous individuals from among the clergy and church people. The proportion of those to be taken was set at one out of every three or two out of every four, depending on the people. Those who were literate were allowed to remain with their fathers in the churches, so that the churches would not be deprived of people to take part in the services.

This decree provoked strong protests. Because the protests came from the clergy, they produced a disquieting impression on Tsar Alexis. In the beginning of the next year, a new decree was forthcoming: "We, the great sovereign, do hereby command protopopes, priests, deacons, and all church people to be informed that we do not order their children to be conscripted into service. We do order that they serve God's churches in an ecclesiastical capacity, or that certain of them engage in worthy and legitimate occupations. The clergy are to deter their children, brothers, and nephews from becoming involved in any kind of reprehensible or thievish activity. They are to provide instruction in all kinds of reputable work, so that in the future there will arise no inclination to enter upon a criminal career. Should any of the children or other kinsmen desire of their own accord to enter our service, they are not to be impeded."

Only Nikon, Joseph of Kolomna, and other like-minded prelates could have complained about the destitution of church property, which was in fact far from being despoiled. It was only to be expected that terribly difficult times, such as prevailed during the entire reign of Tsar Alexis, should expose the monasteries and episcopal houses, as well as the landed estates of laymen, to a considerable amount of economic pressure.

Immovable property belonging to the monasteries remained untouched, nor was its extension curtailed. However, grants of immunity were abolished. These were charters that had been given to bishops and monasteries, allowing them to engage in various enterprises free of duty payments. Monasteries now were assessed sums of money to pay the salaries of military personnel. Thus in 1655 the tsar wrote to the Tikhvinsky monastery: "We have been informed that you are in possession of a substantial amount of money in your monastery. Therefore we have commanded that 10,000 rubles be taken from you for the payment of men in military service. You are not to consider this as an affront to you. When the need for military service is over, we shall command that the money be returned." The government furthermore sent military servicemen who had been seriously wounded in battle to the monasteries, where they were to be fed and clothed. Finally, an order was issued that exempted all elderly men who had been in crown service from having to make donations to the monasteries when being tonsured as monks. All others had to give such a donation.

Laymen sometimes concluded the following interesting sort of agreement with a monastery: "So-and-so has made a donation to the Tikhvinsky monastery of a chestnut gelding worth 10 rubles and money in the amount of 2 rubles. When at some future time he arrives to reside in the monastery by virtue of his donation, we, the hegumen and brethren, shall accept him and care for his welfare as for the rest of the monks. But if it should happen that God summons his soul and he is unable to follow the life that he has arranged through his donation, then we shall enter his name in the litany and in the list of the departed for eternal commemoration."

MORALS AND CUSTOMS

It was said earlier that sharply critical comments concerning moral deficiencies could exert no immediately beneficial influence because the conditions that had produced the deficiencies could not suddenly be made to vanish. Those conditions consisted of stagnation, inflexibility, a narrow outlook, the existence of but few interests that raise humankind above the trivialities of daily existence, cleanse the moral atmosphere, provide a person with the necessary rest, harmonize his energies, and revive them. In a word, there existed a lack of enlightenment. The absence of food for the spirit inevitably facilitated the predominance of materialistic propensities and views.

The church condemned such tendencies and ideas, demanding that they be changed. Neither its censure nor its bidding was effective. The church tried to instill the notion that marriage was a sacrament to be approached with reverence, but society looked upon it in a different light, as expressed in "the absurd, dissonant ditties and ribald sayings" that accompanied a bride and groom to church. Foreigners described with amazement how men and women bathed together in common bath-houses, a custom that long persisted in spite of the church's strenuous efforts to eradicate it. This practice best explains the reaction that mani-fested itself in the confinement of women to the *terem*, the women's quarters ordinarily found in the homes of wealthy and notable persons. The one phenomenon necessarily gave rise to the other. On the basis of testimony to which complete reliance can be given, there was no place, either in the East or West, where the vile sin against nature was treated so lightly as in Russia. Sometimes the consequences were horrible.[19]

The pious Tsar Alexis considered it his duty also to exercise care for the spiritual salvation of his subjects. He required that commanders forcibly compel military servicemen on a campaign to go to confession. Needless to say, he likewise imposed the same requirement on civilians. In 1659 an order was sent to the crown chancelleries stipulating that chancellors, clerks, junior boyars, and people of all ranks were to go to confession and observe the fast during Holy Week. Next year a decree called for a list to be sent to the Monasterial Chancellery[20] of those who failed to go to confession, concerning whom another decree would be issued indicating their loss of the tsar's favor, without mercy. Also in 1660 it was ordered that everyone observe the period of St. Philip's fast, preceding Christmas, and attend church services every day. Some years earlier, at the beginning of Alexis' reign, a decree was promulgated en-joining everyone from working on Sundays or important holy days and ordering a cessation of labor on Saturdays at the time that church bells sounded vespers.

People were not to work—but what was there to do? The crown, which took upon itself obligations *in loco parentis* with respect to its subjects, whom it regarded as children, forbade a host of entertainments and widespread superstitious practices: "On Sundays, important holy days, and on days honoring the great saints, the people shall go to church and stand still during services. Mummers and fortune tellers are not to be invited to private homes. The following activities shall be avoided: gazing at the new moon in hope of receiving special favors; swimming in rivers and lakes during thunderstorms; washing with rainwater caught dripping from silver during a storm with the expectation of acquiring a fair complexion; trying to foretell the future from the shapes taken by poured wax; playing at dice, cards, chess, or knucklebones; leading bears about on a leash or prancing about while brandishing branches or trees; singing impious songs at weddings or uttering obscene words; engaging in fistfights; playing on swings; jumping in place on wooden planks; wearing masks on one's face; or bedecking devilish mares with finery. Anyone who fails to obey shall be beaten with rods. Asiatic balalaikas, musical pipes, horns, psalteries, and other musical instruments shall be searched out and burned."

Through such enactments the crown undertook to impose a monastic atmosphere upon the observance of holidays by a society which for obvious reasons openly exhibited a strong predisposition for sensual pleasures. The prospect of punishment with rods confronted equally those who sang unbecoming songs at weddings, those who, as they led bears about on a leash, indulged in the most immoral performances in front of children, and those who played on swings or at chess! Nor were the threats merely idle words on paper. In 1669 the great sovereign commanded that the table attendant Prince Grigory Obolensky be sent to jail for the reason that on Sunday his servants and peasants performed manual labor in his yard and he, Prince Obolensky, had been overheard uttering vulgarities. Unfortunately, later history was to show how little were rods and jail effective in rooting out past habits that disgraced the Russians. It is to be hoped that other means will be effective in ridding the people of such habits.

Besides prohibiting indecorous behavior, the crown also forbade the most innocent pastimes. But rods and jail did not stretch far enough to become a deterrent to the worst vice of all, against which passionate cries were raised and of which everyone took note. There was no punishment for drunkenness. The phenomenon of intoxication, widely prevalent in early Russia, serves to indicate better than anything else the kind of society with which the historians in the case has to deal.

Any human being, in order to revive and bring into balance his personal powers, must of necessity on occasion cast aside the ordinary cares of daily life and enter into another world, altering his physical activity and mental state. An educated person, to whom is open the wide variety of God's world and man's work, finds such transitions easy and natural. But to a person constantly trapped in an environment of but few outstanding events, typical of a poverty-stricken life, there usually comes to beckon the promise of passing into a different and more exciting state by artificial means, whether spirits, opium, or whatever. He seeks to find a synthetic joy by creating a festive state of mind, so that he can be transported into a different, fantastic world where he can forget himself. Even the pious and moral Tsar Alexis sometimes took pleasure in escaping this way. On 21 October 1674 the sovereign held an evening meal in his pleasure house. Present at the dining table, besides the tsar's confessor, were the chancellors of the council and the boyars, who were on this occasion permitted to forgo the customary obligation of observing each other's relative rank according to the system of precedence. After the meal the tsar allowed himself to be entertained by all manner of games. He played the German organ and musical pipes. They blew horns, played the pipes, and beat upon tambourines and drums. The tsar gave his leave for the confessor, chancellors of the council, and the boyars to take part in the revels, and he had them served until they became inebriated. They departed between eleven and midnight.

The main evil in a society of this kind was that, in a moral sense, a person came into it like a child who has been prematurely delivered. The early Russians did not have the advantage of being exposed to the necessary transitional period between infancy and social life which today in Russia is characterized by the existence of learning, or that which is most admirably conveyed by the word "education." In early Russia people entered society directly from a state of infancy, the cultivation of their mental faculties failing to correspond to their physical growth. It is not surprising that they were ushered into society principally in terms of their physical side.

Quite possibly some will assert that, even in the early period prior to the reforms of Peter the Great, the Russian people did provide their children with instruction and that there did exist educated, well-read persons among them. There can be no doubt but that some did indeed engage in study and that there were literate individuals even among the peasants. Still, there were to be found illiterate persons among the higher classes. This better than anything else indicates the haphazard arrangement of the educational porcess. The point of the entire question is not whether people were being given instruction, but whether any significant number of them were, in what, and how.

It had been a long time since the first remarks were heard about the desirability of opening educational institutions in which more would be taught than just reading and writing. Not before the end of the seventeenth century, however, was a concerted effort made to found such an institution. The chief obstacle to the undertaking was a lack of teachers arising from the fear that persons who were not Orthodox would be selected to carry out this sensitive function.

Before the establishment of the Academy,[21] Russians wishing to educate their children brought teachers into their homes. The tutors usually belonged to the West Russian gentry. But did many wealthy individuals actually hire such tutors? Even the instances when this did take place pertain to the time immediately prior to the reforms of Peter the Great; and persons receiving their education in this manner spent the active phase of their lives in Peter's reign.

Ordinary people of limited means who desired to see their children educated had no recourse but to send them to a school run by some teacher. Here were taught reading and writing. Furthermore, before giving his lesson, a conscientious teacher would read from an *azbukovnik*, or primer. These contained collections of precepts on how pupils were to conduct themselves in school and grandiloquent disquisitions on sundry points of wisdom. Sometimes they included instructional material, explaining elements of grammar and rhetoric. In the primers, a school was referred to as "a temple of learning," which accurately summed up the chief characteristic of the old Russian educational institutions. Their complexion was also evident from instructions imparted in the primers: pupils, upon being dismissed to go home, were not to leave their assignments in the books; they were not to hurl their books on the benches, but give them to the prefect or student monitor, who was supposed to put them away where they belonged. The pupils were obliged, according to the primers, to carry water to school, extend formal greetings to the teacher on Sundays, and bring him food and drink. A primer, in providing a modicum of information, was a luxury. It supplemented the regular course of instruction in the Book of Hours and the Psalter. A good teacher read from it daily to his pupils. Yet, even these superficial schoolbooks, containing the totality of educational wisdom, did not appear until quite late.

The chief and invariable purpose was to learn reading and writing in order to gain the opportunity of "attending to affairs." The authors of the primers knew very well this goal of the students, or more correctly, their parents. They held out as an inducement to the study of the alphabet, the Book of Hours, and the Psalter the promise that, upon completion of studies, all printed and handwritten books would become comprehensible to the pupils, who would be able "to understand all legal documents and contracts, as well as the proper manner of their composition and arrangement."

At how early a stage relative to their education young people in old Russia used to take their place in life and begin their careers can be seen in the example of a certain youth named Alexis, son of one of the best-educated magnates of the period, Prince Vasily Golitsyn. He was already going on military campaigns and submitting petitions with respect to landed property at the same time that he was only starting to write his first syllables.

On one hand the early Russians commenced their life in society very early, indeed prematurely, as regards their preparation, education, and the development of spiritual capacities; on the other, they became independent very late because, instead of the broad moral guardianship of society, they found themselves under the narrow tutelage of the extended family, particularly their senior kinsmen. It is easy to understand how this kind of protracted dependence affected an adult man who was already the father of his own family.

There existed, then, two conditions which created adverse effects on the social development of the early Russians: the absence of education, which released them, still childlike, to assume their role in the community, and the long period of wardship by the family, which kept them in the status of minors. This latter restriction, incidentally, was inevitable because, in the first place, the individual Russian at the outset of his personal career was indeed an adolescent, and secondly, society itself was incapable of furnishing him with moral guidance. Prolonged dependence made him first and foremost servile in his attitude toward authority of any kind. Yet this did not in any way preclude the coexistence of infantile willfulness and petty tyranny.

It has been observed that people who have been under continuous oppression are the ones most likely to make their own power felt over those who stand lower and weaker. Children can be merciless in their treatment of a captured grasshopper, dog, or cat. A slave is pitiless toward an animal or another slave who is beneath him. There is bound to prevail a natural inclination to exercise one's power over the weak if it is not checked by moral restraints and if, instead, daily instances of uninhibited violence are to be seen. This explains why in early Russian society the relations of a man toward his wife, kin, and children were not noted for any marked degree of gentleness. A person who had not left the wardship of the family grew to manhood and was given an unfamiliar status, which he was unaccustomed to accept in a free context. A young man upon being married encountered for the first time another person—weak, docile, and inarticulate—who was placed under his full authority and whom he was expected "to teach," which meant to beat. It little mattered that the officially-approved handbook, *Home Manager,* insisted upon moderation in administering such beatings.[22]

The consequences of such advice can be fairly well foreseen. This is particularly true if, as often happened, an unattractive girl was surreptitiously substituted at a wedding for the beauty who had earlier been put on display as the prospective bride, the identity of the replacement being concealed by heavy veils until the end of the ceremony. A contemporary observer, Grigory Kotoshikhin,[23] noted that "in all the world there is no such fraud perpetrated with young girls as in Muscovy."

Attempts even were made to carry out such subterfuge with the examination of potential brides for the tsar. In 1670 the boyar Bogdan Khitrovo made the following disclosure: "Doctor Stefan came to me and said that three days before, on Tverskaia Street, he had met Ivan Shikhirev, who told him that his niece, Beliaeva, had been taken to the palace as a candidate in the selection of a bride. She was brought before the boyar Khitrovo, who made note of her hands and declared they were ugly. It was after this appraisal that Shikhirev met Doctor Stefan and asked him to help his niece, since she did not have a patron at court, by giving a favorable judgment concerning her hands when the time came for him to examine the candidates."

The doctor answered that he was not called upon to perform such services and that, in any event, he would be unable to identify the niece from the rest of the young ladies.

To this, Shikhirev replied: "As you begin to examine her hand, she will press your palm with her finger, and in this way you will recognize her."

Upon being confronted with the charge, Shikhirev confessed.

The distorted relations between a morally immature husband and an even less mature wife sometimes led to efforts by the husband to rid himself of the wife and vice versa. These attempts reportedly often led in the last resort to the use of poison. However, it cannot be determined with absolute certainty whether this was indeed done with any great frequency. It is sufficient to point to another means whose use at the time is more readily ascertainable. This consisted of tonsuring into the monastic rank. A wife who left her husband to become a nun was thereafter referred to in relation to him as his adopted sister. Similarly a married man who became a monk was called, in reference to his wife, an adopted brother. One such adopted sister submitted a complaint that her adopted brother, having disencumbered himself of her, beat and tortured her, put her sometimes into the cellar and at other times into the stable, which was covered with stinging nettles, and hitched her to the plow. It was revealed that she had been tonsured against her will in a deserted hut and not in a convent, that none of her relatives had been present at the ceremony, and that no one had a certificate attesting to the tonsure.

In the event that a wife murdered her husband, the Code of 1649 prescribed that the criminal be punished by being buried alive up to the head in the ground, there to remain until dead. She was to be punished without mercy. Even if the children of the murdered man and her close relatives did not wish her to be punished, she nevertheless was to be shown no pity whatsoever.

The Code made no reference to the punishment of a man for the murder of his wife. To be sure, cases of this kind did appear in the courts. In 1664, after a certain Ivan Dolgov slew his wife for infidelity, he was punished with the whip and released on bond. Yet the Code of 1649 contained nothing about this kind of matter. Consequently the provincial governors did not dare to prescribe punishment in such cases, preferring to send them to Moscow. There the cases were examined in terms of applicable precedents, comparisons being made with the circumstances under which similar crimes had been committed in the past.

In 1674 a peasant named Bazhenov in the county of Totma confessed to having killed his wife because she had hidden from him one and a half yards of coarse heavy cloth. That, he stated, had been her only offense. Otherwise he had lived with her in mutual harmony. When questioned under torture, he did not change his testimony. The governor requested a decision from Moscow, where it was ordered that a list of precedents be prepared. A search of the records revealed that a musketeer named Eremeev, who had killed his wife while intoxicated, had been punished by death. Another musketeer, also while intoxicated, had stabbed his wife for using foul language. In this latter instance, there did exist cause for the murderer's action and, consequently, it was decreed that his left hand and right foot be severed from his body. The same penalty was decreed for Bazhenov, after which he was to be released without bond, "since he had killed his wife over a minor matter."

Besides the aberrations and crudities of family relations, an adverse influence was exerted on public morality by the widespread prevalence of violence. People became accustomed to cases of brutality, robbery, and murder. This grew into a calamitous habit, for the horrible became, with frequent repetition, less repugnant. Under these circumstances, people began to rely for their personal safety either on their own strength or on chance, but not on society or the crown. It becomes clear, then, why there should have taken place a weakening of social ties, why people should prefer to live in the forests instead of as part of society, and why they should begin to act accordingly.

Life in the capital itself did not guarantee security. In the West a traveler of the Middle Ages would behold and tremble at the sight of a fearsome castle, the nest of a robber baron, perched ominously atop a cliff. In seventeenth-century Moscow, the taller a house and the bigger it was, the more danger it posed to a passerby. This was not because the master of the house, a boyar or lord-in-waiting, would fall upon him to seize his valuables, but because that same master had numerous domestic servants, kept in idleness and poorly paid, who were used to fending for themselves at the expense of passersby, whether they were merely pedestrians or had business with the master.

The servants of Prince Yury Romodanovsky lured the master silversmith with his wares to a country house and beat him to death. They confessed, moreover, to the murder of 20 people and implicated their counterparts in the palace. On Dmitrovka Street, pedestrians, riders, and passengers were never safe from attack by the servants of the boyar Rodion Streshnev or of the princes Golitsyn and Tatev. The government had to dispatch as many as 300 musketeers against bandits on the road to the village of Kolomenskoe outside Moscow. In 1675, with a view to preventing further murders and major robberies from being committed from ambush in the vicinity of Moscow, it was decreed that roads leading out of the city should be cleared of brush and other obstructions up to 700 feet along the sides for a distance of 35 miles. If this was the situation in and around Moscow, one can only imagine what it must have been like farther away, where the peasants would get drunk and promptly set out upon plunder, and where even the prior of a hermitage would engage in robbery and concealment of stolen goods.

The specific punishments pronounced upon thieves and robbers followed a curious pattern. In 1663 the death penalty was abrogated and replaced by the severing of a foot and the left hand. In 1666 the death penalty was restored. Later, the severing of limbs was reintroduced.

It was not only because of robbery that seventeenth-century Russians felt apprehensive and vulnerable. They were surrounded by dangers of another kind, against which there was no protection. This, for instance, is the kind of calamity that came to beset the town of Shuia: "From numerous cities and counties there arrive in Shuia men, women, and maidens. They come to the miracle working icon of the Smolensk Mother of God, bringing with them persons possessed by unclean spirits. During the prayer services, the possessed dream up different sorts of mischief and pour forth invective against various people of the county for having corrupted them. A certain Irina Maurina shouted such accusations against Fedka Yakimov, whereupon Yakimov, in compliance with a decree from the tsar, was taken to Suzdal and executed with cruel death."

Measures were taken to guard against defilement. Knowledgeable persons, capable of diverting all manner of evil, were invited to add their incantations to the traditional blessing of a bride and bridegroom by their parents. But even this did not help: "We had a wedding ceremony at which my brother was married. At the wedding, a deep despondency came upon our mother and her daughter-in-law. They began to scream that they had been defiled by evil spirits. To protect the marriage from all evil, an incantation was recited by Grishka Panin, a townsman of Shuia. On the day after the wedding, the prison warder Palatov came to our house. He took from us the promise of 10 altyns and 4 dengas, a hat, two finger rings, a width of cloth, and a calico handkerchief, whereupon he undertook to relieve our mother and her daughter-in-law of their depression. But he did not succeed in leading them to complete mental recovery."

On a different occasion, another distrubing event agitated that same town of Shuia. All the townspeople were called together to meet in an assembly, at which a query was posed to them in compliance with a decree from the archbishop of Suzdal: "Had anyone of them seen or heard how the cathedral priest Ivan had ridden on the back of a bear?" All the townspeople replied that they had neither been eyewitnesses to such an occurrence nor had they heard anything about it.

In 1674 in Totma a woman named Fedosia was put to death by fire in the presence of a large gathering of people after she had been accused of causing spiritual defilement. Before her execution she asserted that she had not defiled anyone, but had given false testimony about herself during interrogation by the governor because she was unable to stand the torture.

Two further curious instances of fiendish slander will serve as characterizations of this historical period.

In 1671, on the road to Poland, there was apprehended a suspicious individual by the name of Ivan Kleopin, whose interrogation in Toropets led to the compilation of the following official report: "He states that his father is Alexis Kirillov Kleopin of Novgorod and his mother is Maria, wife of Alexis Kleopin, in whose household he resided. However, the identity of his real father is known to Alexis Kleopin. It was one Grigory Abakumov, a cotter of the church of St. Nicholas the Wonder-Worker in the Telbovsky section of Bezhetskaia District in Novgorod, who brought Ivan there from Moscow. Abakumov entrusted the infant to Alexis, who had the baby baptized at his home. When the boy was growing up, Alexis used to call him 'tsarevich.'

"On 6 August, from the church portico in the Telbovsky section of the city, Ivan told six members of the service gentry that he was going to journey to Poland, where he would find support and where he would

become known as Tsarevich Alexis Alexeevich. He would then persuade
the Poles to take up arms and follow him on a military expedition to
Velikie Luki. To this, his hearers replied, 'Well, if you want, go wherever
you please.'

"Ivan on one occasion was told by the wife of Fedor Kleopin, Anisia,
that the priest of the Telbovsky section, Kuzma, had mentioned Ivan in
the course of a conversation and had expressed about him the opinion
that 'He is really quite a great person, but he cannot look after himself.'
But that priest, Kuzma Grigoriev, is a heretic who keeps, and has studied,
heretical books. It was from him that Ivan learned to read and write,
being furthermore introduced to heresy through his contacts with eight-
een members of the service gentry.

"In the Moshensky section of the city, a certain Peter Lupandin referred to Ivan as 'tsar,' whereupon Ivan began to pull Lupandin's beard
for having said it. The comment by Lupandin was overheard by one
Danila Choglokov."

All those implicated by this testimony disavowed any knowledge of
the matter, declaring that they had neither seen nor heard anything. The
priest Kuzma and sixteen other people testified that Ivan was mentally
impaired, suffering from damage to the mind which took place at the
age of six, when he began to be forgetful. After Ivan entered government service, he returned to his true parents and attempted to slash
them with his sword. He did succeed in cutting his brother with it. He
profaned the holy icons and sacred books with blasphemous words. He
gave chase to various people, ran off by himself into the woods, and
said that he, Ivan, was able to grant forgiveness and healing to others.
He tried to commit a violent assault upon his true mother. He cut himself with a knife, hurled himself into a fire, and tore his clothing.

Ivan's foster father, Alexis Kleopin, testified that more than twenty
years earlier Ivan had run away from him in the hamlet where they lived
into the forests because he had become mentally disturbed. Moreover,
he uttered all kinds of obscene words and fancied himself to be an exalted personage, a tsarevich. Finally, Alexis submitted a petition regarding Ivan to the governor of Novgorod, asking that Ivan be brought there
for questioning.

Under torture, Ivan insisted that Alexis Kleopin was truly his real
father and that he had called himself tsarevich because he had become
mentally unbalanced as a result of diabolical slander. He said that he
had set off on the road to Poland for the purpose of inciting the Poles
to launch an attack on Velikie Luki and that he had reviled everyone in
his earlier utterances because he was mentally upset by the atrocious
aspersions made about him and his parentage.

Ivan was hanged.

The second case occurred in Moscow. In 1651 a man named Fedor Shilovtsov was placed under interrogation, during which he submitted information that constituted the basis for the following report: "He was bound over to confinement in the Miracles monastery under the supervision of the priest Ilia. In custody together with him was a foreigner, Krokovsky, who had some kvass that Shilovtsov proceeded to drink. This was followed by a rumbling sound in his stomach; and he believes that, since then, he has been under an evil influence.

"Later, given a leave of absence from the monastery, he went home. Upon returning to the monastery, he began to recite the Psalter, when a loud noise sounded in front of him, as though either an angel or a devil had flown by. And the angel directed him to remove the icon of the Mother of God from the wall because it was wrong to bow before images. He took down the icon and also the cross, and put them on the ground, whereupon the cross began to jump. Seeing this, Shilovtsov stepped upon both the icon and the cross, carrying out this unholy act not impulsively, but at the behest of an angel. For ten weeks or more thereafter, he gave consideration to the thought that it was improper to venerate icons, since God is in heaven, while they are merely divine representations."

The authorities took pains to explain to Shilovtsov that God is invisible and that, when people venerate icons, the honor given the image ascends to that which it represents.

Replied Shilovtsov, "Each person is capable of seeing God with the eyes of reason."

The official report went on to trace the background of this statement: "This theme had been expounded upon for Shilovtsov's benefit in the course of some three or four weeks by the chancellor of the Royal Treasure-house, Zakhar Onufriev, who concluded that the whole matter of icons was being badly managed in Russia, where they can be purchased in the same places that bread and cakes are sold. Ever since then, Shilovtsov has entertained the notion that the veneration of icons is inappropriate.

"His misgivings were exacerbated by the death of his very close friend, Ragozin, who came from the village of Kodashevo near Moscow. Shilovtsov took this very heavily, grieving and weeping for a long time, nearly going out of his mind with sorrow. He began to think about the holy icons and whether it was a salutary practice to venerate them, since they were painted carelessly by men who were ordinary, and sometimes inebriated, to be sold as common merchandise.

"Then, on the occasion of the sovereign's visit to attend church services in the cathedral of the Deposition of the Cloak of the Lord, Shilovtsov began to think to himself: What if he should confess and return the money he had stolen from the mint? Might not the sovereign grant him forgiveness and allow him to speak? Would it then not be possible for him to seize the opportunity and tell the sovereign that God is in heaven, and inquire whether it is right to venerate icons? He would ask the sovereign for evidence to justify the practice. If it should be proved that the veneration of images was indeed a meritorious act, he would then request the tsar to establish an institution designed specifically for the painting of icons, where men of impeccable honor would be employed as iconographers, carrying out their function in accordance with the highest standards.

"When Shilovtsov was placed under confinement in the Miracles monastery and brought to his cell, where there hung an image of the Savior Made-Without-Hands, he gazed upon it and it began to change into pictures of different things."

Similar phenomena also took place at the higher levels of society, where their impact was no less striking. In Tsar Michael's reign an anonymous letter was planted in which the table attendant Ilia Miloslavsky (the future father-in-law of Tsar Alexis) was described as having secreted a magical ring that once had belonged to the famous chancellor Gramotin. For a long time Miloslavsky was kept under guard while a search was made of his possessions. During the next reign, one of Tsar Alexis' kinsmen, the boyar Semen Streshnev, was accused of sorcery, with consequences that were personally devastating. He was deprived of his boyaral rank and exiled to Vologda. Letters also were planted surreptitiously against Artamon Matveev, charging him with sorcery, in an attempt to influence Tsar Alexis' selection of Matveev's ward, Natalia Naryshkin, as his bride.

THE TURN IN A NEW DIRECTION

The economic and moral defects of society came to be recognized. The nation, vital and vigorous, strained to work its way out of the swaddling clothes in which it had been bound too long. The question whether or not to adopt a new orientation was decided. The future lay along the path of change.

The drawing of comparisons and the accumulation of bitter experience had left their mark in the portentous phrase "Things are better elsewhere." Nor would these words cease being repeated, for they urgently pointed to the approaching period of borrowing from abroad and studying under foreigners, a period of spiritual thralldom which, even though it meant political independence and power, would nonetheless be most trying. The situation was unavoidable. But this did not mean that the arduous task could be made easy and peaceful. With the appearance of opposition, a struggle was to ensue that would lead to upheaval. This meant the use of force.

Reforming activity affecting the church was begun by those of the Orthodox faith. How that activity was received, also by the Orthodox, who themselves grew to be considered other than adherents of Orthodoxy, has been described. With regard to education they held fast to the principle that they did not want anyone who was not Orthodox for a teacher. Only learned Greeks and West Russians were acceptable in that capacity. But the heterodox who were entering the country in droves came in a different capacity, as mercenary officers, skilled craftsmen of various kinds, factory owners, and doctors. In the natural course of events the introduction of innovations necessarily proceeded along lines that stressed immediate utility, with the importation of practical skills constituting the first step. Moreover, Civilization already had cast her spell over the Russian people, attracting them by the offer of new pleasures and comforts. The clock, picture, smooth-running carriage, musical instrument, and stage play—these are the things by which the Russians little by little came to be prepared for reforms, like children being coaxed to their lessons with toys. All this was to be seen in Moscow during the reign of Tsar Alexis.

It stands to reason that items from abroad would first appear among the higher classes, in the tsar's palace and the homes of notable persons, where there existed greater familiarity with foreign countries and more wealth for acquiring strange wonders. The common people were forbidden to indulge in music. Indeed, it was ordered that musical instruments be ferreted out and burned. For the minute that music made its appearance anywhere on the scene it invariably became mixed up with some form of superstition and disorder. Of course, when the tsar gave a feast, he "played on the German organ and on musical pipes. They blew horns, played the pipes, and beat upon tambourines and drums." It should not be overlooked that, as early as the reign of Tsar Michael, the tutor of the future Tsar Alexis, Boris Morozov, a man familiar with the West, already had clothing of foreign cut sewn for his pupils, the tsar's sons, and for all the other children studying with them. In Alexis' reign the imitators of Morozov grew in number. The persons closest to the tsar were the leading enthusiasts for things foreign, presenting the tsar with gifts from abroad. Bogdan Khitrovo presented the tsar with a coupé.

Matveev gave him a black German carriage with a shaft bow, clear glass windows, and a top that opened up in two parts. Matveev also gave Tsarevich Fedor a carriage with velvet interior and painted pictures along the sides.

THEATRE AND DRAMA

In all of Christian Europe the origins of dramatic performances, or the so-called "mystery plays," were connected closely with church services, their content consisting of events from sacred history. In Russia this function was served by the *Fiery Furnace* (the story of the Three Children cast into the furnace in Babylon) and the passage of the patriarch on the back of a donkey on Palm Sunday. During Tsar Michael's reign Russian ambassadors returning from Poland told of the theatrical performances with which the Polish king was entertained in his palace. Under Michael's son, similar presentations were staged in Moscow for the great sovereign. The content of the plays was taken from Holy Scripture and their author was usually the monk Simeon Polotsky.[24] Of "comedies" [plays or interludes having a happy ending] with secular content, the work *Temir Aksak* was noted by contemporaries.[25] This book was kept at the palace, in the great sovereign's quarters, but whether it was ever performed is not known.

The actors in the stage plays usually were foreigners or palace servants. In 1674 there was a performance in the village of Preobrazhenskoe in which appeared a cast of foreigners portraying how the head of King Holofernes was struck off by the queen.[26] Musical instruments were played by foreigners and the house servants of Artamon Matveev. Another play, depicting how Artaxerxes commanded that Aman be hanged,[27] was staged by foreigners and Matveev's servants in the presence of the tsar's wife, sons, and daughters. The new art forms being introduced into the country even included the ballet. Just before Lent an entertainment was presented in which foreigners and Matveev's servants danced and played the organ, viols, and other instruments. That the tsaritsa and her daughters were in attendance at these theatrical performances is a circumstance worthy of note, as is also the fact that they accompanied the tsar on his hunting expeditions.

The man in charge of the tsar's foreign entertainers was Johann Gottfried, who had working under him a "master of perspective painting," Peter Ingles.

It became evident with the passage of time that the troupe consisting of foreigners and Matveev's servants was too small for the successful staging of "comedy acts." Consequently in 1673 Matveev ordered that

26 children be selected from the tradesmen in the Burghers' Suburb for training as actors. He had them sent to the master Gottfried in the German Suburb for instruction.[28] Thus it was that in Moscow the creation of a theatrical school preceded the establishment of the Slavic-Greek-Latin Academy! Yet even the number of these thespians was insufficient, so that eventually government clerks were conscripted and sent off to Johann Gottfried to learn the art of acting.

LITERATURE

Although it was a theatrical school designed to provide entertainment for the sovereign that was opened before any other, all indications suggested that the founding of other schools was not about to lag far behind. It was strongly felt that the country had fallen behind. Not only was it strongly felt, but it was also loudly proclaimed that Russians had to learn from others. The approach of a new historical period could be detected in literature as well as in other social and cultural developments.

The way of life of the Russian people before the period of Peter the Great's reform was reflected clearly in its poetry, examples of which by themselves are sufficient to delineate with accuracy the general characteristics of that way of life. Hence, it becomes essential to give some consideration to works of early popular poetry, the more so since those works, created by the people, exerted in their own turn a powerful influence on the life of the people, a phenomenon frequently encountered in history.

THE BOGATYR COSSACK IN SONG AND STORY

If one listens attentively to the long and monotonous song of the Russian people, which commenced in Kiev and Constantinople, passed through Volynia, Galicia, Chernigov, Novgorod, and Moscow, and moved on to Kazan, Astrakhan, and Siberia, it will be clearly seen that this was a people who lived under a set of historical conditions which for the span of eight centuries did not undergo any fundamental change. The favorite figure who captured the imagination of singers was that of the bogatyr or cossack, two words which had the same meaning. As in the tenth century, so in the seventeenth, the Russian world still lay in the Ukraine. Likewise, as in the tenth century, so in the seventeenth, a man would come to feel stifled in his father's house. Such a man, "laden with power, as though weighted with vigor, with strength through his veins flowing free with each heartbeat," would leave home and make his way to the steppes, where it was easier to find someone against whom to pit his youthful strength. Much had changed in the political organization of Russia from the tenth to the seventeenth century, from the times of Vladimir, the warmhearted prince of Kiev,[29] to those of Tsar Alexis, autocrat of all Great, Little, and White Russia. Yet, just as before, bold young men still left home and set out for the steppes to range far and wide, forming along the river Don a military brotherhood of daring rovers where every bogatyr among them could form his own retinue and go forth to accomplish heroic deeds. In this way there was an opportunity for the people, over the course of a whole series of centuries, to sing their song in the same way, because its content was portrayed vividly before their eyes. Nor did the bogatyr disappear when, in the course of time, he became transformed into a cossack.

The form in which early Russian songs about the bogatyrs have come down to the present day is one in which the feats of cossacks are extolled. Those who are acquainted with these songs know that the most prominent place among the ranks of bogatyrs is occupied by Ilia Muromets, who is usually described as an old cossack, and sometimes quite explicitly as a Don Cossack, or even more specifically, as an ataman of the Don Cossacks.[30] "Turbid became the quiet Don, perturbed the cossack brothers; no longer was their ataman among them—gone the old cossack, Ilia Muromets." Robbers, terrified by his strength, beg that he accept them into the membership of his followers, the Don Cossacks.

A young man feels the heavy weight of his own strength, responds to the mood of melancholy inspired in him by the steppes, and says to his mother:

> Oh, my lady, dear mother!
> Grant thy forgiveness to me, and thy blessing.
> Away I must go to the desolate Steppes.
> Driven am I by an urging, the tousle-haired foeman to scatter,
> And put a bogatyr's arm to the test.
> I long with impatience to try, on my own,
> The strength and the prowess of youth.
> How many more years must I live as a child,
> The broad streets familiar treading at home,
> And playing at games with small, simple children?

Until a youth was able to break away into the desolate steppes he must continue living as a "small, simple" child, between which condition and that of manhood there existed no transitional period of education! Fearsome in his aspect was the strong man who, having just torn himself away from the constraints of childhood, had entered the unrestrained freedom of the desolate steppes, where he could "put a bogatyr's arm to the test." Popular songs of the time depicted admirably this restless unchecked energy. These poetic descriptions explain numerous happenings, not only in the early Russian experience, but also in the later history of Russia, which could not all at once overcome all aspects of the past.

It was told, for instance, how Ilia Muromets, resentful at not having been invited to a feast, thought of shooting Prince Vladimir and his princess. Instead, he took aim with his bow at God's churches and miraculous crosses, giving gold domes to the poor folk in taverns for drink.

When Vasily Busalev waged battle against the people of Novgorod, he did not show mercy even to his godfather. Vasily's mother, in order to calm the boisterous bogatyr, approached him from the rear and fell upon his powerful shoulders. At this, the bogatyr exclaimed: "You are a cunning and sly old woman! You guessed how to sap my great strength, by stealthily creeping behind me. Had you approached from the front, I'd not have spared you, my lady, my mother, but would have slain you in place of a Novgorod warrior."

The first task confronting a bogatyr in the steppes was to gather a retinue of other bogatyrs, a band of bold and adventurous young men like himself. The chief occupation of an ataman and his retinue consisted of hunting animals and birds; or they might cut down an oak and fashion a boat in which to head for the sea after fish. Such were the activities that engaged the cossacks in the steppes.

The bogatyr cossack was never anxious to get married and generally did not harbor a very high opinion of women: "A good wife is someone else's stroke of luck; but as for me, I can get along without a bad one." Popular songs mention two types of women: the female counterpart of the bogatyr, who is most often a sorceress, and the "woman," who is confined to the women's quarters. The former, obviously, were not noted to any degree for their feminine traits, but in some of them physical strength was matched with moral power. An example of this type is the "terrible" Nastasia Nikulishna, who wishes neither to endure the death of her husband nor be wed to his slayer. The latter type, or "woman," was depicted in full accord with her confined state, that is, totally without character.

A young maiden was a precious thing, and consequently she was placed under lock and key in the women's quarters, lest she be exposed to some evil influence. The more she was isolated from all kinds of contacts, the greater was her virtue considered to be. In this, indeed, lay all her praiseworthiness, that she was a beauty and well guarded. "She sits in the women's quarters, on the topmost golden floor, behind thirty locks of Damascus steel, where the radiant sun does not warm her or the blustery wind blow upon her or numerous people cast glances." Brothers were given to boasting about their sisters: "What a sister we do have! She ventures not out of the women's quarters, nor does she shed the whiteness from her face or show to others her snowwhite complexion."

In some songs the story is told of arrangements that are being made for the betrothal of such a girl. Suddenly a bogatyr appears and breaks his way into the women's quarters, where she surrenders without the slightest resistance. Later, her former bridegroom arrives, entreats her with the promise of a larger share of wealth, and she passes back to him. But her new husband dies soon after, and the hapless woman finds herself in a most unfortunate predicament:

In my boat I cast off for the far-distant shore;
But, once in midstream, could find land ne'er more.

All the while the bogatyr berates her unsparingly for her infidelity.

The bogatyr cossack was set apart from the crowd. He either left society for the steppes, being conscious of his own strength and superiority, or he was expelled from society, which could not allow him to "put a bogatyr's arm to the test" in its midst. It was unnatural to expect that a bogatyr should have much in the way of respect for the crowd, or that he should take any great pains to be sparing of the common men, the muzhiks. "When the bogatyrs choose to honor the lowly muzhiks, they do so by beating the latter with whips. Bowing humbly before them, the muzhiks cry: 'Thrice cursed shall he be who scraps with you bold ones and starts a great fight.' The muzhiks are then whipped to heart's satisfaction."

Vasily Buslaev was the very type of cossack, or young voyageur of Novgorod, who called together the muzhiks of that city for a feast but gave food only to the brave members of his own retinue, roughly pushing away the muzhiks by the scruff of the neck or their hinder parts.

The bogatyr cossack represented the opposite extreme of the sedentary land-based man, engaged in peaceful pursuits. The adventurer was "laden with power, as though weighted with vigor," and was for this very reason unable to quell his restlessness. He must always be in ceaseless movement, undertaking heroic deeds that saw him wandering from land to land. Unable to abide the stifling city, he could live only in the broad steppes. "Now have departed the mighty bogatyrs for Kulikovo Field.[31] For they cannot live in Kiev, where they prowl along the streets, engaged in tempestuous play, shoving people to and fro. The people could not tolerate these gambols of the bogatyrs. To be shoved by them meant death, and death it was."

Nor was the bogatyr cossack welcome as a provincial governor: "Lord, never let a master become a slave, a slave become a serviceman, a priest become an executioner, or a bogatyr become a governor."

While the landed man toiled, the bogatyr wandered, ranging across the broad plains. Such roving naturally was associated with image of vodka and His Majesty, the Tavern. The bogatyr cossack of the steppes was very well known to the early Russians as an inveterate wanderer and devotee of drink. Ilia Muromets, the most revered of all the bogatyrs, is depicted in popular song as drinking in a tavern with beggars who inhabit the place.

The time would come, however, when strength ceased to flow freely through the veins and one was no longer laden with power. The bogatyr cossack grew old. With the approach of death and final judgment, it became necessary to save one's soul by making amends for having beaten and robbed so many in one's youth. The means for accomplishing this was the monastery. The young bogatyr cossacks are portrayed as mocking the old one: "It's about time, old fellow, that you shut yourself up in a monastery!"

And woe to the old one if, forfeiting this chance, he should instead meet in the desolate plains the monster that is able to deprive him of strength—the monster, Death! He swings his sharp sword, but his arm stiffens and cannot be bent. From his hand the sword falls. Earnestly, the bogatyr prays Death hold off making its claim for perhaps, say, three years, or even three hours, so that he might have time to will his property to the church and give his gold to the poor. But Death answers: "I will give you no time. Your goods are stolen and your gold is ill-gotten. Your soul shall see no salvation." The bogatyr sways atop his faithful mount and falls to the damp earth.

The bogatyr cossack continued to be the hero in popular historical songs for eight centuries because during all that time men of his breed continued to be seen and because, during that entire period, the same kind of struggle went on in the desolate steppes against the nomads of the plains, or "idolatrous pagans" as they were described in the songs.

As inhabitants of the desolate steppes, the bogatyr cossacks were the chief protagonists in that struggle. This constituted the purest, most poetic side of their activity. The warfare in the plains and border regions went on interminably, and always with the same characteristics. This explains why songs about that warfare, extending through eight centuries of time, always told of the same people, and even of the same actions performed by those people.

Persons, places, and events often become merged in popular song under any circumstances. An even greater degree of interfusion than usual took place in Russian popular epics because of the long duration and changeless complexion of the events described in the songs. One and the same thing happened under Prince Vladimir the Saint or Vladimir Monomach or Dmitry Donskoy or Tsar Alexis. Because the first songs to be sung were about Kiev, the warmhearted Prince Vladimir, and a certain group of bogatyrs, the songs that came afterward continued to make reference to the same places and people throughout the entire subsequent endless struggle and the entire series of interminable heroic deeds. Thus Khan Mamai besieges Kiev at the time of the battle at Kulikovo Field. Ermak also is there, having become a nephew of Prince Vladimir.[32]

Besides the struggle with the people of the steppes there were other historical occurrences which could not but fire the imagination of the people and find expression in their songs. Such, for example, was the war with Lithuania. Also impressing itself upon the popular mind was the reign of the first tsar, Ivan the Terrible, who conquered three Tatar khanates and visited terrible punishments upon accused traitors when eliminating treason in Moscow and Novgorod. The following words are put in Ivan's mouth while he is at a feast:

> I bore the imperial mantle away from Constantinople;
> I commanded treason to be expunged from stony Moscow;
> And now the purge of treason in Novgorod I do ordain.

A place came to be reserved in popular song for the story about Ivan's murder of his son. Also memorialized in song were individuals prominent at the Time of Troubles: the mysterious figure of the impostor who became a tsar, his wife, the sorceress Marina,[33] and the favorite of the people, Prince Skopin Shuisky.[34]

Finally, from the period of Tsar Alexis, there was preserved in song the memory of the famous war with Poland over the question of Russian lands. It begins with a description of an assembly. Tsar Alexis emerges from church following a lengthy service, mounts the tribune in Red Square, and delivers an announcement to the boyars, merchants, and soldiers: "Give the sovereign your assistance in thinking of a proper policy. It is urgent that the decision arrived at be sound—not mistaken." The king (of Sweden?) is demanding Smolensk for himself, in exchange for which he will grant lands belonging to China.[35]

The tsar asks whether the exchange should be agreed to.

Speaking for the boyars is the prince of Astrakhan, who says that Smolensk does not belong to Moscow, but to Lithuania. He points out that the city has neither a garrison of musketeers nor a treasury. Therefore, he says, the exchange ought to be made.

These words displease the sovereign, and he turns to the merchants for their advice. But the prince of Bukhara answers instead, repeating the opinion expressed by the prince of Astrakhan.

The sovereign turns to the soldiers. Replying for them is Danila Miloslavsky, who asserts that Smolensk does indeed belong to Moscow and not to Lithuania, that it has many musketeers within its walls, as well as a rich treasury, and that it should be defended. The exultant tsar thereupon makes Miloslavsky the governor of Smolensk, hangs the prince of Astrakhan, and orders that the prince of Bukhara have his head severed from his body.

It is curious to note that, while the crown did in fact allow a free voice to the expression of different opinions in the national assemblies, yet the people, loyal to the traditions of the former urban assembly,[36] could not admit such a freedom into the framing of their fantasies and made the tsar punish by death those whose opinions he did not like.

The appearance in the seventeenth century of a bogatyr cossack, Stenka Razin, the likes of whom had never been seen before, found a most preeminent place in the repertoire of Russian popular songs. Next to Razin even the grand old cossack himself, Ilia Muromets, the most outstanding of the bogatyrs, takes second place, appearing as a mere captain.

Yet, in Great Russia, because of the existence there of a strong government, the new bogatyrs, the cossacks, never played an exceptional or predominant role. The Razins, the bogatyrs who in the early period of the warrior hero had been founders of new states, perished in Great Russia at the hands of the crown. Nor, in any event, were there many Razins. This is why the names of the old bogatyrs came to be preserved in Great Russia.

In Little Russia, quite a different situation prevailed. There, the cossacks roamed widely. The struggle that pitted them against the Crimean Tatars, Turks, and Poles was a matter of primary importance and occupied exclusively the undivided attention and imagination of the people. There the cossack Chmielnicki[37] just barely missed becoming the creator of a new state and founder of a new dynasty. That is why the old cossack Ilia Muromets was, next to Chmielnicki, unable to keep his place even as a captain. The old bogatyrs completely disappeared there. Furthermore the broad plains were filled with commotion and turbulence, an environment unconducive to the maintenance of relics from the past, which were carried away to all four corners by the buffeting winds. In the north, protected by the forests, everything could be safeguarded more easily, even the vestiges of the past.

TRANSLATIONS

Besides their own songs and stories, the Russians avidly listened to and read foreign tales in translation. It did not matter to the people how they came by the stories, so long as they could satisfy their desire to be liberated from the narrow confines of daily life and be transported to a new and different sphere of broader dimensions and dazzling events.

At first the foreign tales were of Byzantine origin, and they entered Russia in South Slavic translations, that is, in Serbian and Bulgarian. Later, in the seventeenth century, west European narratives began to make their appearance, principally by way of Polish literature. Thus the tales of the heroic deeds of Alexander of Macedon constituted for a long time the favorite reading matter of educated Russians. They were well acquainted also in the seventeenth century with the translation into Russian of a work famous in European literature during the Middle Ages, the Trojan history of Guido of Messina.[38]

In west European literature the seventeenth century marked the decline of tales relating the marvelous adventures of heroic knights. This kind of material became the reading matter of common people. In Russia, such chivalric romances in translation from Polish were eagerly devoured during the second half of the seventeenth century by the most educated persons, as evidenced by the significant number of copies which were to be found in the tsar's palace among the books of his sons and which were designated as "entertaining books." This development illustrates the degree of maturity to which the Russian people had attained. They had not progressed beyond the period of childhood, in which fantasy prevails and demands the recounting of wondrous happenings. The chivalric romance was blood brother to the Russian song and poem about the bogatyr cossacks, and it could not but find a hospitable reception in the Russian society of the seventeenth century. The Western hero Buovo d'Antona became the Russian Bova Korolevich.

By way of translations from Polish, Russians in the seventeenth century grew familiar with narratives containing certain moral lessons. At the beginning of that century Fedor Gozvinsky, a translator of Greek and Polish, produced a Russian version of Aesop's Fables, which according to Gozvinsky "tells us much through sound moral advice and gives us sermons beneficial to the conduct of life."

This was not the only translation in the seventeenth century. Also translated at the same time from Polish were the Gesta Romanorum (the "Deeds of the Romans")[39] and the Specula,[40] collections of anecdotes about famous people, particularly from Greek and Roman history, the so-called "Apothegmata." Finally, translations were made, likewise from

Polish, of facetiae, that is, collections of witty or scandalous stories, sharp comments, and jokes (humorous tales). Familiarity with foreign tales did not remain without an effect on Russian literary production, and there can be seen in the seventeenth century efforts to describe the amatory and other adventures of Russian characters. One such narrative that has come down to the present day, a relatively early example, was still associated with those religious conditions in which foreign works made their first appearance in Russian literature. The adventures encountered in line of love and duty by a merchant's son during the reign of Tsar Michael carried the following title: *The Tale of Savva, Son of Foma Gruttsyn, Merchant of the Most Wonderful City of Veliky Ustiug, Which Relates How He Gave the Devil a Written Receipt for His Soul, and How He Was Saved by the Mercy of the Most Blessed Mother of God of Kazan*. Another extant example of Russian tales, *The Story of Frol Skobeev*, is already free of the earlier religious coloration.

The change in direction being taken by society along a new path, so evident in the seventeenth century, was characterized not only by the fact that Western tales were being translated and copied. To be sure, the West attracted the Russians with its comedies for the stage and its humorous stories, but the reorientation was most clearly evident in the Russians' awareness of the need to learn from the West, in the fact that translations also were made of books on grammar, arithmetic, medicine, and cosmography.

A work on Russian geography, *The Great Atlas of the Russian Land*, is known to have existed at the end of the sixteenth century. It was revised and supplemented in the seventeenth century with an explanatory work, *The Book on the Great Atlas*, which described Muscovy along its rivers and roads.

The people most in need of books were those who most frequently came into contact with the Western world and for whom it was urgent to know what was taking place in that world, whose superiority was undeniably apparent. Before all others, those most in need of books were persons in the palace and the Ambassadorial Chancellery. Consequently books were produced in two copies, one to go "upstairs" to the great sovereign, and the other to be sent to the Ambassadorial Chancellery.

An ambassador whose mission took him abroad, usually to Poland, would return with a large number of Polish and Latin books. In 1653 Prince Repnin-Obolensky was sent to Poland. There, by order of the tsar, he purchased the following books: (1) a Slavic-Russian lexicon— for

4½ Polish zlotys; (2) the *Granograph*, or chronicle, of Piasecki[41] –for 10 alotys; (3) a dictionary, or lexicon, published in Gdansk, in three languages, German, Latin, and Polish–for 15 zlotys; (4) Guanini[42] –for 40 zlotys; (5) a Polish Bible–for 50 zlotys; (6) a description of Poland– for 24 zlotys, plus 6 zlotys for binding; (7) an almanac describing the present year, 7161[43] –for a Dutch silver lion dollar. The total expenditure for the books amounted to 25 zlotys.

It would not be difficult to surmise that two of the most noted directors of the Ambassadorial Chancellery, as well as two of the greatest enthusiasts for things Western, Ordin-Nashchokin and Matveev, would also have been the most ardent collectors of foreign books. In 1669 Ordin-Nashchokin had 82 Latin books sent to him from abroad.

GENEALOGIES AND REFERENCES

One problem facing those engaged in conducting foreign relations was the difficulty involved in finding needed references directly from Russian or foreign chronicles, out of which selected extracts had to be made. Before anything else it was necessary to compile genealogical tables, illustrated with portraits of the various rulers and their heraldic devices. Moreover, it was important to provide the tsar and the Ambassadorial Chancellery with information about which Russian sovereigns had engaged in diplomatic relations with which foreign rulers.

Matveev and his associates in the Ambassadorial Chancellery, the subordinate functionaries and interpreters, compiled a book entitled: *The Great Book of State, Being a Description of the Grand Princes and Tsars of Russia, Whence Stems Their Sovereign Origin, Which Grand Princes and Tsars Were in Communication With Which Great Foreign Sovereigns, Both Christian and Moslem, and How Those Great Sovereigns Were Addressed in Their Names and Titles; So Also Are Set Forth All the Portraits and Heraldic Devices of the Grand Princes and Tsars, Ecumenical Patriarchs and Patriarchs of Moscow, the Pope of Rome, and Neighboring Sovereigns.* The portraits mentioned in the title were executed over a period of five months by the iconographers Ivan Maksimov and Dmitry Lvov. The great sovereign ordered that this book be kept in the Ambassadorial Chancellery, but that two identical copies be prepared for him and his son, the tsarevich Fedor, with the addition of all his children and the kings of Poland, beginning with Stephen Abatur (Báthory).[44]

GRIBOEDOV'S HISTORY

The chancellor Fedor Griboedov[45] composed a work along similar lines, entitled: *The History, That Is, the Narrative, or Brief Relation Concerning the Piously Ruling, Hallowed, and Consecrated Grand Princes and Tsars, Who Have Ruled Russia in a God-pleasing Manner*. Griboedov's work consists of a genealogical enumeration of individuals, with the addition of florid praise, the aim of which was to boost the line of Moscow and associate the new dynasty with it.

The listing of sovereigns begins with Vladimir the Saint. As for the shift in importance from the princes of the south to those in the north, Griboedov has this to say: "Upon the passing away to his eternal rest of Grand Prince Vladimir Monomakh, the Russian tsardom began to break up into many local centers of government, so that the primacy of Kiev and its prestige passed elsewhere. The true successor of the Russian fatherland was Grand Prince Georgy Dolgoruky, who was the seventh son of Grand Prince Vladimir Monomakh and who ruled not in Kiev but in Suzdal and also in Rostov, surpassing in honor all his other brothers."

After telling about the ejection from Kiev of Igor Olgovich by Iziaslav Mstislavich,[46] the author says: "Grand Prince Georgy Vladimirovich [Dolgoruky], ruling at that time in the God-preserved city of Moscow, renewed therein the supreme sceptered authority of a pious tsardom, and that illustrious family of tsars governs in glory even unto the present day."[47]

Griboedov enumerates the sons of Georgy Dolgoruky, whereupon he continues: "From them issued forth, as supreme Russian autocrat, the true successor and progenitor of the Russian tsardom, the God-protected Grand Prince Vsevolod.[48] Even then the Grand Princes of Kiev were subject to the sovereigns of the Grand Principality of Vladimir, while the primacy of the city of Vladimir was strengthened by the arrival of the miraculous icon of the Mother of God,[49] which was brought from Vyshegrad by Prince Andrei Georgievich [Bogoliubsky], who thereupon ruled [in Vladimir]. His brother, who was this same God-protected Grand Prince Vsevolod Georgievich, ruled [at this time] in Pereiaslavl. After [the death of] his brother [Andrei], the people of Vladimir called [Vsevolod] to [their] city, and thus a single beloved autocrat came to rule over all the subjects of the Russian land, just as he himself loved them all in exercising his autocratic power."

Yaroslav Vsevolodovich then makes his appearance on the scene as Vsevolod's eldest son. After Grand Prince Alexander Nevsky,[50] the author goes directly to Daniel of Moscow:[51] "For the honor and glory of the grand principality passed at that time to the God-pleasing city of

Moscow." Following immediately after Daniel is Ivan I, the Moneybag,[52] who is himself directly succeeded by Ivan II,[53] with the omission of Simeon the Proud.[54]

The achievements of Ivan the Terrible are described in the following terms: "Besides leading an honorable life and being always girded with zeal for the sake of God, he courageously strove to secure advantageous conquests, annexing the neighboring populous kingdoms of Kazan and Astrakhan, and the land of Siberia. Thus the dominion of the Russian land stretched forth into the vastness, and her people sang for joy, pouring out triumphal praise to God." Ivan's first marriage draws the following observation: "Entering into the state of holy matrimony, the great sovereign, in keeping with his tsarist dignity, chose as his prudent bride, like a bright pearl of precious ruby, the most honored maiden and blessed daughter of the illustrious noble, Roman Romanov." This is followed by a laudatory tribute to Anastasia.

After Tsar Fedor, son of Ivan the Terrible, there is an attempt to delineate the background of the Romanovs. "Through [Fedor's] mother, Anastasia Romanov, the genealogy is reckoned as follows: In the ancient period of the Russian tsardom, there came out of the Prussian land the son of the sovereign of Prussia, Andrei Romanov. The sovereigns of Prussia were kinsmen of Augustus, emperor of Rome."[55]

Griboedov's book, completed in 1669, initially consisted of 36 chapters and concluded with a lengthy account concerning the proclamation of the tsarevich Alexis, son of Tsar Alexis, as successor to the throne. Supplementary material later came to be added concerning the deaths of the tsaritsa [Maria, Alexis' first wife], the tsareviches [Dmitry and Alexis], and of Tsar Alexis himself, as well as about the succession to the throne of Fedor Alexeevich.

GIZEL'S SYNOPSIS

It is most interesting to compare this composition by a Muscovite chancellor with another work contemporaneous with his own, the famous *Synopsis* of Innokenty Gizel,[56] archimandrite of the Kiev Monastery of the Caves. This Little Russian scholar read extensively in Polish books, becoming intimately acquainted with [the chronicle of] Stryikovsky.[57] He displays his erudition by tracing the origin of the Russian people back to Mosoch, son of Japheth,[58] and deriving the names "Russes" from *rasseianie* ["dispersion"] and "Slav" from *slava* ["glory"], which the ancestors of the Russians were supposed to have won through prowess in battle. He speaks of the assistance given by the Slavs to Philip and Alexander of Macedon.

The founders of Kiev, Kiy and his brothers, are descended from Mosoch. Askold and Dir are regarded as descendants of Kiy. The Varangians are referred to by the author as Slavs, but several lines later he says that the Varangian princes came from the Germans. Askold and Dir, mentioned earlier as descendants of Kiy, are described as Riurik's men, and an attempt is made to reconcile the matter in the following say: "Riurik, prince of Great Novgorod, had in his service two distinguished men. Nothing is known about them there, but they came from the line of the founder and first prince of Kiev, Kiy."

After the death of Yaroslav I the author mixes up the princes and events, omitting important occurrences and emphasizing the trivial. He juxtaposes differing accounts of the same events, as when, for instance, he says in one place that Vladimir Monomakh acquired his princely chain, belt, and cap from the governor of Kaffa after meeting him in personal combat, and on another page says that all those things were sent to Monomakh from Byzantium.

As for northern Russia, there is nothing to be found in the *Synopsis*. After the capture of Kiev by Batu,[59] the author proceeds to recount at great length the bloody battles of Khan Mamai. He then returns to Batu and his campaigns in the west. This is followed by a catalog of the northern and southern princes, a description of the transfer of the metropolitan see from Kiev directly to Moscow [without mentioning its presence in Vladimir], the capture of Kiev by Gedimin of Lithuania, the division of ecclesiastical jurisdiction into two metropolitan sees, the establishment of the patriarchate in Moscow, the transformation of the principality of Kiev into a province presided over by a military governor and the annexation of Kiev by Moscow—briefly and in general terms.

BOOKS ON POLITICAL AFFAIRS

Such were the first endeavors, the first incoherent, childish gibberish, of Russian historiography in both north and south. For obvious reasons no particular superiority should be ascribed to either one work or the other. It should be noted, nonetheless, that the monarchical character of the history of northern Russia profoundly affected the written labors of the Musocvite chancellor.

In neither the north nor the south of Russia did contemporaries cease recording the most important general events, occurrences that most attracted their attention or happenings which stood nearest to them in time. However, collected chronicles stopped being compiled in their early form. As new needs arose, works like Griboedov's *History of the Tsars* and Gizel's *Synopsis* came into being. In the sovereign's quarters "upstairs" in the palace, there already were housed books with the generic title *Vasiliologion*, containing lists of Assyrian, Persian, Greek, and Roman rulers, and of the grand princes and tsars of Great Russia.[60] In 1675 Matveev ordered that two more copies of the *Vasiliologion* be made. While Matveev was director of the Ambassadorial Chancellery, the following books were produced: *A Book of Brief Selections on the Nine Muses and the Seven Liberal Arts;*[61] *On the Sibyls;*[62] *A Chrismologion on the Interpretation to Nabuchodonosor of His Dream by Daniel the Prophet Concerning the Four Monarchies;*[63] *The History of the Most Courageous Military Campaigns of the Assyrian, Persian, Greek, and Roman Rulers, and of the Grand Princes and Tsars of Great Russia.*[64]

These works were written and compiled from various books by Nicholas Spafary, a translator of Greek in the Ambassadorial Chancellery, and the clerk Peter Dolgov. At Matveev's initiative, a book was produced that had for its subject matter the single most important event for the new dynasty, the election to the throne of Tsar Michael.

TRANSLATIONS BY SLAVINETSKY AND SATANOVSKY

In 1650 two monks educated in Kiev, Epifany Slavinetsky and Arseny Satanovsky, were summoned to Moscow for the purpose of translating the Bible from Greek into Slavic, and of giving instruction in rhetoric. They were given a salary consisting of a daily allowance of 4 altyns, two cups of wine from the palace, two mugs of honey, and two mugs of beer.

The foreword to Slavinetsky's translation of the Gospel contains the following statement: "At the death of Patriarch Pitirim,[65] the tsar commanded, and the council of bishops confirmed with its permission, that Hieromonk Epifany Slavinetsky proceed with the translation of the entire Bible. The sovereign further commanded that Paul, metropolitan of Sarai, supervise the work and provide those engaged in it with all the necessities. Epifany chose for his assistants Sergy, former hegumen of the Molchinsky Monastery in Putivl; Evfimy, a monk of the Miracles Monastery; Nikifor, a priest and proofreader of books; Moisei, a hierodeacon of Miracles Monastery; and Michael Rodostamov and Flor Gerasimov, copyists engaged in book printing. Father Epifany did not consent to have Simeon Polotsky take part in this labor for the reason that, although Polotsky is educated, it is only in Latin, so that he has not even the slightest knowledge of Greek. Paul made arrangements for the use of his house, called Krutitsy, which is located outside the city of Moscow, atop steep and high hills overlooking the Moscow River. It is a tranquil and quiet location, eminently suited to the task, with fine accommodations, a picturesque garden containing various flowers, trees, and shrubs, and a wellspring from which flows sweet water for the slaking of thirst. All of this is protected by a fence, so that one may think he is in some kind of Paradise." Epifany, who died in 1676, was able to finish translating only the New Testament.

The monks who were given the task of translating the Bible and conducting instruction in rhetoric could not refrain from exceeding the limits of their original assignment. Epifany also translated the section on civil and administrative laws from the first book of Thucydides' *History*[66] and the end of the panegyric to Trajan by Pliny the Younger. Translated from Latin were: a geography in two parts, Europe and Asia; a medical book—the anatomical study of Andreas Vesalius of Brussels;[67] *The Execution of the English King* (Charles I); and lessons in civics and the moral instruction of children.

Satanovsky translated a large collection, *The Royal Garden,* "or the lessons of a certain teacher named Mefret,[68] taken from 120 Greek and Latin writers, including both natural philosophers, poets, historians and physicians, and also theologians and homilists. Likewise described in this book are the names and characteristics, or natural attributes, of numerous animals from the four corners of the world, birds, unusual fish in the sea, snakes and all sorts of crawling creatures, precious stones, pearls, various trees, seas, rivers, streams, forests, and the four elements: water, earth, air, and fire. There are to be found sundry discourses on philosophical and political matters, on the curing of numerous diseases, the customs of different nations, the location of various countries, the height of mountains, diverse seeds, cereals, parables, and a host of other things gathered in a single collection. All this is put together judiciously and conformably with the correct conception of the divine unity of the Holy Trinity and with a proper understanding of the angels and of man, as well as of forces that are either beneficial or harmful to mankind. It furthermore exposes the evil intentions of demons, glorifies God's saints, and censures the heretics with amazing comparisons and testimony from both the Old and New Testaments, supplemented with interpretations by church teachers. The material is organized in such a way, with appropriate references and marvelous astuteness, so as to cover, week by week, the entire year. It is arranged, in groups of two or three items, according to the feast days of the Lord, the Mother of God, and the saints, as well as the entire period of the Great Fast preceding Easter. Every entry is quite extensive. From each one, consequently, it is possible to develop two, three, four, or even five lessons." An order was issued that, for his translation of this book, Satanovsky was to receive an increase in the amount of his salary from the former 4 altyns to 1 grivna daily.

TUTORS

An examination of these books, translated and produced principally for the palace and the Ambassadorial Chancellery, reveals that, as a result of increasing requirements for knowledge, books were needed that would quickly provide indispensable information. For those adults who desired an education, or wished to acquire a reputation for being educated, the most useful books were textbooks or encyclopedias. From a comparatively small number of volumes they could learn as much as possible. The boyar Boris Morozov, when already an old man, complained bitterly in conversation with foreigners that he had not received an education in his youth. An ever-increasing number of people like him naturally began to consider how they might provide an education for their children, who then would be spared having to bemoan the fact that, without guidance or experience, they had to glean on their own whatever they chanced to discover in translated books. Hence, it is not surprising to find that, at first in the palace and later in the houses of prominent individuals, there were to be found tutors, persons who were capable of gathering information of various kinds from a wide assortment of books and imparting it to young people in a lively and simple manner, while at the same time, most important of all, giving them access to the means by which they might later continue their education by themselves or, in other words, instructing them in foreign languages.

SIMEON POLOTSKY

The first, and at the beginning the only, tutors for the tsar's sons were government clerks, who taught them reading and writing. As might be expected, this task was entrusted to clerks who themselves were faultless readers and expert calligraphers, whose personal lives were above reproach, and whose appearance and demeanor were impeccable. In short, these were people who were able "to cross their T's perfectly and execute a bow with consummate grace." Thus the teacher of Tsar Alexis' son Fedor was a clerk from the Ambassadorial Chanceller, Pamfil Belianinov.[69] Yet, by the time of Tsar Alexis' reign, it was becoming impossible to be satisfied with only a single clerk. Consequently there was summoned a tutor of another kind. In this case, with respect to the introduction of education, it would appear that the same expedient was resorted to as was employed generally in other areas throughout the seventeenth century. Foreigners of heterodox religious beliefs were not considered desirable teachers for the young. Hence, there was summoned an educated West Russian monk, Simeon Petrovsky Sitianovich, better known as Simeon of Polotsk, or Polotsky, after the name of his birthplace.

Simeon Polotsky typified the kind of domestic tutor that was in demand among Russians in the seventeenth and eighteenth centuries, and even as late as the nineteenth. He was supposed to impart instruction to children in all subjects, though without compulsion, by making the acquisition of knowledge appear attractive and developing the pupils' taste for it. Besides teaching children, the domestic tutor was supposed to be useful for carrying out other functions about the house. He would compose appropriate speeches or poems on the name days of the master or lady. He would also write stage plays. If someone in the household died, the tutor would have the required eulogy ready to hand. Just such a tutor was Simeon Polotsky, a walking encyclopedia, tireless penpusher, a man able to read about everything, a clever collector from all over of other people's opinions, and a teacher able to present them entertainingly, causing them to be learned through the use of humor. It goes without saying that from such a person there could not be demanded any originality or independence of thought.

Mention has been made of translated encyclopedias, like the *Royal Garden,* collections containing anecdotes about famous persons and noteworthy speeches. Polotsky, who was conversant with Latin and Polish, accumulated from everywhere anecdotes, sayings, and definitions, all of which he put into verse. It was in this form that he expounded the chief events in the Old and New Testaments and the history of the Roman emperors "so that, imparting sweetness to it, the lesson may become more pleasant to the hearts of the pupils, for I hope to induce them to read often and enable them readily to retain in memory what they read."

Let us enter into the classroom of the tsar's son and see what it was that Polotsky presented to his pupil in verse. He speaks to him of citizenship and offers the definitions of seven Greek thinkers, suggesting that they all have merit.

> How it is for a state to be governed well,
> All who live there should know and be ready to tell.
> The seven sages of Greece at no one view could arrive,
> But their ideas together can help a country survive.
> The great, wise Bias gave voice to his word,
> That about any state good reports can be heard,

Which sees that the law is feared like the tsar,
And the tsar, like the law, is held in awe from afar.
Chilo praises the place where the law is observed,
And the orator's squeals remain silent, unheard.
Cleobulus lavishes praise on the city
That extirpates sin with no shred of pity . . . .

In verse, Polotsky paints a picture of the good ruler.

The shepherd who daily tends to his sheep,
Teaches a lesson, what rules we must keep.
"Shepherd" refers to the people who lead,
And to whose commands the flock does give heed.
When a shepherd approaches, the sheep get to their feet,
They rise in his honor, the shepherd to greet.
The shepherd, in turn, watches over his flock,
Bringing back on his shoulder those trapped on a rock.
So a ruler must act at all times, everywhere,
To share with his subjects the cross they must bear.
He ought not deride them, or treat them like dogs,
But love them like children, see them grow straight as logs.
When he looks at his subjects, at himself, and some other,
He should think of the earth as their one common mother.
A shepherd uses his staff for subduing the sheep,
So that peace in the flock and the city they keep.
The guilty are punished, each wrong he makes right,
And to those who may need it, he gives a sound fright.

Likewise in his verses, Polotsky describes the chief virtues of rulers in the order of their importance after the most vital one of all, piety.

A second great virtue for a monarch serene,
Is one that in public most rarely is seen.
Its name is humility, which God loved in the past,
When Jesus the Christ kept it whole to the last.
One thought to the ruler should always be clear,
That he, as a mortal, will not always be here.
Death will arrive, his rule bring to an end,
But he yet can drop pride, idle riches forfend.
A third virtue true is to seek good advice,
Lest through his mistakes he must pay a great price.
A number of eyes see things better than one,
Pride in oneself leads to projects undone.
Counsels well given mean a happy condition,
While thought taken alone yields but weak indecision.

A fourth virtue keeps a good ruler from harm,
He holds fast to justice, like a sword in his arm.
He gives defense to the weak and respect to the strong,
And lets gold ne'er tell what's right and what's wrong.
His judgments are equal for great and for small,
Truth only decides how a sentence will fall.
No spider spins a web tighter than he,
In forming his laws for all equally.
The same justice for all is the principle held,
So that all of the people into one state will meld.

The principles for educating children, as espoused at that time, were also rendered by Polotsky in verse.

As a winnowing fan drives chaff from the grain,
So the uproar of children is dispelled with the cane.
Parents who spare not the rod on their child,
Will not have their appearance in court be desired.
Those children in youth whom the stick well does cure,
Will never, when grown, have to irons endure.
When he saw that his staff had turned into a snake,
Even brave Moses from fear yet did quake.
So likewise a rod is caused to appear,
To a child whose wrongs make its presence draw near.
But if the rod is unused, no cure can begin,
Like a snake it will draw a poor soul to sin.

Although he was a stranger in a strange land, Simeon Polotsky managed to work his way to a high position at court. Moreover, he did so as a teacher who acquired all the advantages accruing to that profession. This was taken as a grave insult to the prestige of the old native teachers, with whom Polotsky could not help but collide. A conflict developed between him and the bishops, who leaned for support on their high rank. Simeon Polotsky placed his reliance on his education, which gave him a strong voice in the resolution of vital problems, and on his position, which he had attained in his rise to the top. Polotsky's struggles led him to a confrontation with Patriarch Joachim himself, the more so since he, Polotsky, was not noted for the humility that was possessed by Epifany Slavinetsky, a modest toiler in his monastic cell.

Patriarch Joachim, as was noted in the case involving the tsar's confessor,[70] had no desire that any member of the clergy should forget about his unequivocal subservience to the primate of the church. Talk began to circulate that Polotsky's teaching was not in all respects correct, a dreadful accusation in view of the suspicions that prevailed at the time about new teachers. In this contest Polotsky was not overcome, thanks to his deftness and his unsusceptibility to such accusations, in contrast to the vulnerability, for instance, of the confessor Andrei Savinov. In the wake of his victory Polotsky expressed his indignation at the empty rumors of the populace, to which the authorities ought not pay the slightest heed, and at the same time he could not keep from berating the bishops.

> Place no faith in the voice of the people uncouth,
> Let actions observed by themselves speak the truth.
> Whoever believes what is borne on the wind,
> Breeds vengeance against him, his words to rescind.

Polotsky also composed a verse about the bishops.

> In thanking the bishops, I would say a short word,
> To give a brief lesson that may well be heard.
> What is needed is more than that truth only be taught,
> A life, when it's holy, with example is fraught.

Whatever Polotsky taught, it was certainly to be expected that he would speak in favor of the new order of things, the very imminence of which imparted to him in Moscow a prestige that he otherwise would not have enjoyed. Among his verses there is an interesting reference to the way in which the spread of education should be facilitated by example from above.

> Francis is known as the first French king
> Who writing and arts to his country did bring.[71]
> (His parents, who lived in barbarity dim,
> Could not disguise their abhorrence of him.)
> When once on the throne, for bright children he sought,
> Who at his command could be earnestly taught.
> In quite a short time, learning spread far and wide;
> The king's own example cast reluctance aside.
> A custom exists for the people to take
> The king as their model, and follow his wake.
> Blest is the kingdom where the morals are strong,
> As set by the monarch, to extinguish all wrong.

Besides his verses, Polotsky also spoke about the importance of liberal education in his sermons. Thus, on Christmas Day, Polotsky delivered a sermon on behalf of the patriarchs of Alexandria and Antioch, in which he exhorted the Russians, in the name of the Divine Wisdom, born that day in Bethlehem, to seek after knowledge, forasmuch as it is the light of the mind's eye and the guide to all of human life. Speaking for the patriarchs to the tsar, he urged him to undertake the establishment of schools, to augment the number of students with his bounty and attention, to search out qualified teachers, and to encourage everyone to a love of labor by the bestowal of due recognition upon those who merit reward.

An enthusiastic advocate of enlightenment, summoned to Moscow for its dissemination, Simeon Polotsky in his sermons proceeded to attack the old teachers, the priests, for their ignorance: "Through their enormous ignorance and complete neglect for the flock entrusted to their spiritual care, a great many mindless persons, like dumb sheep, have lost their way from the true path and have headed toward the abyss of a ruined life . . . . Numerous people who are themselves simply ignorant, who never were students anywhere, presume to call themselves teachers, . . . in truth, they are not teachers, but torturers. It is for this reason that wickedness has become rampant among the people, as is evident by the spread of deception, fortune-telling, sorcery, brigandage, theft, murder, drunkenness, absurd games, robbery, rapine or similar offenses, and finally, even revolt against authority. The chief fault behind all this is the ineptness and negligence of the clergy, who neither teach nor give direction to the souls committed to their spiritual care."

Such accusations of ignorance were not enough to create immediately a priesthood composed of well-informed and competent preachers. Accordingly Polotsky included in his sermons the suggestion that priests ought to read his sermons to their parishioners. It is instructive, however, to glance at the tribulations of one conscientious priest who tried to imitate Polotsky in a far distant corner of Russia.

There lived at one time a certain prominent individual, Grigory Stroganov, "a true inspiration for all Russian notables and men of wealth on account of his piety," who was well-known in the area of Perm for his generosity, hospitality, and love of ecclesiastical splendor. In his own town of Orel he constructed a church, named in honor of the Mother of God. He organized for it a superb choir of singers and began to cast about for a priest. He was told that such a one could be found in Solikamsk, and Stroganov hastened to invite him to Orel, where he greeted the priest warmly and with respect. He also undertook to persuade him to introduce an innovation, the delivery of sermons. The priest had heard that in many cities of "Russia" (thus were the central Muscovite regions called in the area of Perm) clergymen were teaching lessons by way of the spoken word. He accepted the proposal and agreed to imitate the preachers.

He remained uncertain, however, how to proceed. If he took the sermons of Simeon Polotsky, he was afraid that the style would be found inappropriate. The simple folk would find difficulty in comprehending the meaning because of "the loftiness of the words." Were he to take the works of St. John Chrysostom, not only would those who listened be unable to understand them, but even those who tried to read them. Not only laymen, but even priests came out quite frankly in saying that they were incomprehensible. The priest decided in favor of Chrysostom's sermons, but first took pains to rephrase them in a simple style, delivering them sometimes from memory and sometimes from notes.

The undertaking proved to be costly to the new priest. He began to be scolded and laughed at. The parishioners did not refrain from using reproachful words as they urged one another not to listen to his sermons. They shouted: "Up 'til now we have had good and honest priests, who never did this sort of thing. They lived in simplicity and we, in prosperity. For what conceivable reason has this one suddenly taken it upon himself to bring in such novelties?"

This dissatisfaction stemmed from the fact that the previous priests had lived a most remiss existence, without respect for themselves or for their calling. Nor did they know how to inculcate respect for themselves among the parishioners, but pandered to the laymen, who grew accustomed to look upon the priest as "the lowliest slave," and to arrange ecclesiastical rubrics, the order of church services, in whatever way they pleased. The earlier priests had never impeded them.

In the revolt against the innovator of Orel, the other priests in the area took the side of the dissatisfied laymen. The newcomer did not remain long among them. But he did have occasion to thunder at them in his final sermon: "Our pastors do not care for the flock of Christ, but for gold and silver, fine-looking slaves, carriages and horses, buildings and villages, copious quantities of wine, and exquisitely decorated vestments. To me, they appear akin to blind leaders, who consider themselves wise, but who in fact are grossly ignorant. They can be heard to protest: 'What do we need instructive books for? It is enough to know the Book of Hours and the Psalter.' Certainly you speak the truth when you say that it is enough to know what meaning these writings contain. But that knowledge remains far removed from your apprehension of it. Madman! Sitting behind filled glasses in a tavern, you are well able to speak your mind. Sitting in a tavern, you find yourself most capable of engaging in bombast. But in church, suddenly you find yourself voiceless, a prisoner of your own ignorance. Some people say that it is enough for a priest to read from a book before his congregation in church, and they condemn oral instruction, calling it heretical. Madman! Whom is it you place among the heretics? The patriarchs, prophets, and apostles!

"Today, out of desire for power and contempt for the bitter cup of Christ, and for the sake of inebriation and the appeasement of human nature, the reverend fathers and priests have mired their high dignity and merit in dishonor, reproach, and ridicule. All this has not been induced by the tsars and princes, but by base people. It is on account of them that a poor pastor is afflicted by shame, censure, revilement, injury, beating, bonds, and death. As for the rest, I shall keep silent and only with tears confront the question why some evil demon has caused the entire present matter to arise." This preacher put all his sermons together in a single book, to which he gave the name *Statir*.[72]

YURY KRIZHANICH

Next to the two new arrivals in Moscow, the Greek Paissius Ligarides[73] and the White Russian Simeon Polotsky, both of whom loudly expatiated on the absolute necessity for promoting education, a third individual, Yury Krizhanich, should likewise be introduced.[74] At the very time when Russian society began to move ahead, having become aware of the need to go along a new path and yet wavering through uncertainty over how most safely and expeditiously to proceed, there arrived in the country an educated Serb.

An ardent Slavic patriot, Krizhanich since his youth had been deeply aggrieved over the sad fate of the Slavs. He saw in the Russian tsar the only Slavic sovereign competent to extend his hand in assistance to the rest of his kindred people: "To you, Most Honored Tsar, has fallen the lot to be charged with the care of the whole Slavic people. It behooves you, like a father, to devote attention to the gathering together of children who have been dispersed. You alone, O Tsar, have been given by God to us, that you may render assistance to the Slavs beyond the Danube, to the Poles, and to the Czechs. Let them only become aware of their oppression by foreigners, of their shame, and they will begin to give consideration to the enlightenment of the people and to throw off from their necks the foreign yoke. The Slavs beyond the Danube (Bulgarians, Serbs, and Croatians) long ago lost their state, all their power, their language, and all their knowledge. They know not what is meant by national honor. They take no thought about it and are able in no way whatsoever to help themselves. What they need is an outside power so that they can once again be put on their feet and be included in the roster of nations.

"If you, Tsar, are unable at the present difficult period of time to aid them, to restore their state to its former condition and settle things, at the very least you can have the literary Slavic language improved and, by way of suitable instructional books, open the minds of those people. Then they shall begin to understand the idea of national honor and take thought about their own revival.

"The Czechs, and more recently the Poles, have fallen into the same execrable condition as the Slavs beyond the Danube. For although the Poles boast about the deceptive shadow of their state and their independence, it is nonetheless well known that they cannot rid themselves of misfortune and shame. It would be an easy matter for you, Tsar, to support and provide them with a national education."

Krizhanich by his own admission came to Russia in order to accomplish three objectives. First, he wanted to improve the Slavic language, writing for it a grammar and a lexicon. In this way he hoped that the Russians and other Slavs would be able to speak and write correctly and have available to them an abundance of expressions, such as are needed for the phrasing of thoughts in the course of general human interaction. Second, Krizhanich envisioned composing a history of the Slavs, which would refute the lies and slanders of foreigners. Third, he desired to expose the stratagems and misrepresentations with which foreigners deceived the Slavs. Krizhanich succeeded in carrying out the first (as regards the grammar) and last of his intentions.

It is worthwhile to give some attention to his *Political Reflections,* an extensive treatise in which he draws a pathetic picture of Russia's condition.[75] With a view to its improvement, he calls for important reforms, presses for education, and at the same time seeks to arouse the strongest possible distrust and antipathy toward the very people who were able to impart the necessary knowledge and thereby the means for extricating Russia from its lamentable predicament. Those people, of course, were the foreigners, and particularly the Germans, who were seen as innate enemies of the Slavs. It is obvious that, for this very reason, Krizhanich's plan for reform in its most fundamental guiding principle was bound to be unfeasible. It suffered the same fate as the plans, projects, and constitutions which, devised by theoreticians in their studies, lacked any correspondence with the historical laws governing the life of the people.

Nevertheless, Krizhanich's work does possess a certain historical value, for it supplements and confirms the information that is available with regard to Russia prior to Peter the Great's reforms, and in many cases, it explains the lines along which subsequent reforming activity did in fact take place. Krizhanich's book was kept in the great sovereign's quarters; so there is reason to suppose that it did not remain without influence.

If Krizhanich's book had any kind of effect, beyond all else it must have destroyed once and for all in its readers any Chinese-type mentality, the combination of a very lofty opinion of oneself and disdain for other nations. At the same time, it would have wakened in them an awareness of their own shortcomings and the superiority of other peoples, thereby propelling them toward changes which naturally had first to be implemented through imitation.

"The greatest harm for the common welfare stems from ignorance of oneself, when people esteem themselves and their customs too highly and when they regard themselves as strong, wealthy, and knowledgeable, without actually being so."

The Russian people were burdened with terrible poverty. In this respect Krizhanich cited the example of the wealthiest countries in the West and gave the reasons for their prosperity. England and the Netherlands had been able to amass such enormous riches because the mentality of the people there was ingenious, the seaports and trade were superb, handicrafts of all kinds flourished, and the economy thrived as a result of extensive maritime commerce. Even more glorious and fortunate was the country which, in addition to the aforementioned conditions, enjoyed good laws, as for example, France.

And what of Russia? Notwithstanding her immeasurable length and breadth, she was locked in from all sides for purposes of trade, possessed but few commercial cities, and had no valuable manufactures. The minds of the people were obtuse and inert. They displayed no skill in trade, agriculture, or domestic management. Not among the Russians or Poles or any other Slavs did there exist any idea how to conduct distant trade, either over land routes or on the seas. Russian merchants failed even to devote themselves to any study of arithmetic, so that it cost foreign merchants not the slightest effort to deceive them. The Russians were without ability to devise anything new for themselves unless shown how. They had no books on agriculture or other occupations. They were lazy and unproductive, incapable of furthering their own interests if not compelled to do so by force. Their language was poor, poorer indeed than all the other major European languages, so that it was little wonder their minds were dull and sluggish. After all, what cannot be put into words cannot be conceived of by the mind. The Russians did not know history. Unable to hold any sort of political discussion, they were held in contempt by foreigners.

In the style and cut of clothes does the mentality of a people find expression. Russian clothing was ugly and uncomfortable, for which reason foreigners called them barbarians, and especially on account of their unkempt hair and beards. Cropped heads made them loathsome and ridiculous, like some kind of wild apparition. They ate with filthy manners and found their mouths a convenient hiding place for coins. A muzhik would grasp a full pitcher and dangle his fingers in it as he passed it to a guest. Kvass was sold in a disgusting fashion and the dishes were never washed.

The king of Denmark had this to say about the Russian envoys whom he received: "If those people ever come to me again, I shall have to build them a pigsty, because wherever they stay for a while, no one can live for half a year afterwards on account of the stench."

Inability to give expression to thought, slothfulness, intoxication, and wasteful extravagance were the main inherent characteristics of the Russians. It was especially the last trait, prodigality, that gave rise to cruelty towards the people. There was to be found in the Russians no natural courage, no gracious pride, no vivacity. They were unable to carry themselves with pride. The Turks and Tatars, even though they might be defeated on the field of battle, would not allow themselves to be killed without exacting a toll. Rather, they stood and defended themselves to their last breath. But Russian military men, when defeated, would cease to defend themselves and allow themselves to be cut down like men already dead.

The great national fault of the Slavs was their inability to maintain a balance in exercising authority. They did not know how to keep within moderate bounds in anything, to follow the middle path between two extremes. Instead, they wandered about the outer fringes and precipices. Their government was either utterly without order, so that there reigned individual willfulness and disorder, or else it was excessively harsh, severe, and truculent. In the entire world, no government was so disorganized and chaotic as in Poland; yet there existed no government so stern as in Russia.

Such despicable morals had taken root among the Russians that to other people they appeared fraudulent, untrustworthy, inclined to theft and murder, awkward in conversation, and physically dirty. Where did all this originate? From the fact that every place was filled with taverns, customs barriers, franchise-holders, debt collectors, and secret informers. People everywhere were restricted, unable to do anything freely or enjoy the work of their hands without interference. Everyone had to act and trade furtively and silently, in fear and trembling, trying to keep himself concealed from so vast a crowd of officials and agents. Meanwhile those same officials and oppressors of the people, provided with inadequate salaries, could not fulfill their duties as they should, so that simple need forced them to solicit bribes and accept gifts from criminals. Accordingly the people grew accustomed to do everything surreptitiously, like thieves, in fear and guile. They forgot all idea of honor, turning into cowards during wartime. They developed a disinclination to take part in any friendly social activity, and drifted into immodesty and impurity. They did not know how to value integrity or be discriminating about people. The first question with which they approached a stranger was, "Do you have a wife?" And the second, "How much of a salary do you get from the tsar? How much property do you have?" They bathed themselves shamelessly in front of everyone. If they found themselves in need of someone, they were without limit in the degree of self-abasement to which they would sink.

The Italians, Spaniards, and Turks were thrifty and sober. The Germans were thrifty, but they were also heavy drinkers. All the Slavs were extravagant and loved to have feasts. Still, not among the Germans or the other Slavs or anywhere in the entire world, except in Russia, was there to be found such abhorrent drunkenness. Along the streets, in the filth, lay men and women, laymen and clergy, many of whom died through intoxication.

The Russians had to follow the example of the Turks in learning from them the lesson of sobriety, modesty, and proper judgment. To be sure, the infidels engaged no less than the Russians in the sin against nature, but at least they observed a certain reserve. None of them would think of bringing it up in conversation, boasting about it, or reproving someone for it. If someone accidentally betrayed himself, he would not remain unpunished. In Western countries such criminals suffered death by burning. In Russia this vile sin was treated as a joke. Publicly, in waggish exchanges of humor, one person bragged about this sin, another chided him, while a third offered to commit the sin, provided only that the criminal act be done in front of everybody. It was absolutely essential in this country to develop some means of raising the level of shame against sodomy, of public sobriety against inebriation, and of justice against the officials about whom Isaiah said, "Thy princes are faithless companions of thieves."[76]

This, then, is the wretched picture that is painted of the nation's bankruptcy in its economic and social aspects by a Slavic patriot who cannot be suspected of being indifferent toward or taking perverse delight in the maladies afflicting early Russia, as might be surmised in the case of some German traveler. In reading the Serb's description of those scourges, one feels that the author's heart was deeply anguished by the fulfillment of his sad obligation to reveal them. His purpose in writing was not just to level accusations, but along with bringing the evils to light, to show the means for alleviating them.

The first and most important way was through education. This meant surrounding oneself with inanimate advisers, books, since there were few good advisers among living persons: "Books are not carried away by desire, hatred, or love. They do not feign affection, nor do they fear to bear witness to the truth. It is a good thing for most people to acquire learning through practical experience. But this is not the case with the highest authorities. A private person learns through his mistakes. Errors made by a sovereign, however, lead to irreparable national harm. Sovereigns should, therefore, learn from good teachers, books, and advisers, and not from experience. Let no one tell us that the road to learning has been closed to us Slavs by some decision made in Heaven, as though we cannot and must not acquire knowledge for ourselves. Other people did not attain to knowledge in a single day or year, but through studying bit by bit from others. Thus also can we in the same way proceed to learn, if only we want and try.

"Now is precisely the time to start studying, because God has raised a Slavic state in Russia such as has never existed before among our people, and it is well known that the cultivation of learning by a people begins in their period of greatest political strength. Some persons will be heard to object, saying that heresies arise among the learned, and that therefore learning ought not to be pursued. To this I reply that heresies arise also among people who are unlearned. Mohammed was not a learned man. He wrote utter foolishness in his books and, moreover, planted the most widespread heresy in the world. And in Russia, has not heresy sprung from witless muzhiks who have had no contact with books. Heresies are eradicated by learning; through ignorance, they remain rooted for centuries. People are known to die from fire, water, and iron; yet it is impossible to live without them. Likewise is learning essential for people."

Krizhanich was not satisfied with the diffusion of enlightenment as the only means for curing Russia's ills. He made other proposals as well, indicating in them the path along which reform in Russia indeed eventually did proceed. "In Russia," he says, "there exists a complete autocracy. By the tsar's command everything can be corrected and whatever is beneficial can be introduced. Consequently the reform must be put in motion from the top, from the autocratic authority. The Russians themselves will not wish to promote their own welfare unless they are coerced."

How was the autocratic sovereign to embark upon reform? For improving commerce he had to forbid any merchant without a knowledge of reading and arithmetic to have a store with merchandise. Merchants were supposed to have their own elected judges and directors, and decide certain minor lawsuits themselves. The procedure by which they submitted petitions to the great sovereign was to be made easier, and they were to be protected from oppression by the governors. For introducing and developing manufactures, a special chancellery was needed with these as its only functions. It was necessary to have translated into Russian books on manufactures and agriculture. Highly-skilled artisans had to be summoned from abroad, with the right of free return to their homeland, but not before they imparted their skills to Russian youths. The guild system had to be introduced. It was necessary to develop manufactures, so that raw materials brought from foreign countries could be worked by Russian craftsmen. Conversely, the export of raw materials abroad was to be strictly forbidden, subject to severe penalties for any violations. The tsar had to take all trade with foreigners into his hands. Only in this way was it possible to work up an inventory of the merchandise, so that too many Russian goods which were not in surplus would not be sent abroad, and unneeded foreign goods would not be imported.

Russia was only thinly settled and had a smaller population than desirable because of the following reasons. The first was that the Crimean Tatars depopulated the land with their interminable incursions. On all Turkish naval vessels, it was almost impossible to find any oarsmen other than Russians. In all the cities and small towns of the Turkish Empire, there were such large numbers of Russian prisoners of war that the Turks usually asked whether anyone at all remained in Russia. The second reason was that foreigners in Russia not only exported grain and depleted the land with their industries, but they had taken control of all branches of commerce and seized for themselves the highest positions in military service. The third reason for the scanty population lay in the severity of the government. The fourth was the scarcity of stone, with which it would be possible to construct substantial buildings. The fifth reason was the expulsion of people to Siberia and the Ukraine.

In order to increase the size of the population, the government must promote more marriages, especially by regulating the amount of money that priests received for performing weddings, lest this be an inconvenience for poor people. The crown must insure that newlyweds in cities and villages would have housing available for them, so that poverty and the lack of living quarters did not deter them from marriage. Extravagant expenditures on wedding feasts by the poor should be prohibited. Peasant girls were not to be allowed to wear expensive clothes and accessories.

The author is generous in his expostulations against Russian clothes and beards, through the wearing of which he says the Russians expressed their desire more to imitate Asiatic barbarians than educated Europeans.

This, then, was the reform program drawn up by the educated Serb, Krizhanich. It would be very easy for anyone to conclude that Peter the Great in his reforms acted under its influence. However, there is no intention here to suggest that a direct connection existed. Nevertheless a comparison of Krizhanich's program and Peter's activity is very important because it shows that the path of reform chosen by Peter was not a consequence of his own caprice or personal idiosyncracies, but resulted rather from the general views of the best people, the knowledgeable authorities, of that time.

It is apparent that, in one respect, Krizhanich's program could not be carried out. The Russian people during the period of Peter's reform were unable in fact to reconcile the contradiction which in theory appeared to be undergoing resolution. As has been mentioned, Krizhanich tried to imbue the Russians with the consciousness of their own defects. He demonstrated how the west Europeans had far outdistanced them and advised the Russians to learn from the foreigners, not only for the sake of acquiring knowledge, but also to gain acquaintance with their customs and mores. The Russians should translate their books and invite their artisans. Yet, at the same time, Krizhanich exhorted the Russians to shy away from the west Europeans as from the very worst possible enemies.

The author saw the contradiction that was involved here and, to extricate himself, demanded that the Russians learn to tell the difference between imitation and subjection to the influence of the individual being imitated. He insisted that, while adopting civilization, they be able to distinguish the good from the bad. In other words, the Russian people were to leap across a period of several centuries from the lowest level of education to the highest, from infancy to complete maturity. But people accomplish such leaps only under the quills of theoreticians who do not wish to know either history or existing reality.

In Krizhanich's opinion, foreign merchants were under no circumstances to have in Russia any houses, stores, warehouses, or cellars, nor were the Russians to admit into their country any commercial agents, consuls, or residents: "Our Slavic people are everywhere submitted to the following execrable condition: Everywhere on our shoulders sit the Germans, Jews, Scots, Gypsies, Armenians, and Greeks, all of whom such our very life's blood out of us. The contempt with which foreigners treat us and the reproaches they hurl at us stem from two causes: first, our ignorance and neglect of knowledge; and second, our irrationality, or foolishness, on account of which the foreigners rule over us, deceive us at every turn, and make of us whatever they wish, wherefore they call us barbarians."

Failing to comprehend the historical law, in accordance with which a less-educated people is inevitably subjected to the influence and even the rule of a better-educated people, Krizhanich confused effect with cause and disgraced the Slavs by ascribing to them as an inborn defect the characteristic of mental detachment, which was in truth merely the necessary consequence of the first cause that he proposed, and the only real one—ignorance. Demanding the exclusion of foreign merchants from the interior regions, Krizhanich insisted that not a single foreigner be admitted to service or given the rights of citizenship. Once accepted into various posts, the Germans would only bring evil. Peter Basmanov, a boyar and the favorite of False Dmitry I, had been a German, as also had been Michael Shein, who led Russian forces to disaster under Smolensk! It was not against only Germans that Krizhanich took up arms. He spoke with equal, if not greater, fervor against the Greeks.

The false position in which Krizhanich found himself in Moscow derived from the circumstance that, while being a fellow Slav, he was at the same time a foreigner, a Latin, a Catholic priest. Before Krizhanich arrived in Russia there existed the realization that it was necessary to learn from foreigners, but the main stumbling-block to this lay in the fact that the foreign teachers were not Orthodox. To obviate any danger to the faith, exploratory efforts were made to acquire the needed learning from one's own people, not in an ethnic sense, but as co-religionists. Thus, invitations were sent to Little Russians and Greeks. And so it was that, at the very moment when the authority of the Greeks had reached its apogee in Russia, when there existed a desire to learn, but also a determination to preserve the purity of the Greek faith, there arrived in Moscow an educated Slav who offered his instructional services, but who could not satisfy the principal requirement by which he could be accepted as a teacher—being an Orthodox of the Greek faith. Krizhanich could not conceal that he was a Catholic, and what was even more, a Catholic priest. The educated Serb had not come at the right time and, as an uninvited teacher he was dispatched to Siberia. It is possible to suppose that Krizhanich's deprecatory tirades against the Greeks came to be written in consequence of his misfortune, which he apparently attributed to the Greeks. But one may assume with even greater likelihood that, as a Catholic priest, Krizhanich could not check himself, even while in Moscow, from writing against the Greeks as schismatics or giving vent to other denunciations which must have deeply embarrassed the contemporary Russians.

Krizhanich contrasted the Greeks and Germans in the sense that these inherent enemies of the Slavs were leading them to two opposite extremes: "The Germans bring us poisonous innovations; the Greeks, irrationally condemning everything new, offer their inanities under the illustrious name of antiquity. The Germans sow heresy; the Greeks, even though they taught us the true faith, have tacked a schism onto it. The Germans offer us both good and satanic knowledge; the Greeks praise ignorance and consider every kind of knowledge to be heretical. The Germans think that salvation can be attained solely through preaching; the Greeks disparage preaching and regard silence as being most salutary. The Germans shout that it is not allowed to judge anyone; the Greeks, just the opposite, insist that it is necessary to judge people without giving them a hearing" (a comment that can be construed as an allusion to the author's own fate).

Krizhanich enumerates at length the abuses in which members of the Greek clergy allowed themselves to indulge when they came to Russia, seeking donations without sometimes exercising much discrimination in regard to the means for enlarging the amounts requested. Incidentally, Krizhanich relates a curious episode in which he was involved personally: "A certain Sophronius, styling himself as the metropolitan of Philippopolis and Drama, but known commonly as Sophronius of Macedonia, pressed me to write for him a set of forged charters in the name of Patriarch Ioannikios, attesting that he, Sophronius, had been sent by the patriarch for the general needs of the church. When I did not agree to this, he and another metropolitan wanted to knife me, but I broke away and fled to the city clerk. Yet, I must confess that afterwards, fearing for my life, I did compose for him the charters he wanted."

The existence of such abuses was not unknown in Russia, and measures were taken against them, with tight restrictions imposed on the admittance of those seeking donations. But it was also very well known in Russia that the most prominent of the Greek arrivals in Moscow were not at all propagators of ignorance who considered silence better than preaching. As mentioned, Krizhanich in his Catholic zeal did not nettle merely the Greeks, but the Russians as well. He declaimed against those writings, held sacred by the people, which contained adverse comments about Catholicism—for example, the *Life of St. Sergius.* In another regard, he advanced the notion that Russians were more sinful than the

Poles and therefore were suffering military defeats at their hands. Finally, Krizhanich permitted himself to strike out directly at Orthodoxy as being "destructive of ecclesiastical monarchy, which was founded by Christ as the best type of government, and establishing in its place an ecclesiastical administration headed by many ecumenical hierarchs."

The learned Serb came to Russia as a spokesman for enlightenment, which was supposed to open the minds of all Slavs. But Russia, in moving towards enlightenment, wanted first and foremost to remain Orthodox. The learned Serb, wishing by way of enlightenment to open the minds of his borther Slavs, was unable to do this very thing himself. He could not grasp the contradiction that inhered in his own moral outlook, that he was both a Slavic patriot and a Catholic.

Exiled to Siberia for un-Orthodoxy, Krizhanich wrote there a work which is most valuable for its portrayal of conditions in Muscovy and for its statement of the inevitable approach of reform. At almost the very moment that Krizhanich was beset by troubles in Moscow, a certain clerk, Grigory Kotoshikhin (Koshikhin), fled abroad, where he composed an equally valuable description of Muscovy.[77] Both these episodes serve as signs of the times.

AVVAKUM: BOGATYR OF THE OLD BELIEF

At the same time that clamor grew ever louder in Moscow about the necessity for change, the adoption of learning, and the promotion of arts and crafts, other voices were raised against the innovations and the movement of the people in a new direction, which was seen as leading to the reign of Antichrist. These voices belonged to the Old Believers. They sang their own historical song, telling about the siege of Solovetsky monastery and how Tsar Alexis commanded his governor, Saltykov:

> March you to the sea, the blue sea,
> To the island, the great island,
> To the monastery, the noble Solovetsky Monastery:
> Destroy you there the old faith,
> The true faith,
> And plant you there the new faith,
> The false faith.[78]

Of all the literary works produced by the Old Believers, about which no mention has yet been made, there is one of outstanding importance. This is the description of the experiences of Archpriest Avvakum, written by himself.[79] Its importance lies in the fact that, better than any other work, it transports the historian back to the Russia of the seventeenth century, from which we who live in the present day have moved so far and whose events we understand only with much difficulty, attributing to persons of that period our own traits, views, and aspirations.

We have had occasion to learn what it meant to be a "strong man" in early Russia. We have seen how the strength of bogatyrs was contrained but weakly in the absence of shaping or direction through education. The whip and the rod alone can never replace such shaping and direction. As soon as the bogatyr broke away from the whip and rod of his father's house and began to flex his muscles, what was left to hold him in check? Even his own mother had to creep to him furtively from behind in order to calm his frenzied strength. The details of Nikon's life explain a great deal concerning the appearance of those bogatyrs in the midst of a society which had not formed the moral restraints necessary to clamp their primordial vitality. Until the historian begins to consider the seventeenth century and to understand that Nikon was a bogatyr dressed in the miter and vestments of a patriarch, he will fail to grasp the true meaning of the man. Only then will Nikon cease to astound him by his strength—and his weakness.

Together with the patriarch-bogatyr, the seventeenth century also produced a bogatyr-archpriest. This happened as a consequence of the unbridled vigor of a man who became the avowed enemy of Nikon and spokesman for the schism. In his valuable autobiography Avvakum does not appear alone. He is surrounded by a whole bank of bogatyrs who, lacking self-control like himself, broke with Nikon's church reforms and unyieldingly supported traditional religious practices, such as making the sign of the cross with two fingers and singing the double alleluia.[80]

At this point it would not be amiss to mention a special kind of bogatyr, the holy fool, who also was "laden with power, as though weighted with vigor" and who freed himself of this burden by walking barefoot in the freezing cold, clad only in a shirt. The crowd, seeing such a display of strength, was quite ready to believe in the feats of Ilia Muromets and Dobrynia Nikitich as narrated in song and story. In Avvakum's autobiography the historian furthermore meets with the familiar governors of old, zealots in pursuit of the pleasure they derived from making others feel their power. Likewise encountered in the book are the governors of Siberia, those Russian Cortezes and Pizarros who went off in search of new lands and grew utterly uncontrollable in the midst of ferocious beasts and savages. Finally, there is to be found the untamed fury of the crowd, which so readily vents itself in violence.

THE LIFE OF AVVAKUM

"My birthplace," says Avvakum, "was in the region of Nizhny Novgorod (the same as Nikon's), beyond the Kudma river, in the village of Grigorovo.[81] My father (a priest) was partial to alcohol; my mother was prayerful and observed all the fasts, always instructing me in the fear of the Lord."

Avvakum's lively and impressionable nature was exhibited early. While yet a child he saw in his neighbor's yard a dead domestic animal. This so upset him, that he could not sleep that night. He rose and started to pray "in the recollection of death, that I too shall die."

Misfortune descended upon Avvakum in childhood, and he was driven away from his relatives after his father's death. Yet, this only tempered the strength of the young bogatyr. At the age of twenty he was ordained a deacon, and two years later, a priest. His fanciful personality soon made an appearance. Avvakum became distinguished for his energetic activity and zeal in fulfilling his obligations. This attracted many parishioners to his side. But this same strength led him into conflict with other forces.

Avvakum took to disputing with persons of importance, and it is well known what such persons were like in the seventeenth century. One of them, angered at Avvakum for interceding on behalf of a young girl whom he had taken away from her mother, came to church with a crowd and crushed the priest half to death. Another time, the same individual beat Avvakum inside the church, dragging him by his legs in his vestments. A different man of local importance likewise became infuriated at the priest. He hastened over to Avvakum's house, beat him, and gnawed the fingers of his hand. Later, running into Avvakum on the road, he shot at him with two pistols but, fortunately, both misfired. This particular individual eventually succeeded in seizing Avvakum's house and robbing him of everything, down to the last piece of bread for the road.

At this time a child was born to Avvakum, who set off wandering with his staff, his wife, and his unbaptized child. After having the child baptized along the way, they arrived in Moscow.

There Avvakum came into close acquaintance with the most prominent members of the white clergy, the tsar's confessor Stefan Vonifatiev and the archpriest, Ivan Neronov. They saw in Avvakum a powerful personality and told about him to the sovereign, who was most favorably disposed toward individuals of strong character among the clergy, whom he was in fact trying to seek out.

Vonifatiev and Neronov sent Avvakum back to his former residence, where he found the walls of his house destroyed. He tried to settle down but could not live in peace for long: "There arrived in my village dancing bears with drums and tambourines, and I, a sinner, zealous for the sake of Christ, chased them off. In a field I myself smashed the masks and drums of many mummers, seizing from them two large bears, one of which I hurt badly, though he later recovered, and the second of which I released into the field."

There came sailing down the Volga, to Avvakum's misfortune, a certain Vasily Sheremetev, who was to take over as governor in Kazan. Complaints were lodged with him about the zealous priest. The boyar summoned Avvakum to come aboard his craft, where he sharply upbraided him. But this did not spell an end to the troubles. Sheremetev was accompanied by his son, Matvei. The Sheremetevs were strongly inclined to admire foreign customs and manners, and Matvei exemplified this by shaving his beard. When the elder Sheremetev, after having inveighed against Avvakum over the matter of the bears, ordered the priest to give his blessing to the son, the zealous follower of Christ, upon beholding the indecent face, declared that he would on no account comply. Instead he began to censure him on the basis of the Scriptures. The boyar grew terribly angry and commanded that the accuser be hurled into the Volga, a stern order that was, by the way, not carried out. Avvakum escaped with being tormented and ousted.

Avvakum could not long reside in his village. He was ejected for a second time. So, once again, he trudged off to Moscow, where the sovereign ordered that he be installed as archpriest in Yurievets-on-the-Volga.[82] There Avvakum came into conflict not with the governor, but with another power—the local community. Within eight weeks the new archpriest was able to arouse against him the clergy and laity, both men and women. A huge crowd assembled at the patriarchal chancellery, where Avvakum attended to church matters. Dragging the archpriest out, they brought him into the middle of the street where they beat him with rods and stamped upon him. After beating him nearly to death, they threw him under the corner of a house. The governor came running to the resuce with a force of cannoneers. Grabbing hold of Avvakum, he placed him on a horse and took him home. Around the house he stationed the cannoneers. This turned out to be a wise precaution. The crowd drew near the archpriest's house. Above the din the voices of the priests and women in particular could be heard shouting: "Kill the thief, the whoreson! We'll hurl his body into the ditch for the dogs!"

That night, leaving behind his wife and children, Avvakum fled with two others along the Volga to Kostroma, where he found the same story repeated. The residents of that city had expelled their own archpriest, Daniil. By way of explaining these events it must be recalled that people like Vonifatiev, Neronov, Avvakum, and Daniil were the most advanced individuals of the time. As innovators, they aroused strong feelings against themselves.

In Moscow, the tsar's confessor and the tsar himself greeted Avvakum reproachfully for having quit his cathedral church. Nevertheless they did not return him to Yurievets, but allowed him to stay in Moscow. There, together with other progressive individuals, he was entrusted with the correcting of books. How things turned out is a matter of record. Avvakum and his associates within the progressive element became leaders of the Old Ritualists, and Avvakum with all his might declaimed against the new ways. In this, he collided head on with Nikon.

Let him tell in his own words about this clash: "I was taken from vespers by the musketeers and chained up for the night in the patriarchal court. When Sunday morning came they put me into a wagon and took me from the patriarchal court to the Androniev monastery in Moscow, where they threw me in chains into a dark chamber carved out beneath the ground. There I sat for three days without eating or drinking, straining against my chains to perform my genuflections and knowing not whether I made them to the east or west. Not a single soul came to see me, but only mice and cockroaches, while crickets chirped and fleas were plentiful. In the morning the archimandrite arrived with the brethren and let me out. They reproved me for not having obeyed the patriarch and for having opposed and spoken out against his writings.

"After I had been seized, they also apprehended Login, the archpriest of Murom. At the cathedral church, in the tsar's presence, (Nikon) tonsured (him) into the monastic rank during the divine liturgy. After his tonsure, they removed from his his cassock and caftan. Login became inflamed with the zeal of divine fire and, denouncing Nikon, spat into his eyes across the threshhold of the altar. Removing his belt, he ripped off his shirt and hurled it into Nikon's eyes inside the altar.[83] What happened next was miraculous! The shirt blossomed out and spread over the paten on the altar table like the sacred cloth cover for the paten and chalice.

"And they brought me to the cathedral church for tonsuring. The sovereign, leaving his place in the church, approached the patriarch and requested that I not be tonsured. They exiled me to Siberia with my wife and children."

Avvakum was, in general, treated with considerable lenience in comparison with other proponents of the schism. Later, as will be seen, he became the object of much consideration by way of efforts at persuading him to abandon the schism, or at least not to voice his advocacy of it so vehemently. The reason for this was that Avvakum enjoyed a spotless reputation for his pious life, and obviously, it was a matter of great difficulty for the pious Tsar Alexis to persecute such a person.

In Tobolsk, Avvakum was received well. The archbishop granted him a post in one of the churches, and the governor of Tobolsk, Prince Khilkov, greeted the zealous priest with respect. Yet, during one of the archbishop's absences from the city, the spirit of the bogatyr again revealed its strength and again incited against itself a still different force.

The archbishop's secretary, Ivan Struna, whose imperious self-will knew no bounds when the archbishop was away, developed a desire to torment without reason the deacon of the church where Avvakum served as priest. The deacon fled from the secretary, went to the church, and there placed himself under the priest's protection. But Struna had no intention of letting the deacon evade his wrath so easily. At vespers he burst into the church with a crowd of some twenty people and, in the choir, took hold of the deacon by the beard. Avvakum broke off the vespers and came running to the deacon's aid. Snatching the deacon away, he then grabbed hold of Struna, whom he forced to sit in the center of the church and, "for having created a disturbance in church, whipped him soundly with a belt." Struna's followers ran off in all directions, while the secretary, under the archpriest's belt, begged forgiveness.

This, however, did not end the affair. Other priests, monks, and Struna's kinsmen raised a hue and cry through the entire city over Avvakum. At midnight a mob brought a sleigh in front of his house, broke into it, and having seized the archpriest, intended to drown him. Writes Avvakum: "I suffered a whole month from them as I tried to hide in various places—going sometimes to the church at night, sometimes to the governor, and sometimes even asking to be lodged in jail when they did not let me find sanctuary anywhere else."

While in Tobolsk, Avvakum's passionate devotion to the old books began to wane: "I went to the cathedral church for matins and engaged in light conversation with the people there in the presence of the governor. In church, I took note how they performed the office of oblation, whether they prepared the altar-breads according to the traditional or the new manner. Standing next to the table of oblation and watching the ritual, I took the officiants to task. But as time went on, I became accustomed to their practice and ceased to reprimand them."

Unfortunately, one night Avvakum had a dream in which he was told, "Hearken to this, my warning, lest you become completely estranged from me."

To Avvakum's mind, this was the voice of Christ Himself, threatening to punish him for his lapse into the spirit of Antichrist. Accordingly he did not go to church for the divine liturgy, but took himself off to dinner at the house of the governor, Prince Khilkov, to whom he revealed his dream. The nobleman began to weep. Avvakum thereupon apparently hastened to make amends for his sin of weakness. As a result, a decree arrived ordering his removal from Tobolsk to the Lena river.

In Yeniseisk, while he was still en route, another decree was received, changing his destination to Dauria.[84] There he was to be enrolled as chaplain in the regiment of the governor of Yeniseisk, Afanasy Pashkov, who was then seeking new lands to be brought under the great sovereign's authority.

Pashkov did not at all resemble the earlier governor, Khilkov. Says Avvakum: "At the place called Long Rapids, he began to push me off the raft. 'It is your fault that the raft moves so badly. You are a heretic! Off with you into the mountains, and travel not with cossacks!'

"Oh, what misery! The mountains are high and the thick forests, impenetrable. A stone cliff stands like a towering wall, the whole of which can be viewed only by bending one's head as far back as possible. Those mountains are infested with large snakes. They also contain geese, ducks with red feathers, black crows, and grey jackdaws. In those mountains are also to be found eagles, hawks, gyrfalcons, turkeys, pelicans, swans, and an enormous multitude of other wild birds. Upon those mountains wander many wild animals—wild goats, deer, bison, elk, boars, wolves, and wild sheep. They all passed right before my eyes, but not one of them could I catch. It was into those hills that Pashkov wanted to cast me out, to find my home with the birds and beasts.

"I wrote him a short letter, of which this is the beginning: 'Oh, man! Despise not to fear God! The heavenly hosts do quake before Him. You alone dare hold Him in contempt.' Some few other things were written there, and I sent the letter to him.

"Not long afterward, some fifty people came running. They took my raft and hurried back to him. As they arrived with the raft, his agents took hold of me and brought me before him. He stood there with his sword, quivering with anger, and bellowed at me like a wild animal. He struck me on one cheek, then the other, and then upon my head, knocking me off my feet. Grabbing a chain, he hit me three times on the back as I lay on the ground. Then, after stripping me, he gave me 72 lashes with the whip, also upon the back."

Fortunately for Avvakum, a protector was found who took his side. This was Yeremei, Pashkov's son, who tried to persuade his father not to sin by beating the archpriest. Yeremei did so, however, with insufficient prudence, approaching his father directly from the front, instead of from behind, with his entreaties. The old man lost all control of himself. Drawing his sword, he began to chase after his son, who was only scarcely able to escape.

After this episode, Pashkov himself fell victim to a stroke of bad luck when his raft ran onto some rocks and could not be dislodged. Yeremei took advantage of the occasion to speak to his father: "Father! It is for your sins that God punishes you. You needlessly beat the archpriest with a whip. It is time, my lord, to seek forgiveness."

The old man roared at Yeremei like a wild creature. Yeremei saw what calamity was about to befall and stepped away towards a pine tree. Clasping his hands, he prayed, "Lord, have mercy!"

The old man picked up a pistol, took aim at his son, and released the firing mechanism. Misfire. He pulled the trigger a second time. Again, misfire. A third time again he pulled it. And for a third time, another misfire. In a violent fury, the old man hurled the firearm to the ground. The young man picked it up, pointed it off to one side—and it fired.

The father sat down on a chair. Leaning upon his sword, he pondered. Soon he began to weep, saying: "I have sinned, doomed wretch that I am! I have spilled innocent blood. Needlessly did I beat the archpriest. It is for this that God punishes me!"

At that moment, his raft suddenly broke loose of the rocks on which it had been caught. Pashkov called his son to him and said: "Forgive me, Yeremei. You speak the truth!"

The son replied, with a deep bow: "God will forgive you, my lord. I am guilty before God and you."

Avvakum concludes: "Yeremei is exceedingly wise, for his own beard was already turning grey, and yet he greatly reveres his father and fears him."

The archpriest later was brought to Fort Bratsky. There he was thrown in jail and given a cell covered with straw: "I lay on the straw like a little dog. Sometimes they fed me; sometimes, not. There were many mice, and I struck at them with my priest's cap—the fools would

not give me a stick. I wanted to shout at Pashkov 'Forgive me!' But
God's will prevented me. It was ordained that I be patient. He had me
transferred to a warm hut.

"In spring we once again set out on our journey. Oh, what a time!
Two of my little sons died from want. With the rest, I continued to
suffer as we wandered about the mountains and sharp cliffs, naked and
barefoot, surviving on grasses and roots. For my children and little pile
of baggage, I was given two tired old horses, while my wife and I continued on foot, hurting ourselves on the ice. The country was barbarous.
The natives were hostile. We dared not lag behind the rest of the company, and yet we were scarcely able to follow behind the horses. My
poor wife would trudge and trudge, and then fall down. It was very
slippery.

"Once, as we shuffled along, she fell, and another frail figure stum-
bled over her, whereupon he also fell. They both cried out, but neither
could get up.

"The muzhik shouted, 'Oh, little mother, my lady! Forgive me!'

"My wife replied, 'What are you doing, old man? You have crushed
me!'

"I approached. The poor woman complained to me, 'Is this agony
going to last much longer, archpriest?'

"And I answered, 'Markovna! Until our very death.'

"Sighing, she answered, 'Very well, Petrovich. Let us walk on.' "

The time arrived when it became the archpriest's turn to become depressed and obtain encouragement from his wife.

"For ten years," says Avvakum, "Pashkov tormented me, or else I
tormented him, I don't know which. God will disentangle it." An order
finally arrived directing Avvakum to go to Russia, and the archpriest set
off. Upon arriving by water at the Russian cities, he discovered, as far as
the church was concerned, "that he was doing no good, but rather that
a riot was breaking out."[85]

"Greatly saddened, I sat down and began to consider: 'What am I to
do? Am I to preach the Word of God or go into seclusion? My wife and
children have tied me.' "

"And seeing that I was depressed, my wife came up to me with kind-
ly concern and said: 'Why, my lord, have you turned so sorrowful?'

"I explained to her in detail: 'My wife! What am I to do? The winter
of heresy is at the door. Shall I speak out or remain silent? You have
tied me!'

"She answered: 'Lord, have mercy! What are you saying, Petrovich?
Go, go to the church! Speak out against the shameless heresy!' "

Avvakum likewise describes an interesting domestic scene.

"In Moscow I had a frenzied man, named Filip, who was chained to the wall in a corner of the house because he was possessed by a fierce and cruel devil. He kept striking out and fighting so violently that the house servants could not cope with him. When I, a sinner, came with the cross and holy water, he became docile and, as though dead, fell before the cross of Christ.

"One day I returned from visiting Fedor Rtishchev in a most depressed state of mind, having contended strenuously with heretics at his house about the faith and the law.[86] At that moment a disturbance was taking place at home. My wife had gotten into an argument with the widowed house servant, Fotinia. Upon entering, I beat them both and treated them roughly. Right then, the devil began to make himself felt in Filip. Breaking his chains, he went into a frenzy and shouted so horribly that all the people of the household were struck with terror. Without having purified myself, I came up to him and wanted to calm him down, but it did not turn out as before. Grabbing hold of me, he began to beat and flay me. Then he hurled me away and said, 'I am not afraid of you.'

"I became filled with deep remorse. 'The devil, I say, has taken over my will.'

"After lying down for a short while, I managed to collect myself in my conscience. Rising up, I sought out my wife and with tears begged her forgiveness. Bowing to the ground before her, I said: 'I have sinned, Nastasia Markovna. Forgive me, a sinner!' She bowed to me.

"I likewise asked Fotinia to grant me her forgiveness. Thereupon, lying down in the middle of the room, I bade each person to give me five blows with the whip upon by accursed back. There were about twenty people in all, and every one of them—my wife, my children, and the rest—abided by my behest, weeping as they did so.

"When they had finished whipping, I besought their pardon. The devil, seeing his inevitable downfall, once more departed out of Filip. I blessed him with the cross, and he recovered."

Avvakum was received in Moscow with utmost cordiality. It was thought that this strong personality could be dissuaded from the schism by the warmth of affection. Says Avvakum: "They received me like an angel of God. The sovereign and the boyars were all glad to see me. I stopped by to see Fedor Rtishchev. He came out of his room himself to greet me and receive my blessing. He engaged me in lengthy conversation, not letting me go home for three days and nights and informing the sovereign about me afterwards.

"The sovereign forthwith summoned me for an audience and spoke gracious words: 'Are you faring well, archpriest? God grant that we meet again.'

"And I, facing him, kissed his hand and pressed it, saying: 'The Lord lives and so is my soul alive, sovereign tsar! As for the future, let it be as God wills.'

"He gave a gentle sigh and departed for wherever he had to go. And there were other things that happened also, but why say much? All that is now past.

"He ordered that I be installed in the guest quarters of a monastery in the Kremlin. While passing on outings by my house, he often exchanged greetings with me, bowing low and saying: 'Grant me your blessing and pray for me.' Riding by on horseback he would dip his cap, at other times taking off his fur-lined hat. As he passed by in a carriage, he would look out the window in my direction, whereupon all the boyars in the train of his entourage would also ask, over and over, as each of them passed by: 'Archpriest! Bless us and pray for us!'

"How shall I not feel sorry for the tsar and those boyars? It is sad to see how generous they were, giving me a place anywhere I might desire. They suggested that I become one of the confessors, so that I would be joined with them in faith. However, I saw that all these things were like dross, in order that I might gain Christ.

"They perceived that I was showing no signs of coming over to their side. The sovereign then ordered the boyar Rodion Streshnev to try to persuade me to keep silent. And I responded in such a way as to gratify him, for the tsar, who has been enthroned by God, treated me with kindness. I expected things to improve only slightly. But they promised that, at the beginning of the year, during the feast of St. Simeon, I would be given a position correcting books in the printing house. I was very pleased, for this was closer to my desires than even the post of confessor. The tsar graciously vouchsafed that I be given 10 rubles. The tsaritsa likewise sent 10 rubles; the confessor, Luka, also 10 rubles; Rodion Streshnev, also 10 rubles. And our old friend, Fedor Rtishchev, instructed his household treasurer to provide me with a compensation of 60 rubles. There is no need to talk about the other gifts and payments that were made! It seemed that everybody was carrying and dragging in every conceivable thing.

"While in Moscow I stayed continually at the home of my dear friend, Feodosia Prokofievna Morozova, for I was her confessor, as well as her sister's, Princess Evdokia Prokofievna (Urusova). Moreover, I also frequented the home of Anna Petrovna Miloslavskaia and visited at Fedor Rtishchev's to contend with those who had estranged themselves from the church. I lived this way for half a year.

"Yet it became evident to me that, insofar as the church was concerned, I 'was doing no good, but rather that a riot was breaking out.' And so, once more I began to criticize. I wrote at quite some length to the tsar that he should strive to seek after ancient piety, protect our one common mother, the Holy Church, from heresy, and install on the patriarchal throne someone who was an Orthodox believer instead of a wolf and apostate, like the pernicious and heretical Nikon. From that point on the tsar began to feel disturbed about me. He did not like it when I again started to speak out; he liked it only when I kept silent. But that was not how it was to turn out for me. And the church authorities, like goats, started to spit upon me and decided once more to banish me from Moscow, for many persons there came to see me and, upon seeing the truth, refused to attend their fraudulent church services anymore.

"Accordingly, I received a reprimand from the tsar: 'The ecclesiastical authorities make complaint against you, that you have emptied the churches. Go forth once more into exile.'

"I was taken to Mezen.[87] In the towns along the way, I gave instruction to God's people and castigated those who were blemished brutes. Thus they brought me to Mezen, where they kept me for a year and a half before sending me back to Moscow.

"Upon my return to Moscow they sequestered me under supervision in the Pafnutiev monastery, where repeated messages arrived, saying over and over: 'Must you long torment us? Join with us, dear Avvakum!' I rejected them as though they were devils, even as they pried their way into my eyes.

"I then wrote them a declaration filled with defiance. They got me out of Pafnutiev monastery and took me again to Moscow where in the patriarchal reception chamber the ecclesiastical authorities disputed with me. They brought me to the cathedral church. There, during the divine liturgy, upon completion of the great entrance,[88] they tonsured me and the deacon Fedor, after which they pronounced a malediction. Thereupon I uttered a malediction on them in return. How grievously forlorn was that divine liturgy for me. They took me away by night to the monastery of St. Nicholas-on-the-Ugresha, where they kept me for seventeen weeks in a frigid room. The tsar himself came to the monastery, walked about near my cell, and after staying a little while, left the monastery again.

"When they tonsured me, there took place a great disturbance in the palace involving the late tsaritsa. She, dear woman, stood up for us and dissuaded them from imposing punishment on us. It is for this reason that they took me to Pafnutiev monastery, where, locking me up in a dark room, they kept me in irons for a little more than a year.

"They then conveyed me from Pafnutiev monastery to Moscow and placed me in a guest house. After waiting a long time at the Miracles monastery I was brought before the ecumenical patriarchs, whose presence was augmented by all our leading hierarchs, sitting there like foxes.

"I talked about a good many things from the Scriptures with the patriarchs. Finally, they issued their final statement to me: 'Why are you so obstinate? Everyone—Palestinians, Serbs, Albanians, Wallachians, Romans, and Poles—all make the sign of the cross upon themselves using three fingers. You alone stand upon your obduracy and cross yourself with two fingers. Such conduct is improper.'

"And I had this to say to them in reply concerning Christ: 'Ecumenical teachers! Rome fell a long time ago and continues to languish without recovery. The Poles suffered ruin together with Rome, remaining to the end enemies of the Christians. And among yourselves, Orthodoxy is blemished. You have become powerless as a result of the might of the Turkish Mohammed. In the future, come to learn from us. By the grace of God, we have an independent, sovereign state. Prior to the appearance of the renegade Nikon, Orthodoxy in our Russia under the pious princes and tsars was pure and undefiled, and the church was not torn by dissension. . . .'

"I stepped over to the doorway and lay down on my side. 'You go ahead and sit down, but I shall lie down,' I told them.[89]

"They started to laugh: 'You are a fool, archpriest, and fail to show respect to the patriarchs.'

"And I answered: 'We are fools for Christ's sake. You are distinguished, and we are unhonored; you are strong, and we are weak.'

"They clamped me into chains. Then they took me to the Vorobiev Hills, and later to the monastery of St. Nicholas-on-the-Ugresha. There, the sovereign sent me the regimental commander Yury Lotukhin for the sake of receiving a blessing, and we discussed a number of things. Again they moved us to Moscow, to the guest house of St. Nicholas monastery, and once more took written depositions from us concerning the true faith.

"Later, the tsar's gentlemen-in-waiting Artamon (Matveev) and Dementy (Bashmakov) were sent to me many times, relaying messages from the tsar: 'Archpriest, I am aware of your pure, blameless, and God-like life. I, together with the tsaritsa and my children, ask your blessing. Pray for us. Please listen to me. Do come to some accommodation with the representatives of the ecumenical church, even if only in small degree.'

"And I replied: 'Even if God should will that I must die, I shall never enter into agreement with apostates. You are my tsar. What do those foreigners have to do with you? They lost their own emperor and have wandered here so they might swallow you.'

"And so once more, with my brothers being punished while I remained unpunished, they sent me to Pustozorie."

To the very end, Avvakum remained steadfast. Here is his confession: "Although I am not an intelligent man, and certainly am not in the least an educated person, yet this I do know, that the whole Church, transmitted by tradition from the Holy Fathers, is holy and undefiled. I hold this unto death, even as I received it. I shall not remove the bound of things eternal. Thus was it laid down before us; so let it lie even unto the ages of ages."

THE CONSTANT SISTERS

Avvakum's wife lent support to his zeal, but this was not the only such instance in the history of the schism. The noblewoman Feodosia Morozova, the widow of Gleb Morozov, brother of the famous Boris, enjoyed considerable prestige at court.

"At home, she was waited upon by some 300 servants, besides which she also had 8,000 peasants, as well as a multitude of friends and relatives. She rode about in an expensive carriage, finished in mosaics and silver, drawn by six or twelve horses with jingling chains, followed by some hundred servants and slaves, both male and female, who safeguarded her dignity and safety."

This wealthy and celebrated noblewoman, together with her sister, Princess Evdokia Urusova, became such ardent disciples of Avvakum that a whole host of deprivations and sufferings could not overcome their firm determination. In virtue of their position it is easy to understand what kind of support both these sisters were able to extend to the schism as they gathered about themselves the most active of its proponents. It is also easy to appreciate how little pleasure this must have afforded the tsar, who made use of all the means at his disposal to dissuade them—entreaties, threats, punishments—all to no avail.

"Senseless fanatic" is what Morozova was called by Tsar Alexis, who considered her sister, Evdokia, to be less temperamental and, indeed, humble. But this supposedly meek woman, as often happens, bolstered the "fanatic" with her firmness.

At her interrogation, in answer to a question posed to her by Metropolitan Paul of Krutitsy as to whether she would be willing to receive Communion in accordance with the same service books as used by the sovereign, the tsaritsa, and the tsarevnas, Morozova gave the following reply: "I would not receive Communion. I know that the tsar takes Communion according to the revised service books of Nikonian publication. The enemy of God, Nikon, has spewed forth his heresies like spittle, and you now lean down to lick it up. It is clear that you are just like him."

The sisters were shut away in different places. Patriarch Pitirim ventured to make representations on their behalf before the tsar: "With respect to the widowed noblewoman Morozova, I suggest you command that her house be restored to her and that she be given a hundred peasants for the needs of her household. As for the princess, my advice is that she be returned to the prince. This would render the whole affair more seemly. After all, it is only a question of balky women. What kind of thought are they able to give to the issues?"

"I would have done that long ago," answered the tsar, "but you have no idea how rabidly intransigent that woman is. If only you could have seen how that Morozova argued, and continues to argue even now. She made a lot of trouble for me and caused many difficulties. If you do not believe what I say, go and find out for yourself. Just summon her for a personal audience and ask a few questions. Then you will find out how unbending she is. Begin to chastise her, and then you will really get a taste of her sweet pleasantries!"

The patriarch had a taste of her sweet pleasantries and beat a hasty retreat. The sisters were subjected to torture in the palace. At a meeting of the sovereign's council, the question was raised whether Morozova should be consigned to the flames.

"The boyars could not reach an agreement. Then Dolgoruky, with a series of brief comments, removed their indecision."

The schismatic women were carted off to Borovsk and locked in a prison cell hewn out of the earth. Urusova could not endure the rigors of confinement and soon perished. Morozova followed not long afterward.

NEW SKILLS, NEW FOREIGNERS

New teachers came from everywhere. In the palace and in the churches, from monastic cells and from Siberian exile, they propounded the need for change and the indispensability of knowledge. Those stung by the exhortations, the insulted former teachers, who had occupied the leading place in society and who had aroused a strong reaction against the innovations which they themselves introduced, rose up in opposition to the changes being promoted by their rivals and declared that no changes of any kind should be allowed. "It was laid down so before us; let it lie thus even unto the ages of ages."

At the time when the old and new teachers, clad in priestly vestments and monastic habits, were disputing about the two and three-fingered sign of the cross, when the Russians grew divided in a ferocious struggle, when the compromise with knowledge, the effort to introduce learning through Orthodox teachers without doing violence to Orthodoxy was far from being as successful as might have been wished, when the old teachers accused the Orthodox Greeks and Orthodox Little and White Russians of being heretics and Latins at that very time there arrived still newer teachers of a different sort, who were unwelcome both to the old and the new teachers in churchly garb.

The newcomers were non-Orthodox foreigners. They came and found a hospitable reception because, before grammar and rhetoric, it was essential for the Russians to learn how to lead a military attack. They arrived because of the obvious state of economic bankruptcy, arising out of the Russians' lack of skill in manufacture and commerce, and the inaccessibility of the sea. They entered because of the law which dictates the precedence of objective over subjective reality. Some attention should be devoted to these new teachers to see what kind of people they were and what kind of life they led in the German Suburb, which played such a consequential role in the process of reform.

Reference has been made to the employment of mercenaries and their historical significance. These hired military troops were recruited from among those who had willingly or unwillingly taken leave of their own countries, or in a word, from among those who constituted the cossacks of Western Europe. For the cossacks of Russia it was the wide steppes that served as a free and untrammeled refuge. On those plains they could roam at will, give but nominal recognition to the authority of the Russian crown, and take up arms against it at the first hint of disagreement, all the while maintaining their status as Orthodox Russians. In Western Europe there were no plains where a cossackdom could be formed. Consequently the west European cossacks were left with two alternatives. They could either sail across the ocean to discover and conquer new lands, which for the Western cossacks in the New World

corresponded to the activity of the Eastern cossacks in the land beyond
the Urals, or they could take up the eternal occupation of retinues made
up of bogatyr cossacks: "to serve the seven kings in the seven hordes,"
seek a good salary, and gather some plunder in the service of various
sovereigns. By the seventeenth century, one such sovereign was the tsar
of all Russia.

The character of these Western cossacks, who appeared in Moscow
under the name "service foreigners," is explained by their origin and
activity. Emigrating either by choice or otherwise, the service foreigners
changed their allegiance and colors depending on where the most lucrative rewards could be found. A motley band of arrivals from different
lands and peoples, they were cosmopolitans par excellence, distinguishable by an easygoing morality and by their attitude of utter indifference
for the fate of the country within whose boundaries they chanced temporarily to settle. More money and greater plunder remained always
their main aim. It was hard to find among them anyone with an academic education; such persons would not have wandered off to join bands
of mercenaries. But generally they were vivacious people, intelligent,
widely traveled and broadly experienced, having much to say about any
number of things, pleasant and cheerful companions, given to enjoying
a full and happy life with plenty of carousing through the wee hours of
the morning, free of any responsibility, living day by day, and quite accustomed to sharp reversals of fortune: here today and gone tomorrow.
Today, a victory with much booty; tomorrow, a battle lost, booty gone,
and detention in captivity as a prisoner of war.

Such were the people who regularly were called to Moscow during
the seventeenth century. At first the increased numbers of foreigners
in Moscow elicited a strong protest and many complaints from the
priests. Hence, the government adopted a policy of isolating foreigners
and settling them in a special suburb. It seemed that Russia was sealing
herself off from foreigners, but this was merely an appearance. Russia
was changing her orientation from East to West, and the German Suburb
represented the West. History was on the side of the German Suburb.
Old Moscow would soon defer to its outlying district, the German Suburb, just as old Rostov earlier had deferred to its outlying dependent
town, Vladimir. It would not be long before the German Suburb, acquiring its own palaces, attracted the tsar and his court away from the
Kremlin. The German Suburb was a stepping-stone in the direction of
St. Petersburg, just as Vladimir had been a stepping-stone towards
Moscow.

PATRICK GORDON'S DIARY

The service foreigners of the German Suburb did not pass their time immersed in silence. One of the most outstanding among them habitually wrote down day-by-day his adventures and experiences. He left behind a most interesting record about himself, his associates, and Russia prior to Peter the Great's reforms. This is the diary of Patrick Gordon.[90]

By birth, Patrick Gordon was a Scotsman and a Catholic. The latter circumstance barred his access to the university in his native land. In his state of idleness the young man fell in love, but could not marry the object of his passion. Partly it was this and partly it was Gordon's longing for freedom that impelled him to leave his homeland, the more so as he had nothing there to lose. He sprang from the cadet line of the family of Gordon, being himself a youngest son. And so, the young Gordon went abroad.

He initially entered the Jesuit college in Braunsberg, but soon found that the cloistered life did not suit his character. In 1655 he joined the military forces of the Swedish king, Charles X Gustavus, who was then fighting the Poles. The next year Gordon was captured by the Poles and given his release on condition he enter Polish service. Later the same year he fell into Swedish hands and returned to duty on their side. As a hired officer he was not paid a salary. However, he did not overlook any favorable opportunity to support himself through plunder, guarding his booty by night in a forest, like a robber, and noting in his diary, for example, that he was able, though not without some difficulty, to appropriate some horses from two peasants.

Gordon served in the Scottish military company, which was noted for its pillaging. In 1658 he was captured a second time by the Poles and found a place in their service. "After all, Gordon's chief aim," he says of himself in the third person, "was to seek his own fortune, which now became difficult to do in Swedish service because the Swedes had hanging around their neck the emperor, the Polish and Danish kings, and the Russian tsar. To be sure, for an honest man service with the Swedes was first-rate. The people are fair and give every man his due on the basis of his achievements. But it is also possible to find one's fortune with the Poles. The Polish generals deal arrogantly with foreigners, but the rest of the Polish nobility and those who are educated treat us well."

Still, Gordon was unsuccessful in trying his luck among the Poles. And so, in 1661, he entered Russian service with the rank of major. In September he arrived at the German Suburb in Moscow. At first, Gordon found himself dissatisfied in his new surroundings. He was summoned to appear before the head of the Chancellery for Service Foreigners, the boyar Ilia Miloslavsky, the tsar's father-in-law. Miloslavsky ordered Gordon to take a lance and a musket and demonstrate his skill with them. Gordon replied that, had he been told about this in advance, he would have brought along his orderly, who, it might be assumed, was more thoroughly versed than he in handling weapons. He added that such skill was of minimal importance to an officer, since his main task was directing his soldiers. The boyar declared that all service foreigners arriving in Russia, even those holding the rank of colonel, had to demonstrate their proficiency with the lance and musket. There was nothing to be done about it. Gordon took up the lance and musket, and upon departing, left the boyar quite satisfied.

Soon afterwards, the veteran seeker after booty ran head on into another notorious group of adepts in the field of self-aggrandizement: the Muscovite bureaucrats. In compensation for having left service elsewhere and entering Russia, Gordon was to receive an allowance of 25 rubles in money and 25 rubles in sables. The foreigner was not familiar with the custom that, in order to receive this allowance, he had first to present a gift to the chancellor. Gordon showed up to collect his allowance; the chancellor, citing various trivial reasons, refused to give him anything. Gordon resorted to threats. No success. He went to the boyar in charge to lodge a complaint. The boyar ordered the chancellor to issue the allowance. Still the chancellor refused. Gordon approached the boyar a second time. Arriving still a third time with his complaint, he told the boyar straight out that he could not understand who had greater power, the boyar or the chancellor, since the latter apparently thought nothing of ignoring the boyar's commands. The boyar grew angry and called for the chancellor. When he arrived, the boyar seized him by the beard and gave him a good thrashing, warning that the whip would be next if Gordon showed up once more with his complaint. The chancellor came up to Gordon and belabored him with verbal abuse. Gordon answered in kind and wound up threatening to demand release from service.

Indeed, Gordon began to give serious consideration to ways and means for getting out of Russia. The salary was minuscule, and even that paltry amount was paid in copper coins (4 kopecks being equivalent to one of silver). It was impossible just to live, much less stash anything away for the future.

In the Chancellery for Service Foreigners it was discovered that Gordon intended to ask the boyar for his release. The authorities were

thrown into consternation and gave him a written authorization for payment of the money and sables. Gordon's stubborn streak now showed.
He declared that he no longer wanted the allowance but desired to gain
his release. The Russians undertook to persuade him that, by requesting
to resign, he was sealing his own fate. For, it was pointed out to him, he
was a Catholic who had but recently arrived from Poland, against which
a war was in progress. Should he seek to go back now, it would be clear
that he had come to Russia on a mission as a spy. Instead of obtaining
permission to depart, he would more likely be granted the opportunity
of becoming acquainted with Siberia. Gordon felt a wave of apprehension, accepted the allowance, and remained in Moscow at the German
Suburb.

In the German Suburb rather curious occurrences sometimes took
place. There, as in all other outlying districts of the city, the duty for
maintaining security was entrusted to a police sergeant, who was given
the following instructions: "You are to exercise a close watch over your
district and preserve strict security. You shall order that regimental and
battalion commanders, officers of lower rank, merchants, residents of
every kind, and foreigners not keep for purposes of work in and around
their houses, without proper written certification, any Russian fugitives,
persons only recently baptized into the Orthodox church, White Russians, or vagrants; that they not participate in duels or engage in murder
or fighting of any kind; that they not trade in commercial alcoholic
beverages, spirits, beer, or tobacco; that they not admit or receive robbers or prostitutes; that, without making application at the Chancellery
of the New Quarter, they not keep any alcohol on their premises; but
that for work in and around their houses they hire unbaptized foreigners
of various faiths."

Yet, as mentioned earlier, little heed was paid by soldiers to orders
about spirits, and their foreign officers peered through their fingers at
this. On one occasion, the authorities in Moscow found out that some
soldiers were storing wine at a certain house in the German Suburb.
A government clerk arrived with a detachment of musketeers to investigate. He uncovered the wine even though the soldiers had been able to
hide it in the garden. The musketeers confiscated the wine and took
several soldiers into custody. However, other soldiers appeared, freed
their comrades, retrieved the wine, and pushed the musketeers back to
the city gates. At this point reinforcements arrived to aid the musketeers,
and the soldiers in their turn now retreated. Soon they received additional

numbers, so that before long some 800 soldiers confronted 700 musketeers. A battle began in the narrow streets, in the course of which the soldiers forced the musketeers back to the gates of the White City. But to the assistance of the musketeers came 600 of their comrades, led by the commander of the Kremlin guard, and they cut off the soldiers who had entered the White City. Twenty-two men were arrested, beaten with whips, and exiled to Siberia.

Playing at cards was likewise prohibited, and the soldiers played secretly at night. A Russian captain, Spiridonov, once caught some of them and, as was the custom of the authorities in those days, made of the occasion an opportunity to enrich himself. He took not only all the money at stake on the table, but also an additional 60 rubles from the soldiers who were there. About all this he said not a word to his commanding officer, Gordon. The latter sent for Spiridonov and gave him a severe dressing down, warning him of harsh penalties in the future. The captain, unaccustomed to such delicate persuasion, flew into a rage. Gordon then resorted to prompting of a different kind. He grabbed Spiridonov by the head, hurled him to the floor, and beat him so badly with a cudgel that the unfortunate wretch was barely able to get up. The captain lodged a grievance with the colonel, but since no witnesses had been present, Gordon denied the charge. The captain went to the boyar with his complaint, and again Gordon issued a denial.

The landlord of the house in which Gordon lived wanted to be rid of his tenant, and the petitions he submitted to the authorities concerning this were granted. Gordon was twice sent written notices to vacate his quarters, but he paid no attention to them. Then, while Gordon was seated at dinner one day, a government clerk entered his room with an order to move elsewhere immediately. The clerk was accompanied by some twenty trumpeters, most of whom had remained downstairs.

"Show me the order," Gordon insisted.

"I will not show it to you," replied the clerk. "You have already hidden two earlier notices, or maybe you tore them up."

"I am not leaving these quarters until you show me the order," declared Gordon.

The clerk directed the trumpeters to take away Gordon's trunk, while he picked up the regimental colors. Gordon leaped from the table. With the aid of his orderly and two officers who were dining with him, he chased the clerk out of the room and down the stairs. But the clerk joined up with the rest of the trumpeters, and again headed upstairs for Gordon's room. Gordon and his comrades, enjoying the advantage of height at the head of the staircase, repelled their adversaries all the easier because the trumpeters were armed only with staffs. Hearing the commotion, other soldiers came running. They attacked the clerk and the trumpeters, who quickly retreated. The soldiers pursued them to the Yauza Bridge and took away their caps. The whole affair came to naught because, luckily for Gordon, Miloslavsky had picked a quarrel with Rtishchev, to whose chancellery the clerk belonged. Meanwhile, Gordon changed residence.

Once he had decided to remain in Moscow, there was nothing to be done but try to come to some accommodation with the existing customs. Gordon invited all the clerks in the Chancellery for Service Foreigners to his lodgings for a feast, and presented some of them with two sables, some with one. From then on he enjoyed their full favor and respect. Whatever business he had to transact at the chancellery was handled efficiently and expeditiously.

Yet, despite this, Gordon still was unhappy in Moscow. A man was used to acquiring valuables with a weapon in his hands, and here it was necessary to bestow gifts upon people who caught sables with their paws! He could not break out to the West. Perhaps it might at least be possible to go farther east. Fedor Miloslavsky was just then being granted an appointment as ambassador to Persia, and Gordon began to make inquiries about accompanying him as a member of his staff. Realizing that requests without some additional sweetening were unacceptable, Gordon took 100 zolotoys to Miloslavsky himself and 20 zolotoys to his majordomo. But the money was wasted, for it proved impossible to arrange the matter. Here the foreigner had been recruited for military service, and now he wanted to leave with the ambassador to Persia, where it was perfectly possible for the Russians themselves to go. And what then? He might take it into his head to leave there, or perhaps transfer his services to the shah!

Although the police sergeants in the German Suburb were given instructions to prevent incidents of dueling, nevertheless the foreigners gave scant attention to this prohibition. In 1666 Gordon had a duel with a Major Montgomery,[91] with whom he had quarreled at a feast given in his lodgings for palace servitors on the tsar's name day.

The service foreigners did not always come to loggerheads with each other only at feasts, under the influence of alcoholic spirits. On his return from the military campaign of 1676, Gordon, who was by then a colonel, learned that some of the dragoons in his regiment wanted to lodge a complaint against him. They were being incited to this by a

General Major Trauernicht. Coming across Trauernicht at the home of Prince Trubetskoy, Gordon sharply lectured him in the presence of many colonels. He accused Trauernicht of having joined forces with the scum of his regiment and inducing them to seek redress against him. Trauernicht said nothing. But next day he marched the soldiers to the Chancellery of State Service and Appointments to file a grievance against Gordon. A few days later, a Colonel Scheele,[92] a relative of Trauernicht, came to Gordon and proposed that, if Gordon were to pay Trauernicht 300 pounds, he would bring the matter with the dragoons to a close. Gordon responded to the offer with a threat.

When Gordon discovered that the case was being sent to the tsar the next day, he had 20 rubles delivered to the chancellor of the council. The chancellor promised to take Gordon's side. Also on his side was a military governor, the chief commander himself, Prince Grigory Romodanovsky. When the case was reported to the tsar, Romodanovsky declared that everything contained in the petition was a lie and that the crux of the matter lay in the fact that Gordon insisted upon strict discipline, not allowing his subordinates to steal or straggle. "I say this," added the prince, "not because Gordon gave or promised me anything, but because I know his diligence in the service of His Tsarist Majesty."

The peasants of twenty hamlets in which Gordon's regiment had been stationed submitted a deposition under the signatures of three priests stating that they had no reason whatsoever to complain about Gordon. The plaintiffs, seeing that the case would not end in their favor, offered to make peace with Gordon if he gave them five rubles. Gordon answered that he would give them five rubles if they told him the names of all their accomplices, so that he might know who were his friends and his enemies in the regiment. Otherwise, not a kopeck would he give them. The dragoons refused.

APPENDIX 1

MONETARY CONVERSION TABLE

1 ruble = 1 zolotoy = 2 efimoks = 10 grivnas = 100 kopecks = 200 dengas
1 altyn = 3 kopecks = 6 dengas

While subject to fluctuations, the above equivalent values for individual monetary units were generally applicable in Muscovy from the fifteenth to the seventeenth century. Deviations from these values and equivalences for other periods can be found in the footnotes. It should be noted that, in the Muscovite period, rubles, grivnas, and altyns were not actual coins, but monetary units used for accounting. The grivna once had constituted a form of specie in early Russian history, but disappeared, except in name, as a consequence of economic and political disintegration. The ruble and altyn started to be minted as coins in 1704, after the period covered in the present work. It is apparent, then, that this list includes no Russian coins of large denomination. The absence of such coins from circulation explains why foreign coins, particularly the zolotoy and efimok, played an important part in the Muscovite monetary system.

APPENDIX 2

LIST OF CHANCELLERIES MENTIONED

Ambassadorial Chancellery — *Prikaz posolsky*
Chancellery of Cannoneers — *Prikaz pushkarsky*
Chancellery of Commercial Affairs — *Prikaz kupetskikh del*
Chancellery of Financial Control — *Prikaz schetnyi*
Chancellery of Military Tenures — *Prikaz pomestnyi*
Chancellery of Musketeers — *Prikaz streletsky*
Chancellery of Reiters — *Prikaz reitarsky*
Chancellery of the Apothecary — *Prikaz aptekarsky*
Chancellery of the Exchequer — *Prikaz bolshoy kazny*
Chancellery of the Horse — *Prikaz koniushennyi*
Chancellery of the New Quarter — *Prikaz novy chetverti*
Chancellery of the Royal Household — *Prikaz bolshogo dvortsa*
Chancellery of the Royal Treasure-house — *Prikaz kazennogo dvora*
Chancellery of State Revenues — *Prikaz bolshogo prikhoda*
Chancellery of State Service and Appointments — *Prikaz razriadnyi*
Chancellery for Criminal Affairs — *Prikaz razboinyi*
Chancellery for Galicia — *Prikaz galitskoy chetverti*
Chancellery for Kazan — *Prikaz kazanskogo dvortsa*
Chancellery for Kostroma — *Prikaz kostromskoy chetverti*
Chancellery for Little Russia — *Prikaz malorossiisky*
Chancellery for Novgorod — *Prikaz novgorodskoy chetverti*
Chancellery for Service Foreigners — *Prikaz inozemnyi*
Chancellery for Siberia — *Prikaz sibirsky*
Chancellery for State Storehouses — *Prikaz kazennykh zhitnits*
Chancellery for Stonework — *Prikaz kamennykh zhitnits*
Chancellery for the Collection of Provisions for the Musketeers —
    Prikaz sbora streletskogo khleba
Chancellery for the Commemoration of Souls — *Prikaz panafidnyi*
Chancellery for the Principality of Smolensk —
    Prikaz kniazhestva smolenskogo
Chancellery for Ustiug — *Prikaz ustiuzhskoy chetverti*
Chancellery for Vladimir — *Prikaz vladimirskoy chetverti*
Judicial Chancellery of Moscow — *Prikaz sudnyi moskovsky*
Judicial Chancellery of Vladimir — *Prikaz sudnyi vladimirsky*
Monasterial Chancellery — *Prikaz monastyrsky*
Privy Chancellery — *Prikaz tainykh del*

NOTES

Additional information on personalities and topics found in the text and notes is available in Joseph L. Wieczynski, ed.; *The Modern Encyclopedia of Russian and Soviet History* (MERSH) and Harry B. Weber, ed., *The Modern Encyclopedia of Russian and Soviet Literature* (MERSL), both published by Academic International Press.

CHAPTER I

1. The battle on the Catalaunian Plains, near Châlons-sur-Marne, marking Attila's defeat, took place in A.D. 451. The Crimea was annexed by the Russian Empire under Catherine the Great in 1783.

2. Ferdinand the Catholic, as Ferdinand V, held the throne of Castile jointly with Isabella from 1474 to 1504. As Ferdinand II, he was also king of Aragon from 1479 to 1516. The final war against the Moors ended with the conquest of Granada in 1492.

3. Ivan III, called "the Great," was grand prince of Moscow and all Russia from 1462 to 1505. The traditional date for the overthrow of the Tatar yoke is 1480.

4. The Tatars swept into Russia from Asia in 1237-1238, conquering almost all of it by 1240. The Chuvashes and Cheremis are Finnish peoples of eastern Russia. The Bashkirs, who occupy an area between the Volga river and the Ural mountains, are considered to be tatarized Finns. Finnish tribes occupied northern Russia long before the arrival of the Tatars, and in large areas of the north their presence antedated the arrival of the Slavs.

5. Translation of *rod*. Technically, a family structure reckoned on only one line of descent is called a sib. If a sib is matrilineal, it is known as a clan; if patrilineal, a gens. In the present translation the word "clan" is employed instead of "gens" because of its greater familiarity. Where so used, it always refers to a patrilineal clan. In later portions of the present work, where the transformation of this primitive social unit is indicated, the term *rod* is translated as "extended family" or simply "family."

6. This famous passage from the Russian Primary Chronicle refers to the disappearance of the Avars, or Obry, an Asiatic people who established a nomadic empire from the Danube to eastern Russia in the second half of the sixth century A.D. The later extension of their empire to the west was destroyed by Charlemagne at the end of the eighth century. For the full reference to the Avars in the Chronicle, see S.H. Cross and O.P. Sherbowitz-Wetzor, trans., *The Russian Primary Chronicle, Laurentian Text* (Cambridge, Mass., 1953), pp. 55-56, referred to hereafter as *Chronicle*.

7. A Turkic-speaking people from Asia, the Khazars (for whom Soloviev uses the name *kozary*) in the seventh century A.D. established a thriving commercial

state extending from the lower Volga to the northern Caucasus. They provided stability in the area until their rule was broken by the Russians in approximately 967.

8. Soloviev points out (see p. 37, 90) that in early Russian history the word "boyar" (*boiarin*, probably of Old Turkish origin) designated a man who, of his own volition and only for so long as he wished, held a high position in a prince's retinue, which gave him the right to act and be heard in an advisory capacity. During the Muscovite period the term referred to a member of the service nobility of the first rank, appointment to which was formally made by the tsar. In this translation (see p. 94) Soloviev lists the names of families with the right to pass directly to the rank of boyar and those who had first to enter the second highest rank, that of lord-in-waiting (*okolnichii*). Soloviev also mentions the way in which new boyars were created and describes the response to this policy by boyars with older hereditary claims to the rank (see pp. 95-98). It may be noted that in Russia only the rank of prince (*kniaz*) was fully hereditary in the sense that it was acquired by an eligible member of a princely family independent of the tsar's consent.

9. Soloviev's phrase is *variago-russkie kniazia*. The traditional date for the arrival of the Varangian Russes, as given in the Russian Primary Chronicle, is 862 (*Chronicle*, p. 59). Whether they were Scandinavians or Slavs, or a combination of both, or whether the event took place at all, has been the subject of considerable debate in Russian historiography.

10. *Webster's Third New International Dictionary* (hereafter *Webster's Third*) provides an anglicized form for *bogatyr*, defining it as "one of the legendary medieval heroes of Russia." However, it does not appear to have been used in this sense until about 1240. For a brief discussion of the word's possible etymology and its use in Russian oral literature, see I.F. Hapgood, *The Epic Songs of Russia* (New York: Charles Scribner's Sons, 1916), p. xxii, n. 1. See also George P. Majeska, "Bogatyri," in Joseph L. Wieczynski, ed., *The Modern Encyclopedia of Russian and Soviet History* [MERSH] (50 vols., Gulf Breeze, Fla.: Academic International Press, 1976-), 4, 15-17.

11. *Webster's Third* provides an anglicized form for *muzhik*, defining it as "a Russian peasant." In the present work Soloviev often contrasts it with *muzh* (literally "man"), here translated as "magnate."

12. Oleg is described in the Russian Primary Chronicle as having begun his rule in Novgorod in 879. In 882 he moved to Kiev, where he reigned as grand prince until 912. See *Chronicle*, pp. 60-69.

13. Soloviev's transcription of the passage is: *Tut vek pro Dobryniu starinu skazhut, sinemu moriu na tishinu, vam vsem, dobrym liudiam, na poslushanie.* In M.A. Poltoratskaia's *Russkii folklor* (New York, 1964), p. 124, there is a comparable passage from a bylina [epic song] about Dobrynia Nikitich: *To starina, to i deianie: / Sinemu moriu na uteshenie, / Bystrym rekam slava do moria, / A dobrym liudiam na poslushanie, / Veselym molodtsam na poteshenie.* However, in contradistinction to Soloviev's description of the passage as an introductory formula, in Poltoratskaia's anthology it stands as a coda marking the end of the bylina. On the bylina, see D.N. Pushkarev, "Bylini," in MERSH, 6, 69-71.

14. The Russian Primary Chronicle is one of the earliest indigenous written sources for the history of Russia. Originally thought to have been the work of a

single monk, Nestor, it was shown by later scholarship to be the work of different individuals. The beginning of its compilation has been traced to the second decade of the twelfth century. Its coverage of events begins with the year A.D. 852 and extends to 1116. For an analysis of its authorship and composition, see *Chronicle*, pp. 3-50.

15. Yaroslav, known as "the Wise," inherited Novgorod in 1015 upon the death of his father, Vladimir, who introduced Christianity into Russia on a large scale. In 1019, after warfare with his brothers, Yaroslav gained the grand principality of Kiev, where he reigned until his death in 1054. The period of his rule marked the zenith of early Russian history, with Kiev preeminent as a political, cultural, and economic center.

16. In the Russian Primary Chronicle, under the entry for the years 860-862, Riurik is described as the eldest of three brothers summoned by the native Slavs and other Finnish tribes to rule over them. He established his capital in Novgorod, where he remained until his death in 869. See *Chronicle*, pp. 59-60.

17. The incident referred to by Soloviev is mentioned in the Russian Primary Chronicle under the year 945. Igor, grand prince of Kiev from 913 to 945, is described as having demanded from the Slavic tribe of Derevlians an additional tribute besides the regular payment he had collected already. Thereupon the Derevlians ambushed him and the small part of his retinue with which he had visited them. See *Chronicle*, p. 78.

18. In about the year 991 a highly articulate pagan priest named Bogomil succeeded in causing a widespread resurgence of paganism in Novgorod. The grand prince of Kiev, Vladimir, who had introduced Christianity some three years earlier, sent his uncle to Novgorod to bring about the restoration of the Christian faith, which apparently was carried out with the use of force. See S.M. Soloviev, *Istoriia Rossii s drevneishikh vremen* (Moscow, 1959), 1:186; hereafter referred to as Soloviev, *Istoriia*.

19. Sviatoslav, grand prince of Kiev from 962 to 972, conducted an aggressive policy of expansion that saw Russian conquests in the east along the Volga, in the south along the coast of the Black Sea, and in the southwest across the Danube river. For a time, before being expelled by Byzantine forces, he considered establishing his new capital in Bulgaria.

20. The Kiev Monastery of the Caves (*Kievo-Pecherskaia lavra*) was founded in 1051 by monks who had clustered in the caves of a hill not far from the princely residence of Berestovo. The monastery soon became an important religious and cultural center.

21. The "invitation of the princes" refers to the episode described in notes 9 and 16, and is dated in the Russian Primary Chronicle under the year 862. The death of Grand Prince Yaroslav occurred 192 years later.

22. The period referred to by Soloviev extends from 1054 to 1174. Andrei Bogoliubsky, prince of Rostov and Suzdal after 1157, moved his capital to the city of Vladimir in the north, enhancing its prestige greatly after the capture of Kiev in 1169 during a civil war. See David M. Goldfrank, "Andrei Bogoliubskii," in MERSH, 1, 218-221.

23. Vladimir Monomakh, grand prince of Kiev from 1113 to 1125, left a testament, or instruction, to his children. It is included, apparently as an interpolation, in the Laurentian text of the Russian Primary Chronicle following the events of 1096 (*Chronicle*, pp. 206-15).

24. In Soloviev this final sentence reads simply, "–thus spoke Igor's retinue." Sveneld was one of Prince Igor's generals. Granted permission to collect his own tribute, he used part of it to reward generously those who accompanied him. The complaint of Igor's retainers, and the unfavorable comparison they drew between their own wealth and that of Sveneld's men, led Igor to his disastrous encounter with the Derevlians (see note 17).

25. The episode with the spoons is related under the years 994-996 in the Russian Primary Chronicle. See *Chronicle*, p. 122.

26. A grivna constituted the basis of the old Russian monetary system. The word originally referred to a neck ring, such as worn by a chieftain. There were three units of grivna: gold, silver, and marten skins. The early silver grivna took the form of a hexagonal bar of silver, elongated at each end, weighing approximately one troy pound. As a unit of money, the grivna equaled half a pound of silver until the second quarter of the twelfth century, when its value began to decline. From the fifteenth to the seventeenth century, one grivna was valued at 20 dengas, and 10 grivnas were equivalent to one ruble.

27. The term *veche* is here translated as "urban assembly."

28. In 1068 rebellious elements in Kiev overthrew Grand Prince Iziaslav and released from prison Vseslav, whom they proclaimed their new ruler (see *Chronicle*, pp. 148-49).The Polovetsians, known also as Cumans, were a Turkic people who are recorded in the Russian Primary Chronicle as having first invaded Russia in 1061 (see *Chronicle*, p. 143). They remained in the steppes thereafter until driven out by the Tatars in the second quarter of the thirteenth century.

29. The Great Water Route, or Greek Road, consisted of a series of rivers, lakes and fords connecting the Baltic and Black seas. The southern part of the route, including the portion below Kiev, consisted of the Dnieper river and the Black Sea. Extensive commercial expeditions were launched every year along this road, with its southernmost terminus in Constantinople.

30. The reference is to Prince Oleg (see note 12).

31. In this sentence Soloviev is of course dealing with an earlier period (when the Slavs were compelled to move northeastward into the east European plain) than in the preceding paragraph (when he describes the second prince as moving from north to south).

32. Andrei Bogoliubsky contended with Mstislav of Kiev over Novgorod. It was this struggle that had as one of its consequences the sack of Kiev by Andrei's forces in 1169 (see note 22).

33. Yaroslav, son of Grand Prince Vsevolod of Vladimir, held Pereiaslavl as his hereditary principality in the north. He also acceded to the princely throne of Novgorod at the invitation of its townspeople, with whom he maintained stormy relations. On one occasion Yaroslav seized some 2,000 merchants from Novgorod while they were in Torzhok. Later he had additional confrontations with the great commercial city of the north. (For Soloviev's account of these conflicts, see his *Istoriia*, 2:32, 46.) After the death of his elder brother at the hands of the invading Tatars in 1237, Yaroslav became grand prince of Vladimir until his own death in 1246.

34. Translation of *oprichniny* (sing. *oprichnina*).

35. In 1245 Pope Eugene IV appointed a Franciscan friar, Joannes de Plano Carpini, to undertake the first formal Catholic mission to the Tatars. His journey

to Mongolia and back took him twice through Kiev and its environs, whose devastation he vividly described in his history of the Mongols and description of Tartary.

36. Vsevolod "the Big Nest" (from the large number of his offspring) was grand prince of Vladimir from 1176 to 1212.

37. The system of precedence (*mestnichestvo*) was a method for appointing individuals to civil and military posts in Muscovy. Eligibility was determined by a complicated set of calculations that took into consideration a person's genealogical standing within his own family and the relative standing of families among each other. The system lasted from the second half of the fifteenth century until 1682, when it was formally abolished.

37. Dmitry "of the Don," or Donskoy, was grand prince of Vladimir and Moscow from 1359 to 1389. Dmitry compelled the other Russian princes of the northeast to recognize him as their "senior brother," thereby elevating his own preeminence among them and that of his capital city, Moscow. In 1380 Dmitry inflicted the first major defeat upon the Tatars by a Russian force at Kulikovo Field near the headwaters of the Don river, from which he gained his epithet.

39. The Golden Horde was the name used in the Russian sources to designate the part of the Mongol empire, with its capital at Sarai on the Volga, which came to be established in Russia after the invasion of 1237-1240. Later, as the empire broke up into its component parts, the name continued to be employed in reference to an independent Tatar state until its extinction in 1502. After the Tatars had conquered Russia they imposed a heavy tribute, payable apparently in silver. At first, special Tatar officers performed the task of collection. In 1328, however, the grand prince of Vladimir was designated tribute collector by the Tatar khan. In that same year (or possibly in 1332 according to some opinion), the prince of Moscow received the khan's appointment as grand prince of Vladimir. The combination of these offices and functions heightened the influence and increased the material resources of the prince of Moscow.

40. Vasily Veliaminov, the last commander of Moscow's city militia, died in 1374. Grand Prince Dmitry Donskoy thereafter refrained from filling the vacancy.

41. The reference is to Vasily II "the Dark" (so-called, according to popular tradition, because he was blinded by his cousin in a civil war), grand prince of Moscow from 1425 to 1462.

42. Riurik (said to have died in 879), the traditional founder of the first Russian ruling dynasty, is juxtaposed here with Gedimin (who died in approximately 1340), prince of Lithuania, under whom that country became a great power in Eastern Europe. In Moscow the princely descendants of Riurik and Gedimin contended with each other for rank and honor under the system of precedence in the service of the grand prince of Moscow (who, of course, was considered as belonging to one branch of the Riurik dynasty).

43. The term *okolnichii*, the court rank next below that of boyar, is translated as "lord-in-waiting." For Soloviev's description of the qualifications required for admission into this rank and the functions associated with it, see p. 90 of the present translation.

44. The term *dumnye liudi* is translated as "councillors." See p. 51 of the present translation.

45. During the interregnum in Poland-Lithuania from 1572 to 1574 the name of Ivan the Terrible's son, as well as that of Ivan himself, was brought up as possible

successor to King Sigismund II. The negotiations proved fruitless with respect to the selection of a Russian candidate.

46. In 1472 Ivan III married Zoe Paleologue, niece of the last emperor of the Byzantine Empire. After the fall of Constantinople in 1453, Zoe's father, Thomas, had maintained his position as despot of Morea until 1460, when he fled with his children to Rome. Zoe, having converted to Catholicism, lived under the protection of the pope, whose representatives, perceiving a favorable opportunity for missionary activity and the possibility of engaging Russian support against the Turks, were instrumental in arranging the marriage with Ivan. Upon her arrival on Russian territory Zoe converted to Orthodoxy, at which time she received the name Sophia.

47. The reference is to Vasily III, grand prince of Moscow and all Russia from 1505 to 1533.

48. The boyar Ivan Bersen-Beklemishev wrote disapprovingly about the way Vasily III conducted affairs of state, not in traditional consultation with the boyars, but with people of unimpressive background whom he personally selected and met in private.

49. Ivan IV "the Terrible" succeeded to the throne of the grand principality of Moscow in 1533 upon the death of his father, Vasily III. In 1547 he was crowned tsar and continued to reign until his death in 1584.

50. During Ivan the Terrible's reign, Muscovy from 1565 to 1572 came to be divided geographically and administratively into two separate regions, both eventually about equal in size. One part consisted of a Regular Administration (*Zemshchina*) in which the traditional organs of state administration continued operating in their customary manner. The other became subject to the Extraordinary Administration (*Oprichnina*) in which the tsar was free to select as officials those whom he personally favored without regard to long-standing claims concerning precedence. After 1572, when Ivan had strengthened his political power at the expense of the nobility, no further reference to the Extraordinary Administration is made in the sources. In its place, mention is made of the tsar's "court" (*dvor*).

51. Some historians place the beginning of the Time of Troubles, a calamitous period for the Muscovite state, in 1598. Soloviev favors the year 1604. Its arrival was heralded by the extinction, with the death of Tsar Fedor in 1598, of the Muscovite branch of the ruling line of Riurik. Numerous crises followed: a long series of severe famines, the appearance of impostors claiming to be the legitimate tsar, social unrest, internal rebellion, and foreign invasion—including occupation of Novgorod by Swedes and Moscow by Poles. The western, central, and southern parts of the Muscovite state were severely affected. In response to calls for national unity from ecclesiastical authorities, order was restored with cossack assistance by a militia from the free cities of the north. The period ended in 1613 with the election of Tsar Michael by a national assembly, marking the start of the Romanov dynasty.

52. During the Time of Troubles the village of Tushino near Moscow became the temporary "capital" of an impostor claiming to be Dmitry, the son of Ivan the Terrible and legitimate heir to the throne. A considerable traffic developed between the Kremlin and Tushino as noblemen, bureaucrats, and clergymen sought to discover which of the two centers of power held greater advantages.

53. Afanasy Lavrentievich Ordin-Nashchokin (ca. 1605-1680) was born in Pskov, the son of a member of the service gentry. After his period of education,

which included the study of foreign languages, he entered state service, fulfilling both military and civil duties. He held high diplomatic posts and was elevated to the rank of boyar. From 1667 to 1671 he served as director of the Ambassadorial Chancellery. One of the leading progressive thinkers of the time, he was very much interested in carrying out military and economic reforms along Western models. Soloviev devotes considerable attention to Ordin-Nashchokin's efforts later in the present work, where he also indicates his significance as one of the persons in influential positions who began promoting reforms along new, predominantly secular lines.

54. Artamon Sergeevich Matveev (1625-1682) was a noted diplomat and government official. For his services the tsar raised him to the rank of boyar. Matveev strongly promoted a foreign policy that envisioned annexation of the entire Ukraine by Muscovy. He replaced Ordin-Nashchokin as director of the Ambassadorial Chancellery. As guardian of Natalia Naryshkin, he introduced his ward to the widowed Tsar Alexis. A marriage was arranged, from which union a boy was born in 1672 who was to become Peter the Great. As mentioned later by Soloviev, Matveev also supervised the composition of various books useful for conducting foreign relations.

55. As the leading ecclesiastical dignitary of the Russian church from 1308 to 1326, Metropolitan Peter is regarded as having made a crucial decision in transferring his residence from the city of Vladimir to Moscow, whose reputation he also advanced by selecting it as the place of his interment. Alexis, discussed at greater length here by Soloviev, was metropolitan from 1353 to 1378 and eventually was canonized a saint by the Russian church. The accession of Jonas to the metropolitan see in 1448 marked an important departure from customary procedure. It was accomplished by the Russian bishops, in cooperation with Grand Prince Vasily II, without the usual authorization from Constantinople. Accordingly, it signified the beginning of an independent Russian church.

56. Sergius of Radonezh (ca. 1321-1391), born near the city of Rostov the Great, came from a boyar family. About 1345, together with his brother Stefan, he founded Holy Trinity monastery, which came to have a similar importance in relation to Moscow as the Monastery of the Caves held for Kiev. He assisted Dmitry Donskoy in preparing with his benediction of Russian military forces to contend successfully against the Tatars at Kulikovo Field in 1380. After his death Sergius was canonized a saint by the Russian church, and the monastery he founded came to be known as the Holy Trinity-St. Sergius monastery.

57. In 1469 the patriarch of Constantinople authorized the installation of an Orthodox metropolitan in Kiev, who would remain subject to his, the patriarch's jurisdiction. Moscow, which since 1448 had its own independently elected metropolitan, refused to recognize the authority of the new metropolitan in Kiev. Thus, two metropolitans of Russia came to exercise ecclesiastical control in separate obediences. As Soloviev indicates later, the existence of the second metropolitan see sometimes played an important role in the relations between Russian principalities, as when Novgorod sought to extricate itself from growing ecclesiastical domination, which meant also growing political domination, by Moscow.

58. Prince Vasily Patrikeev opposed the growth of absolutism under Grand Prince Ivan III. For his opposition he was compelled to take monastic vows (whereupon he became known as Vassian or, popularly, Vassian Kosoy) and exiled from the capital. He returned under Ivan's successor, Vasily III, and supported the

position of those who advocated the independence of the church as opposed to the development of close ties between it and the state. At the same time he argued against the large landed estates owned by monasteries, pointing to the distressing conditions under which peasants lived there. He did not take a similar stand with respect to the abolition of landed estates in the hands of laymen. Consequently, even though a monk, Vassian has been regarded as a spokesman for the interests of the boyars and princes. His death occurred sometime before 1545.

59. Ivan Sanin, who assumed the name Joseph upon becoming a monk, was born about 1440, the son of a wealthy landowner in the principality of Volokolamsk. There, not far from Moscow, he founded in 1479 a monastery which came to bear his name. Early in his career Joseph opposed the increasing concentration of monarchical power in Moscow. Later he switched his position and became the leading ideological supporter of it. He also favored ownership of large landed estates by monasteries, arguing in part that this was a necessary precondition for fulfilling their charitable functions. His position, that of the so-called "possessors," came to prevail at a church council in 1503, where the objections of the "non-possessors" under the leadership of Nilus Sorsky and Vassian Kosoy, were repudiated.

60. The point made by Soloviev's reference to Alexis, Vassian, and Joseph appears to be that whenever persons of noble birth or high social standing entered the church administration or even simply the monastic rank, they tended to preserve their original class viwepoints and habits of outspokenness. However, their numbers were small. Consequently, although individual exceptions did exist, their influence was sporadic.

61. The parochial, or secular, clergy (which was not required to take monastic vows and whose members, indeed, had to be married before ordination) was known in Russia as the white clergy, as opposed to the black (monastic) clergy. Bishops and other ranking church officials normally were drawn from the latter category.

62. Vasily I, son of Dmitry Donskoy, was grand prince of Vladimir and Moscow from 1389 to 1425.

63. In 1375 Cyprian was elevated to the rank of metropolitan and spent his first fifteen years in that capacity in Lithuania. Thereupon he came to Moscow, where he continued to serve as metropolitan until 1406. He later was canonized by the Russian church.

64. The primate of the Russian church was elevated from the rank of metropolitan to patriarch in 1589, a change effected largely at the initiative of Boris Godunov. As the foremost state official in the reign of Tsar Fedor I, Godunov undertook to conduct negotiations with the patriarch of Constantinople and bring them to a successful conclusion.

65. This method of appointing officials to lucrative local posts was known as kormlenie, literally "feeding." Its abolition was begun by the central government in the reign of Ivan the Terrible.

66. The legal condition of pledged dependence was known as zakladnichestvo.

67. See note 37.

68. These are translations of the Russian terms sosedi, podsosedniki, and zakhrebetniki, respectively.

69. Tsar Alexis occupied the throne of the Muscovite state from 1645 to 1676.

70. See note 40.

71. The tribune in Red Square (*Lobnoe mesto*) was erected in 1534. Used originally by the tsar and ecclesiastical dignitaries as a dais from which to address the people, it was designated officially in 1685 as a place of execution.

72. The Shuiskys were a prominent boyar family, whose lineage was traced to Riurik. After the extinction of the Moscow branch of the Riurik dynasty, the Shuiskys strongly opposed the candidacy to the throne of Boris Godunov, whose family had entered Muscovite service at a comparatively recent time and whose genealogy traced back to the Tatars. After Godunov's election Vasily Shuisky apparently was actively involved in a conspiracy to overthrow him by asserting the legitimacy of an imposter claiming to be Dmitry, son of Ivan the Terrible. The plan worked, but only initially. Godunov died, the impostor was killed, and Shuisky acceded to the throne as tsar in 1606. However, he did not succeed in establishing a Shuisky dynasty, or even in keeping himself on the throne for long. Because of internal turbulence and foreign invasion, Shuisky was deposed in 1610 and confined to a monastery.

73. Boris Godunov held the position of chief regent during the reign of Tsar Fedor I (1584-1598). After Fedor's death a national assembly was summoned at which, with the support of the clergy and military servitors, Godunov was elected tsar. Natural calamities, internal disturbances, opposition from the boyars, and the appearance of an impostor claiming the throne marked the turbulent end of Godunov's brief reign. He died in 1605.

74. Tsar Michael, first of the Romanov dynasty, was chosen to occupy the throne by a national assembly in 1613. His reign lasted until 1645.

75. The term *sobory* (sing. *sobor*), literally "councils," is here translated as "national assemblies." Soloviev gives additional attention to these gatherings on pp. 101-2, where they are referred to as councils or extraordinary meetings (*chrezvychainye soveshchaniia*). Nowhere in the present work does Soloviev specifically use the term "national assembly" (*zemsky sobor*). It is, nevertheless, employed at this point in the translation because of its familiarity.

76. *Webster's Third* gives "voivode" as an anglicized form of *voevoda*. The term refers to military governors of districts or provinces, who performed a variety of functions: military command, financial administration, police, and justice. The use of voevodes for local administration became particularly prevalent after the Time of Troubles when the institutions of local self-government, which had begun to appear throughout the Muscovite state in the reign of Ivan the Terrible, proved inadequate in the face of foreign invasion and internal rebellion. See pp. 119-40 for a detailed description of the characteristics and functions of the military governors.

77. Moscow experienced violent unrest in 1648 (which resulted in the summoning of a national assembly and enactment of the code of 1649) and in the "copper riots" of 1662 (arising from the government's debasement of the coinage).

78. The reference is to the account in the Russian Primary Chronicle about the revenge wrought by Grand Princess Olga upon the Derevlians for the death of her husband, Igor. In the Chronicle, passing reference is made to the capital city of the Derevlians, Iskorosten, whose wooden construction rendered it particularly vulnerable to destruction by fire. See *Chronicle*, p. 81.

79. Ivan the Terrible engaged in a long conflict, the so-called Livonian War, against Poland-Lithuania and Sweden. After a quarter century of occasionally

intense, but mostly sporadic fighting, treaties were signed with Poland-Lithuania in 1582 and Sweden in 1583 that wiped out all gains made by the Russians during the war and frustrated Ivan's principal aim of obtaining direct access to the Baltic Sea. Unlike the peoples of Asia, the enemy in the West proved to be far more formidable because of superior tactics, organization, and technology. The weakness of Russian arms would be a telling factor in the subsequent Time of Troubles.

80. Soloviev develops this point further on pp. 206-8.

81. Ermak, son of a cossack and a Danish slave girl, escaped as a young man from sentence of death for horse stealing. He was hired by the powerful Stroganov merchant family to protect their vast holdings and enterprises beyond the Volga from the Tatars. In 1582 Ermak led a force of some 800 freebooters to the central course of the Ob river, where he captured the capital of the Siberian khanate, presenting his newly-won prize to the tsar, Ivan the Terrible.

82. A man of obscure origins (the Muscovite government officially maintained that he was a certain Grigory Otrepiev, a renegade deacon from the Miracles monastery in Moscow), the Impostor, or False Dmitry, claimed to be the youngest son of Ivan the Terrible and legitimate heir to the throne. Aided by a boyar faction in Moscow which opposed the coronation of Boris Godunov, and with the backing of Polish magnates, False Dmitry raised an army of cossacks, Polish adventurers, and a growing number of malcontents as he crossed the border from Poland-Lithuania into Muscovy in 1604. The following year he was crowned tsar, but his reign was brief. He was overthrown and killed in 1606 after losing his support among the boyars.

83. After the coup d'etat that overthrew the first False Dmitry, a second False Dmitry arose among the cossacks. For a time he presided as "tsar" at his capital in the village of Tushino on the outskirts of Moscow (see note 52). After abandoning it in 1609 when his situation became precarious, he retired to the safety of Kaluga, about 90 miles southwest of Moscow.

84. Stenka (or Stepan) Razin came to be celebrated in popular songs and stories for the rebellion he led in 1670-1671. The movement started with discontented elements among the cossacks along the lower Don river, but spread to become a general uprising, attracting masses of Russians and non-Russian natives. Eventually Razin was apprehended by regular cossack leaders and handed over to government authorities for execution.

85. See note 81.

86. Kondraty Bulavin and Emelian Pugachev were rebel leaders during the reigns of Peter the Great and Catherine the Great, respectively. For a time it appeared that Pugachev's widespread rebellion of 1773-1774 might bear threateningly on Moscow itself.

CHAPTER II

1. The belfry of Ivan the Great, which today rises to a height of 320 feet, was completed under Boris Godunov in 1600 as part of his program of public works.

2. The term *veliky gosudar,* a traditional designation for the tsar, is translated as "great sovereign."

3. In 1571 a large Tatar force attacked Moscow, broke through its outer defenses, burned the city outside the Kremlin, and carried off some 150,000 captives.

4. In 1703 Peter the Great constructed his new capital, St. Petersburg, in the delta of the Neva river.

5. For sixteen months in 1608-1609 a force of some 30,000 men belonging to the second Flase Dmitry besieged Holy Trinity-St. Sergius monastery without success.

6. The musketeers (*streltsy*, literally "shooters") were founded about 1552 by Ivan IV as Muscovite infantry regiments. They resided in special districts assigned to them in various cities, where they constituted a police force during peacetime. Besides their salaries from the state, which were not only insufficient but also often pocketed by their commanders, the musketeers received an income from activity in petty trade. The regiments of musketeers continued an often turbulent existence until their abolition by Peter the Great.

7. *Webster's Third* gives "kvass" as an anglicized form of *kvas*, a mildly alcoholic beverage made from bread or grain, sometimes with the addition of raisins.

8. In Russia the observance of Palm Sunday traditionally has been celebrated with willow branches in place of palm leaves.

9. The feasts of the Dormition (known as the Assumption in the West) and of St. Peter are celebrated on 28 August and 12 July, respectively (as adjusted for the twentieth century from 15 August and 29 June according to the Julian calendar).

10. The Hall of Facets (*Granovitaia palata*), built between 1487 and 1491 and finished in faceted white stone, is one of the oldest civil buildings in Moscow. It contains a single chamber, 29 feet high, with 530 square yards of floor area.

11. Kitai-gorod was a walled district in Moscow that adjoined the Kremlin and included Red Square. Its name, which came to be used in the sixteenth century, derives from *kita* (meaning "thatch") and referred to the original defensive wall around the area, consisting of an earthen rampart reinforced with thatch. This type of construction was later replaced by stone walls.

12. White City (*Belyi gorod*) refers to the district of Moscow which was enclosed by a large wall, interspersed with 28 towers and nine gates. It was constructed between 1586 and 1593 at an average distance of approximately 1.2 miles beyond the Kremlin. The wall ran in a semicircle to the north, with the Moskva river to the south completing the system of defense. Towards the end of this volume Soloviev mentions White City in connection with disturbances involving foreigners in Muscovite service.

13. Soloviev deliberately uses the word for slaves, *kholopia*.

14. Ivan Gramotin was a Russian diplomat who became chancellor of the council under the first False Dmitry. He went on to serve the second False Dmitry. Later he became an agent for the king of Poland, in whose campaign against Moscow he took part. Apparently while in Poland he became closely acquainted with Philaret, who was the father of the future tsar, Michael, and who was later himself to become patriarch of Moscow. With such powerful support, Gramotin after the Time of Troubles managed to preserve his position as keeper of the seal and chancellor of the council. He died in 1638.

15. Andrei and Vasily Shchelkalov were influential chancellors prominent in the area of foreign relations during the reign of Ivan the Terrible.

16. A church council in 1666-1667, attended by the patriarchs of Alexandria and Antioch, divested Nikon of his patriarchal rank. For a further discussion of Nikon, see pp. 178-82.

17. The Privy Chancellery (*Prikaz tainykh del*), founded in 1654, originally functioned in the area of the tsar's private matters. For Soloviev's description of its origin and functions, see p. 117.

18. See note 54 of Chapter I.

19. A person named Peter, for instance, would be referred to, and would refer to himself, in official correspondence as Petrushka (Little Peter). The practice of using diminutives this way, though not of course informally by individuals, was abolished by Peter the Great on 30 December 1701 (Soloviev, *Istoriia*, 8:88).

20. Before the consolidation of the Muscovite state at the end of the fifteenth and beginning of the sixteenth century, numerous Russian princes ruled over their independent principalities as over hereditary estates, succession to which typically proceeded by way of apportionment from father to all the sons. Moscow itself for a long while constituted such a patrimonial principality, or appanage (*udel*).

21. At the beginning of the seventeenth century, during the Time of Troubles, a number of impostors besides False Dmitry appeared among the cossacks with fanciful dynastic claims to the disputed Muscovite throne. Among them, in Astrakhan, was an individual posing as a Tsarevich Augustus.

22. In 1649, during the reign of Tsar Alexis, a new code of laws was enacted, which continued to form the basis of Russian jurisprudence until 1830. Clearly partial in terms of drawing legal distinctions between classes, it favored the interests of the service gentry and merchants as against those of the clergy and peasants.

23. Prince Valdemar was the son of the king of Denmark, Christian IV. This episode, which took place in December 1643, is described by Soloviev in *Istoriia*, 5:236.

24. The formula in Russian is: *Gosudar ukazal i boiare prigovorili.*

25. Soloviev's rendering of this formula is: *Po ukazu v. gosudaria i po prikazu diakov sdelano to-to.* Some Russian historians (e.g., Nicholas Zagoskin) have held that, with respect to decisions in council, the determination by the boyars carried equal force with the tsar's command. Soloviev here points out that commands from the tsar and orders from chancellors, which can in no way be regarded as having equal force, were also placed in formulaic juxtaposition.

26. The Russian phrase as given by Soloviev is *vznosit dela k boiaram vverkh.*

27. Soloviev's terminology is *chrezvychainoe soveshchanie* (translated as "extraordinary meeting") or *sobor* (translated as "assembly").

28. Since 1569, with the Union of Lublin, Poland and Lithuania had been united in a single state. Hence the alleged injustices of the Polish king called for a campaign against Lithuania, which was geographically adjacent to Muscovy.

29. The terms *vybornye liudi* and *sovetnye liudi* are here translated as "elected representatives" and "advisers," respectively.

30. The term *deti boiarskie* is translated as "junior boyars." In the early period of Russian history the term was applied to lower-ranking members of the princely retinues who held posts appropriate to "children (sons) of boyars," the literal meaning of the term. In the fifteenth and sixteenth centuries, it came to refer to a category of service people whose function often was that of provincial cavalrymen.

31. For the early period of Russian history it is correct to translate *dvorianin* as "courtier." For the Muscovite period, starting with approximately the middle

of the fifteenth century, a more appropriate translation is "member of the service gentry."

32. See note 25 of Chapter I.

33. The reference is to Ivan Pososhkov (1652-1726), son of a silversmith. He became noted in the reign of Peter the Great as a writer on the economic foundations of the state. In the aftermath of the miserable showing by Russian armed forces at the siege of Narva in 1700, he wrote a work entitled *On Military Conduct (O ratnom povedenii)*, from which Soloviev excerpts the passage quoted in the text.

34. The Russian phrase is *byt u del i kormitsia*, "to administer official business and receive subsistence."

35. The contemporary Russian phrase was *ustroeny vechnym zhitiem.*

36. This select regiment of musketeers was known as *stremennyi*, "of the stirrup," referring to its customary proximity to the tsar's conveyance.

37. An alphabetical list of chancelleries mentioned by Soloviev, together with their Russian names, is contained in Appendix 2.

38. See note 54 of Chapter I.

39. The cossack hetman Ivan Samoilovich actually promoted Ukrainian unification under Moscow. Later, accused of treasonable relations with the Crimean Tatars, he was exiled to Siberia, where he died in 1690.

40. In 1667 a treaty signed at Andrusovo, a village just south of Smolensk, ended a long series of wars between Muscovy and Poland-Lithuania over control of the Ukraine. The new border was fixed for the most part along the Dnieper river, with the territory east of it, the so-called "right-bank Ukraine," passing to Moscow. Poland also ceded Kiev for two years, but the Muscovite presence there became permanent. The successful negotiator for Tsar Alexis at the numerous sessions prior to the signing of the treaty was Ordin-Nashchokin.

41. If Soloviev is correct, this is a rather curious metaphorical reference to the eye, usually thought of as observing rather than being observed.

42. The Russian text reads *Prikaz kamennykh zhitnits*, literally "Chancellery for Stone Storehouses." The reference is probably to the *Prikaz kazennykh zhitnits*, which is here translated as "Chancellery for State Storehouses."

43. Two hundred fifty to 350 chetverts. One chetvert equals half a desiatin, and one desiatin equals about 2.7 acres. In the Muscovite period chetverts were computed in "three fields," which means that one chetvert was equivalent to 1½ desiatins, or approximately 4.1 acres.

44. Lukh is located approximately 200 miles northeast of Moscow.

45. Tikhonova Pustyn is located about 90 miles southwest of Moscow. Prince Repnin's village, Myt, stood between it and Lukh.

46. In June 1648 a spontaneous popular uprising broke out in Moscow. At the heart of widespread dissatisfaction was the existence of governmental corruption, particularly on the part of powerfully placed members of the tsar's family. Tsar Alexis appeared personally in public to quiet the turmoil. His assurance that justice would be done was followed by the exile and punishment of the most flagrant violators. See also note 77 of Chapter I.

47. The term *meshchane* derives from the Polish *mieszczanin*, "burgher." The word came to be applied to the petty bourgeoisie generally, often with a derogatory connotation.

48. In 1656 the Muscovite government began issuing copper coins as a substitute for those made of silver, a move which contributed to rising inflation and popular

unrest. This measure, combined with the government's later decision to buy back the copper coins at one percent of their face value, triggered the so-called "copper riots" in Moscow in 1662. See also note 77 of Chapter I.

49. Serfdom in Russia was abolished in 1861.

50. Soloviev at this point makes reference exclusively to urban taxpayers. However, the contrast he makes in the following sentence concerning "the two parts of the population" stands out more clearly if the statement here is taken as including all taxpayers generally, both urban and rural.

51. War with Poland-Lithuania erupted in 1654 and lasted until 1667, with an interruption between 1656 and 1658. The conclusion of the war was marked by the signing of the treaty of Andrusovo (see note 40).

52. From 1656 to 1658 Moscow and Sweden fought over the issue of intervention in beleaguered Poland-Lithuania. The war was brought to an end by the inconclusive treaty of Cardis in 1661.

53. The expansion of Muscovy into the Ukraine provoked intermittent conflicts with the cossacks there. The latter sometimes sided with the Poles, as was the case at the time of the Muscovite defeat at Konotop in 1659, which was brought about by the forces of the hetman, Ivan Vygovsky, and his allies, the Crimean Tatars. Moreover, Muscovite proximity to Turkish holdings led to numerous wars with the Ottoman Empire, the first of which lasted from 1672 to 1681.

54. See note 84.

55. Solovetsky monastery, located on an island in the White Sea, became a center of the Old Belief at the time of Patriarch Nikon's church reforms. Its monks, refusing to accept the new printed service books and ritualistic changes, held out against government forces in a siege lasting from 1668 to 1676.

56. The date in the Russian text is incorrectly given as 1762.

57. Ustiug Veliky, once a satellite city of Great Novgorod, is located on the left bank of the Northern Dvina river. In the seventeenth century it was famous for its embroideries, wood carvings, and silverwork.

58. Each urban taxable unit was known as a *sokha* (which, with a different meaning, was also the name for a basic unit of taxation on land in rural areas). The size of an urban *sokha* varied from place to place. Generally, at the beginning of the seventeenth century, it consisted of 40 best households, 50-60 medium, and 70-100 poor ones.

59. Soloviev's figures are: 9,526 chetverts of rye; 7,224 chetverts of oats; and 306 chetverts of barley. As a unit of dry measure, one chetvert equaled approximately six bushels.

60. The sum of 7,656 and 4,705 is, of course, 12,361, or one ruble less than the total cited in the text.

61. The word *kabak* has been translated as "tavern"; the franchised government outlet, *kruzhechnyi dvor*, has been rendered as "liquor warehouse and drinking establishment" or simply as "drinking establishment."

62. The term *vedro* is translated as "bucket." *Webster's Third* defines "vedro" as "a Russian unit of liquid capacity equal to 3.25 U.S. gallons or 2.71 imperial gallons."

63. The term *kruzhka* is translated as "mug," a unit of liquid measure variously equivalent to 1/8 or 1/10 of a bucket (*vedro*).

64. The term *charka* is translated as "cup," equal to 1/16 of a mug (*kruzhka*).

65. The reference is to one *pud* of honey. *Webster's Third* defines "pud" (for which it gives "pood" and "poud" as two other alternative anglicized spellings) as "a Russian unit of weight equal to about 36.11 pounds."

66. The amount in Russian is a *chetverik.*

67. Sophia, daughter of Tsar Alexis and his first wife, assumed control of the government with the aid of her favorite, Vasily Golitsyn, after the death of her brother Fedor in 1682. Her regency was brought to an end in 1689 by her younger half-brother, who was to become known as Peter the Great.

68. Each taxable unit (*soshka*) consisted of 122 acres of arable land. In this instance, the tax assessment was imposed on a total arable land area of 4,026 acres.

69. Kaigorodok (also Kaigorod), a town which was in the eastern part of Muscovy, is located approximately 185 miles northwest of Perm.

70. Shuia is located approximately 156 miles northeast of Moscow. Much of the material used by Soloviev in describing urban organization and city life in the Muscovite period was drawn from the records of Shuia.

71. Actually 99.435 miles. The distance given in the text is 150 versts (a verst being equal to 0.6629 miles).

72. Fedor III, son of Tsar Alexis, reigned from 1676 to 1682.

73. The term *muzhiki gorlany* is translated as "loud-mouthed big shots." Soloviev describes these individuals at greater length in *Istoriia*, 5:315-17.

74. In 1650 both Pskov and Novgorod experienced rioting directed against their upper classes and against exactions imposed by Moscow. A national assembly was summoned, which persuaded the townspeople of Pskov to end their rebellion. Despite their acquiescence, a punitive expedition against them was dispatched from Moscow.

75. The Stenka Kotiatnikov mentioned here by Ordin-Nashchokin is, of course, the same Stepan Kotiatnikov referred to earlier as being the elected chief of local administration in Pskov. Under Ordin-Nashchokin's plan for administrative reorganization, Kotiatnikov would have been responsible for collecting duties on alcoholic beverage sales from private tavern owners.

76. The New Commercial Statute (*Novotorgovyi ustav*) of 1667 consisted of an introduction, 94 articles, and seven supplementary articles dealing with foreign trade. With various additions incorporated after its enactment, the New Commercial Statute remained in effect until 1755, when it was replaced by the Customs Statute (*Tamozhennyi ustav*).

77. Efimoks were large silver coins minted in various cities of central and western Europe. Outside Russia, their common name was thalers. Pegged at 50 kopecks, or half a ruble, for internal circulation, they were widely used throughout Muscovy in the absence of large Russian coins. The silver Lithuanian zolotoy was equal to one ruble according to the rate of exchange prescribed by the New Commercial Statute, as Soloviev describes later in this section. A different valuation of the zolotoy puts it as having been equal to 20 kopecks. See S.G. Pushkarev, comp., *Dictionary of Russian Historical Terms from the Eleventh Century to 1917* (New Haven, 1970), p. 193.

78. Shklov is located on the right bank of the Dnieper river, approximately 22 miles north of Mogilev.

79. One *berkovets* equals 361.13 pounds of potash.

80. The Russian terms are *krestianin, bobyl,* and *zakhrebetnik,* respectively.

81. The reference here is again to the *soshka;* see note 68.
82. The total area involved in the assessment of taxes, based on 240 *soshka* units, was 29,280 acres.
83. The figures quoted by Soloviev are one grivna per chetvert from a total Siberian reserve supply of 2,270 chetverts. In the translation, the conversion to pounds is based on the officially fixed value, prevalent in the seventeenth century, of 48 puds per chetvert. In practice, the value of a chetvert was subject to frequent deviation, and the figures in the translation could conceivably be reduced by as much as half.
84. Verkhoturie is located east of the Ural mountains, beyond Perm.
85. Both these areas are in the northern Ukraine.

CHAPTER III

1. The reference here is to the reign of Ivan the Terrible, under whom Muscovy conquered the Tatar khanates of Kazan (1552), Astrakhan (1556), and Siberia (1582), but whose efforts at expansion westwards were thwarted in the disastrous Livonian War (1558-1583). See also note 79 of Chapter I.
2. The Ukraine, inhabited by a predominantly Orthodox population, lay within Poland-Lithuania, a Roman Catholic state, until a portion of it was annexed by Moscow. See notes 40 and 51 of Chapter II.
3. *Webster's Third* gives "protopope" as the anglicized version of *protopop.* Translated sometimes as "archpriest," it refers to the highest rank of the white, or married, clergy.
4. Russia was affected directly by the attempts to bring about a reunion of the Orthodox and Catholic churches at the Council of Florence (1439) and at Brest (1596).
5. Metropolitan Platon (1737-1812) was one of the leading figures in the field of education during the reign of Catherine the Great. A noted orator, he also served as religious tutor to the future emperor, Paul I. He became archbishop of Moscow in 1775, and was elevated to the rank of metropolitan in 1787.
6. Macarius was metropolitan of Moscow from 1542 to 1563. He exercised considerable influence during the early part of Ivan the Terrible's reign and was the ranking prelate at the Council of the Hundred Chapters in 1551, many of whose decisions were denounced as erroneous by later councils, such as that of 1621.
7. Philaret was patriarch of Moscow from 1619 to 1633. Prior to his enforced tonsure into the monastic rank in 1601 under Boris Godunov, Philaret bore the secular name Fedor Nikitich Romanov. Married to Ksenia Ivanovna Shastova (who later also was tonsured, assuming the monastic name Marfa), he was the father of the future Tsar Michael. After his elevation to the patriarchate, Philaret was involved actively in the administration of both church and state.
8. Joachim was patriarch of Moscow from 1674 to 1690.
9. Possibly a russianized version of "Say."
10. Nikon (1605-1681), born into a peasant family in the region of Nizhny Novgorod and given at baptism the name Nikita (Minov), was ordained into the priesthood at the age of twenty. In 1635 he became a monk and in 1646, as

hegumen of Kozheozersky monastery, he caught the notice of Tsar Alexis, whom he greatly impressed. Thereafter he rose rapidly through successively higher positions in the church hierarchy, being elected patriarch of Moscow in 1652. Once in that office he abandoned his earlier idea of effecting church reforms in accordance with traditional Russian ways and, instead, pushed strenuously for change on the basis of contemporary Greek models, which he came to regard as being in all respects more correct than their divergent Russian counterparts. After coming into conflict with the tsar and numerous state officials over a variety of issues, but principally over the limits of authority proper to church and state, he left Moscow in 1658 and was deposed formally as patriarch by the council of 1666-1667.

11. Philip was metropolitan of Moscow from 1566 to 1568, in the midst of the turbulent period of the Extraordinary Administration (see note 50 of Chap. 1). A scion of the boyar family of Kolychev, Philip assumed an outspoken stance against Ivan the Terrible over the excesses associated with the tsar's effort to strengthen, by violence if necessary, his supreme authority as autocrat. On 8 November 1568 a number of Ivan's followers appeared during the divine liturgy in the cathedral of the Dormition and proclaimed the metropolitan's deposition. He was incarcerated and later exiled to a monastery in Tver, where he was assassinated the following year by one of the tsar's agents, Maliuta Skuratov.

12. Joseph, patriarch of Moscow from 1642 to 1652, launched upon a program of revising church books. The publications issued under his auspices became greatly revered by the Old Believers, who denounced the new standards for correcting the books imposed by Joseph's successor, Nikon.

13. All these accusations, including the charges leveled against Ivan Kokoshilov, are contained in a petition described by Soloviev as having been lodged against Nikon not on the basis of his reforming activity, but on the ostensible grounds of his being an unsatisfactory patriarch. See Soloviev, *Istoriia*, 6:208-10.

14. Actually 5.4 acres. The area mentioned is two desiatins, each of which equals 2.7 acres.

15. As Soloviev describes in another volume, the flower of the Muscovite cavalry, under the reckless command of Prince Simon Pozharsky, was destroyed in a single day by Tatars and cossacks near the Ukrainian town of Konotop on 28 June 1659. Later, in a series of engagements in late September and early October 1660 at Chudnov in the Ukraine, the Muscovites lost an entire army and saw their renowned leader, Prince Vasily Sheremetev, taken prisoner by the Crimean Tatars. See Soloviev, *Istoriia*, 6:50-51, 88-92; see also note 53, Chap. II.

16. This is the year in which Nikon accepted the office of patriarch, having been elected to it by a council in 1652.

17. The patriarchal reserve (*patriarshaia oblast*) was a sizable area under the direct jurisdiction of the patriarch of Moscow.

18. The provision calls for three dengas from each chetvert (about 4.1 acres).

19. See p. 228

20. The Monasterial Chancellery (*Monastyrsky prikaz*), founded in accordance with the principles of the Code of 1649, was a central crown administrative agency staffed by laymen who exercised jurisdiction over all monasteries and clergy, and the peasant populations on their lands. Abolished in 1677, the year after Tsar Alexis' death, it was restored with a revised function by Peter the Great.

21. In 1687, at the initiative of Simeon Polotsky and his former student Silvestr Medvedev (known as Simeon Agafonnikovich before entering monastic life), there

was founded in Moscow the Slavic-Greek-Latin Academy, which had the distinction of being the first institution of higher education in Great Russia. Its name was changed to Moscow Theological Academy in 1814, at which time it was moved to Holy Trinity-St. Sergius monastery.

22. Translation of *Domostroy,* a collection of rules and principles governing the conduct of a townsman in his relations with the secular authorities, the clergy, his family, and servants. Soloviev is one of a number of historians who hold that the *Domostroy* was put into its final form by the protopope Silvester, a contemporary of Ivan the Terrible, from a work originating in Novgorod at the end of the fifteenth and beginning of the sixteenth century. Other authorities consider Silvester the sole author, who composed the work sometime after 1547.

23. Grigory Kotoshikhin, who was born about 1630, served as a clerk in the Ambassadorial Chancellery. He participated in two embassies to foreign countries before taking flight abroad in 1664. After working and traveling in different countries, Kotoshikhin arrived in Sweden in 1666. He was executed next year in Stockholm for murdering the owner of the house in which he resided. He left behind a largely unflattering description of his homeland, *Russia in the Reign of Tsar Alexis (O Rossii v tsarstvovanie tsaria Alekseia Mikhailovicha).*

24. Soloviev devotes considerable space to Simeon Polotsky. See pp. 217-24.

25. It is unlikely that *Temir Aksak* was performed on the stage, since it appears not in the form of a play, but of a tale *(povest),* which may, however, have been read aloud. It is divided into two parts, beginning with a legendary biography of Temir Aksak (Tamerlane) and his conquests. The second part describes Vasily I's campaign against him, the transfer to Moscow of the icon of the Mother of God of Vladimir, and the miracle wrought by it in causing the invader to depart.

26. Soloviev's reference to *Alafern-tsar* apparently relates to the decapitation of Holofernes (Judith 13:1-11). In the biblical version Holofernes is not a king, but the chief general of the Assyrian king, and he is described as having been slain by his Hebrew captive, Judith.

27. In Esther 7, Aman is described as having been hanged on the order of King Assuerus rather than Artaxerxes.

28. The German Suburb *(Nemetskaia sloboda)* was one of several areas in the vicinity of Moscow reserved for the residences of foreigners. Originally founded as a detention center for prisoners of war during the Livonian War (see note 79 of Chapter I), the area later was set apart for people from various countries who entered Muscovite service. Soloviev describes the significance of the German Suburb and the type of person it attracted on pp. 251-53.

29. The epithet in Russian is *laskovyi.*

30. The term *ataman* refers to a leader of the Don Cossacks.

31. This passage manifests the tendency toward anachronism referred to by Soloviev. Kulikovo Field was the location of Dmitry Donskoy's victory over the Tatars in 1380, more than a century after the Mongol conquest. Other parts of the passage refer to the earlier Kievan period.

32. Here again, as described in the preceding note, the events at Kulikovo Field (where Khan Mamai was defeated by Dmitry Donskoy) are jumbled together with the earlier Mongol siege of Kiev. Ermak (see note 81, Chap. I) was, of course, neither a contemporary nor a kinsman of Prince Vladimir.

33. Marina Mniszech, daughter of a prominent Polish magnate, came to Moscow in 1606 where she married False Dmitry I and later was crowned. After her

husband's death she continued to maintain a claim to the Russian throne through her connection with False Dmitry II and eventually through her infant son, Ivan. All her endeavors, however, ended in failure. In 1614 she was apprehended by crown authorities and died under mysterious circumstances in a prison cell.

34. Born in 1586, Michael Skopin-Shuisky became a prominent diplomatic and military figure whose successes on the battlefield during the Time of Troubles enhanced his popularity among the service gentry and townspeople. This apparently gave rise to fearful resentment within a rival faction, and Skopin-Shuisky died under rather clouded circumstances in 1610, possibly of poison.

35. It must be remembered that this is a summary of a popular song which, obviously, takes considerable liberty with historical facts.

36. Unanimity, or as close an approximation of it as possible, was the desired norm in arriving at decisions by the urban assemblies of early Russia.

37. Bohdan Chmielnicki (or Khmelnitsky) was the hetman, or chief, of cossacks in the Ukraine. He led a major revolt against the Poles in 1648 and obtained recognition as a semi-independent ruler. Subsequent defeats impelled him to acknowledge the suzerainty of Moscow. He died in 1657.

38. Guido delle Colonne was a Sicilian poet of the thirteenth century whose chief work, *Historia Troiana,* appeared in Latin about 1282.

39. The tales are not notable for their historical value. They served, rather, as vehicles for edification, each one being accompanied by a moral considered suitable to the story.

40. In the seventeenth century there were several *Specula* (*Zertsala* or "Mirrors") which were available in a variety of Slavic translations. Among them was a collection of tales with 102 illustrations.

41. Piasecki, bishop of Przemyśl in the seventeenth century, was the author of a chronicle which covered the period from 1604 to 1618, from the appearance of False Dmitry to the treaty of Deulino.

42. A certain A. Guanini (*Gvagvin* in the russianized form), who served as commandant of Vitebsk before his death in 1614, wrote a work entitled *Sarmatia,* in which he described the cruelties of Ivan the Terrible.

43. According to the early Russian calendar, adopted from Byzantium and retained until Peter the Great's reforms, yearly calculations were based on the creation of the world, reckoned to have occurred 5508 years before the birth of Christ. Thus, 5508 + 1653 = 7161.

44. Stephen Báthory (1533-1586), prince of Transylvania, was elected king of Poland in 1575. He quickly went on the offensive against Muscovy and brought the long Livonian War to a successful conclusion for Poland.

45. Fedor Griboedov remained in government service as a chancellor from 1632 to 1671. Besides writing his *History,* which he completed in 1669, he was also a member of the commission involved in drafting the Code of 1649. He died in 1673.

46. The expulsion of Igor from Kiev is mentioned under the year 1146 in the Russian Primary Chronicle, which attributes the initiative for the ouster to the townspeople of that city.

47. Prince Georgy Dolgoruky is here referred to as ruler of Moscow. This was true. But the effect of the statement is to enhance Moscow's prestige at the expense of Suzdal, which was actually the capital in which Georgy established himself as its first independent prince. (He also succeeded in becoming grand prince of Kiev.) The last part of this sentence, translated literally, reads: ". . . and now

their illustrious tsarist family governs in glory." This is an apparent attempt to overcome problems connecting with the extinction in 1598 of the Riurik dynasty in its Moscow line. On the whole, Griboedov tries to impart an early predominance to Moscow at a time when it existed merely as a small fortified outpost and to assert a dynastic continuity with the installation and succession of the Romanovs.

48. The reference is to Vsevolod III (see note 36, Chap. I).

49. The icon of the Mother of God of Vladimir, dating to the twelfth century, traditionally has been held as originating in Constantinople. Brought first to Kiev, it subsequently was moved to Suzdal, then Vladimir, and finally Moscow. There, placed in the cathedral of the Dormition, it came to symbolize the spirit of Russian unity. See note 26, Chap. III for the reference to this icon in the tale *Temir Aksak*.

50. Alexander Nevsky (ca. 1220-1263) became prince of Novgorod in 1238. After his father's death, he received permission from the Tatar khan to assume the grand-princely throne of Kiev in 1246 and of Vladimir in 1252. He is noted for his victories over the Swedes (1240), the Germans (1242), and the Lithuanians (1245). As he won these battles in the West, he followed a policy of submission to the Tatars.

51. The youngest son of Alexander Nevsky, Daniel received Moscow as his own separate principality in accordance with his father's bequest. Becoming thus the first prince of Moscow, Daniel ruled until his death in 1303.

52. Ivan I, "the Moneybag," became prince of Moscow in 1325. He was granted a charter by the khan in 1328 (or 1332) to the grand principality of Vladimir. For the significance of this, see note 39, Chap. I. The date of Ivan's birth is unknown; he died in 1340. It should be noted that, in the text, no mention is made at this point, between the reigns of Daniel and Ivan I, of the latter's elder brother Yury (or Georgy), who was the first prince of the Moscow line to be installed, with the khan's permission, as grand prince of Vladimir. He was killed by Prince Dmitry of Tver in 1325 in the capital of the Golden Horde.

53. Ivan II was prince of Moscow and grand prince of Vladimir from 1353-1359.

54. Simeon the Proud, after his installation by the khan in 1341, made reference to himself as "grand prince of all Russia," asserting in this way the growing preeminence of Moscow. He died of the plague in 1353.

55. Needless to say, this genealogical account is more imaginative than historical.

56. Innokenty Gizel (ca. 1600-1683) came from Prussia to the Ukraine, where he converted to Orthodoxy. In 1656 he became archimandrite of the Kiev Monastery of the Caves, having earlier received an appointment as rector of the Kiev Academy.

57. Matvei Stryikovsky (born 1547), was a Lithuanian historian who wrote a chronicle that was translated from Polish into White Russian in 1582 and into Russian in the seventeenth century.

58. Genesis 10:2.

59. Batu led the Mongols in their successful conquest of Russia in 1237-1240. Khan Mamai lived about a hundred years later. See notes 31-32, Chap. III.

60. The full title of the historical compilation produced by Nicholas Spafary in 1673 is: *Vasiliologion, or Enumeration, of Assyrian, Persian, Hebrew, Greek, Roman, and Pious Greek Rulers, and of Grand Princes and Sovereign Tsars of Russia, Who Throughout the Entire World Have Ever Engaged or Are Now Engaged in Glorious and Courageous Wars.*

61. This work was translated by Nicholas Spafary in 1673. The title given by Soloviev is translatable as *The Muses, or the Faces of the Seven Liberal Arts (Musy ili sedm svobodnykh uchenii v litsakh)*. The correct title is the following, which is the one translated in the present text: *Kniga izobrannaia vkratse o deviatikh musakh i o sedmikh svobodnykh khudozhestvakh*.

62. The full title is *The Tale of the Sybils, That Is, Prophetesses (Skazanie o Sivillakh, sirech prorochitsakh)*.

63. This work is a Russian translation from the Greek, with supplementary interpretations, by Nicholas Spafary and Peter Dolgov. The full title is: *Chrismologion, That Is, an Excerpt, from the Prophecy of Daniel Concerning the Dream of Nabuchodonosor, as well as the Four Universal Monarchies (Khrismologion, sirech kniga perecheneslovnaia, ot prorochestva Daniilova, skazanie soniia Navukhodonosorova; takzhe o chetyrekh monarkhiiakh vselennyia)*.

64. This is the same as the *Vasiliologion* in note 60, Chap. III.

65. Pitirim was patriarch of Moscow for an uneventful ten months in 1672-1673.

66. In Thucydides' *History of the Peloponnesian War* the funeral oration of Pericles contains a brief exposition on the principles of government and system of laws in Athens.

67. The reference is to Vesalius' *De Fabrica Humani in Corporis*, 1543.

68. A fifteenth-century German preacher, author of *Hortulus Reginae*.

69. Soloviev's footnote: "As compensation for his service, he received a regular salary of 60 rubles; in his capacity as a clerk of the first rank in the Ambassadorial Chancellery, he received 55 chetverts of rye (a chetvert of rye cost 21 altyns in 1674), a like amount of oats, and 10 puds of salt annually. Moreover the teacher was granted additional amounts of money on great feast days and the sovereign's name day, for a total of 45 rubles." The official conversion rate in the seventeenth century placed one chetvert on a par with eight puds of rye (though numerous deviations from this norm existed). As mentioned elsewhere, a pud equals 36.11 pounds.

70. See pp. 183-84.

71. Francis I, king of France from 1515 to 1547, was noted for his love of the arts and literature. The beginning of the Renaissance in France is customarily dated from his reign.

72. *Statir. Teachings for Sundays and Other Occasions Throughout the Entire Year, Numbering 156, Composed and Written in 1684 by an Unknown Parish Priest of the Perm Eparchy in the Town of Orel (Statir. Poucheniia voskresnye i drugie chrez ves god chislom 156, sochinennye i pisannye v 1684 godu neizvestnym prikhodskim sviashchennikom Permskoy eparkhii v gorodke Orle)*.

73. Paissius Ligarides arrived in Moscow as metropolitan of Gaza. A Greek educated in the Catholic tradition, whose individual loyalties remained uncertain, he came to take part in the deliberations of the church council of 1666-1667, leading to the confirmation of Nikon's reforms and his deposition from the rank of patriarch.

74. Russians customarily referred to Yury Krizhanich as a Serb. He was actually born in Croatia, not far from Karlovac, in 1618. He received a Jesuit education and was ordained a Catholic priest. He made two trips to Muscovy. The first was a brief visit in 1647. He arrived a second time in 1659, entering the tsar's service as a grammarian. In 1661 he was exiled to Tobolsk, where he spent the next

fifteen years. In Siberia he engaged in considerable literary production. Released from exile in 1676, the year of Tsar Alexis' death, Krizhanich left for Poland the following year.

75. Krizhanich's *Politichnye dumy* was written between 1663 and 1666 during his exile in Siberia. This treatise is also variously known as *Politics (Politika)* and *Conversations on Ruling (Razgovory ob vladatelstvu)*.

76. Isaiah 1:23.

77. See note 23, Chapt. III.

78. Solovetsky monastery, located on an island in the White Sea, became a stronghold of the Old Belief. Besieged by government forces sent to enforce the Nikonian church reforms, it maintained a stout resistance from 1668 to 1676. When finally it was taken, the monks were meted out heavy punishments. But their "stand for the faith" had a strong impact on the attitude of the entire north and served as an example to many who rejected the foreign innovations in their religious life.

79. *The Life of Protopope Avvakum, Written by Himself (Zhitie protopopa Avvakuma, im samim napisannoe)*. In presenting selections from Avvakum's auto-biography, Soloviev made use of N.S. Tikhonravov's printed Russian edition (St. Petersburg, 1862). Born in 1620 or 1621, Avvakum Petrovich became a staunch proponent of the Old Belief. After many harrowing experiences, he was ordered in 1682 to be burned. See Joseph T. Fuhrmann, "Avvakum Petrovich" in MERSH, 2, 193-197 and D.N. Breschinsky, "Avvakum Petrovich," *The Modern Encyclopedia of Russian and Soviet Literature* [MERSL], (50 vols., Gulf Breeze, Fla.: Academic International Press, 1977-), 2, 4-10.

80. The manner for making the sign of the cross (whether by bringing together and extending the forefinger and middle finger or joining the thumb, forefinger, and middle finger) and the number of times (whether two or three) that the al-leluia was chanted in prayer services became two of the most visible issues around which seethed the controversy over the maintenance of the true belief as opposed to the introduction of reform. Exactness in adhering to customary ritual became in this case indissolubly tied to concern for preserving the traditional purity of the faith.

81. Grigorovo lies on the right bank of the Volga in the region of Nizhny Novgorod (today known as Gorky).

82. Yurievets-on-the-Volga was at one time an important commercial center in the region of Nizhny Novgorod.

83. In Orthodox churches the altar area is separated from the rest of the interior by a high screen covered with icons. The main entrance into the altar is through the central portal, the Royal Doors. It was at this location in the cathedral that the events described by Avvakum took place.

84. Dauria is a historical region of eastern Siberia, in the vicinity of Lake Baikal.

85. Matthew 27:24.

86. Fedor Rtishchev (1626-1673) was active as a crown official and tutor in the household of Tsar Alexis. He is noted for initiating many innovations, including the establishment of a school in the Andreevsky monastery and opening the first hospital in Moscow.

87. Mezen is a county located northeast of Archangel.

88. The Great Entrance is performed by celebrants of the Divine Liturgy at the beginning of the most solemn part of the ceremony.

89. The sequence of events given here by Soloviev is unclear, being only a partial transcription of the original account. The significance of Avvakum's action can be better understood from the full description of the episode. There, Avvakum tells how the patriarchs had just engaged in a particularly virulent exchange with him, in the course of which all the inquisitors had risen to their feet. As they proceeded to sit down after the altercation, Avvakum decided to follow suit and do them one better.

90. The manuscript of Gordon's diary, written in English, consisted of six volumes in four. Entries covering the years 1667-1677 and 1678-1684 have been lost. An abridged version was published in German (*Tagebuch,* 3 vols., St. Petersburg and Moscow, 1849-1852), subsequently translated into Russian (*Dnevnik,* 2 vols., Moscow, 1892). Fragments from the diary, interspersed with synopses by the editor, are available in English under the title *Passages from the Diary of General Patrick Gordon of Auchleuchries in the Years 1635-1699* (1859; reprint ed., London, 1968).

91. The name is given as *Mongomeri* in Soloviev.

92. The name is given as *Shchil* in Soloviev.

INDEX

Red Square, 64, 81-82, 207, 267, 269
Regular Administration (*Zemshchina*),
53, 264
Reiters, cavalry soldiers, 86, 108-11,
118
Renaissance, 77
Repnin, prince, 126, 271
Repnin-Obolensky, prince, 210
Retinue (*druzhina*), xvi, 26-27, 29-
30, 33-41, 43, 49-50, 52, 54, 57-
58, 60, 63, 67, 73-74, 79, 88, 90,
102-4, 108, 203-5, 250, 260, 270.
See also Cossack military frater-
nity
Ritter, Karl, xv
Riurik, prince, 30-31, 37, 50, 53,
214, 261, 263-64, 267, 278
Rivers: Danube, 41, 224, 259, 261;
Dnieper, 25, 27, 41, 262, 271,
273; Don, 27, 70-71, 203, 263,
268; Kama, 71; Kudma, 236;
Lena, 125, 240; Moskva, 269;
Neva, 78; Northern Dvina, 154,
272; Ob, 268; Oka, 25, 166;
Terek, 116; Volga, 27, 42, 45-46,
58, 70-72, 185, 237-38, 259-61,
263, 268, 280; Volkhov, 154;
Western Dvina, 25; Yaik (re-
named Ural river), 71
Rod (gens), 259
Rodostamov, Michael, copyist, 215
Roman Catholic Church. *See* Church,
Roman Catholic
Roman Catholics, 59, 170, 177, 232-
34, 249, 251 253, 264, 274, 279
Roman emperors, 108, 215, 218
Roman Empire, 23, 31, 35, 52, 60,
70, 103
Romanov, Andrei Ivanovich, tradi-
tionally son of the king of Prussia,
founder of the Romanov family,
213
Romanov, Fedor Nikitich. *See*
Philaret, patriarch of Moscow
Romanov, Roman Yurievich, boyar,
father-in-law of Ivan the Terrible,
213
Roman rulers, list of, 215
Romans, 26

Rome, 59, 246, 264
Romodanovsky, Grigory Grigorievich,
prince, boyar, military governor, 94,
97-98, 256
Romodanovsky-Starodubsky. *See*
Romodanovsky, Grigory Grigorievich
Romodanovsky, Yury Ivanovich, prince,
boyar, 98, 195
Rostov, people of, 32, 45, 58, 85
Rostov the Great, city, 42-45, 58, 185,
212, 250, 261, 265
The Royal Garden, encyclopedia, 216,
218, 279
Rtishchev, Fedor Mikhailovich, 243-45,
255, 280
"Russes," origin of the name, 213
Russia, 27-28, 34, 37-39, 41, 49, 56, 60,
62, 64, 67, 69, 73-75, 78-80, 82, 88,
97, 108, 124, 127, 129, 143, 149,
156-58, 166, 169, 171, 188, 190,
198, 203, 208-9, 215, 222, 227, 229-
30, 233-35, 242, 246, 249, 252-53,
263, 274, 276-78
Russia, eastern, 46, 259
Russia, northern, 32, 44, 49, 57, 59, 74-
75, 97, 166, 214, 259, 280
Russia, northeastern, xvii, xix, 42, 45-
50, 54, 65, 166
Russia, northwestern, 109
Russia, southern, 75, 166, 214
Russia, southwestern, xvii, xix, 41, 45-
46, 48-49, 54
Russia, western, 42, 46
Russia, Kievan, 97
Russia in the Reign of Tsar Alexis, by
Kotoshikhin, 276
Russian Empire, 259
Russian faith. *See* Church, Russian
Orthodox
Russian history, 204
Russian literature, 210-25, 234
Russian people. *See* Russians
Russian Primary Chronicle. *See*
Chronicle
Russians, 25, 54, 57, 61, 73-75, 77, 117,
146, 152-53, 155, 158, 168-70, 173,
175, 177, 189-90, 192, 195, 200,
202, 209, 213, 225-31, 233, 249,
255, 268

THE EDITOR AND TRANSLATOR

Alexander V. Muller is professor of history at California State University, Northridge. He did his undergraduate work at Gonzaga University and the University of Washington, receiving a B.S. degree in psychology. After entering the Army, he served as an officer in the infantry and later in the artillery. Upon return to civilian life, he reentered the University of Washington, where he earned his M.A. and Ph.D. degrees in history. For one year he held the post of predoctoral instructor in history at the University of Washington. At Northridge, where he has served as vice-chairman of the history department, he teaches courses in early and imperial Russian history, Byzantine civilization, the Middle Ages, western civilization, and historiography. He also teaches in the humanities interdisciplinary program. He has translated and edited *The Spiritual Regulation of Peter the Great* (Seattle, 1972) and is the author of "The Inquisitorial Network of Peter the Great" in *Russian Orthodoxy under the Old Regime* (Minneapolis, 1978). Professor Muller lives with his wife, Helen, and two children, Alex and Tanya, in Granada Hills, California.

ACADEMIC INTERNATIONAL PRESS

THE RUSSIAN SERIES

1 S.F. Platonov *History of Russia* Out of Print
2 *The Nicky-Sunny Letters, Correspondence of Nicholas and Alexandra, 1914-1917*
3 Ken Shen Weigh *Russo-Chinese Diplomacy, 1689-1924* Out of Print
4 Gaston Cahen *Relations of Russia with China . . . 1689-1730* Out of Print
5 M.N. Pokrovsky *Brief History of Russia* 2 Volumes Out of Print
6 M.N. Pokrovsky *History of Russia from Earliest Times . . .* Out of Print
7 Robert J. Kerner *Bohemia in the Eighteenth Century*
8 *Memoirs of Prince Adam Czartoryski and His Correspondence with Alexander I* 2 vols.
9 S.F. Platonov *Moscow and the West*
10 S.F. Platonov *Boris Godunov*
11 Boris Nikolajewsky *Aseff the Spy*
12 Francis Dvornik *Les Legendes de Constantin et de Methode vues de Byzance*
13 Francis Dvornik *Les Slaves, Byzance et Rome au XIe Siecle*
14 A. Leroy-Beaulieu *Un Homme d'Etat Russe (Nicolas Miliutine) . . .*
15 Nicholas Berdyaev *Leontiev* (In English)
16 V.O. Kliuchevskii *Istoriia soslovii v Rossii*
17 *Tehran Yalta Potsdam. The Soviet Protocols*
18 *The Chronicle of Novgorod*
19 Paul N. Miliukov *Outlines of Russian Culture* Vol. III (2 vols.)
20 P.A. Zaionchkovsky *The Abolition of Serfdom in Russia*
21 V.V. Vinogradov *Russkii iazyk. Grammaticheskoe uchenie o slove*
22 P.A. Zaionchkovsky *The Russian Autocracy under Alexander III*
23 A.E. Presniakov *Emperor Nicholas I of Russia. The Apogee of Autocracy*
24 V.I. Semevskii *Krestianskii vopros v Rossii v XVIII i pervoi polovine XIX veka* Out of Print
25 S.S. Oldenburg *Last Tsar! Nicholas II, His Reign and His Russia* 4 volumes
26 Carl von Clausewitz *The Campaign of 1812 in Russia*
27 M.K. Liubavskii *Obrazovanie osnovnoi gosudarstvennoi territorii velikorusskoi narodnosti. Zaselenie i obedinenie tsentra*
28 S.F. Platonov *Ivan the Terrible* Paper
29 Paul N. Miliukov *Iz istorii russkoi intelligentsii. Sbornik Statei i etiudov*
30 A.E. Presniakov *The Tsardom of Muscovy* Paper
31 M. Gorky, J. Stalin et al., *History of the Civil War in Russia* 2 vols. Out of Print
32 R.G. Skrynnikov *Ivan the Terrible*
33 P.A. Zaionchkovsky *The Russian Autocracy in Crisis, 1878-1882*
34 Joseph T. Fuhrmann *Tsar Alexis. His Reign and His Russia*
35 R.G. Skrynnikov *Boris Godunov*
43 Nicholas Zernov *Three Russian Prophets: Khomiakov, Dostoevsky, Soloviev* Out of Print
44 Paul N. Miliukov *The Russian Revolution* 3 vols.
45 Anton I. Denikin *The White Army* Out of Print
55 M.V. Rodzianko *The Reign of Rasputin—An Empire's Collapse. Memoirs* Out of Print
56 *The Memoirs of Alexander Iswolsky*

THE CENTRAL AND EAST EUROPEAN SERIES

1 Louis Eisenmann *Le Compromis Austro-Hongrois de 1867*
3 Francis Dvornik *The Making of Central and Eastern Europe* 2nd edition
4 Feodor F. Zigel *Lectures on Slavonic Law*
10 Doros Alastos *Venizelos—Patriot, Statesman, Revolutionary*
20 Paul Teleki *The Evolution of Hungary and its Place in European History*

FORUM ASIATICA

1 M.I. Sladkovsky *China and Japan—Past and Present*

THE ACADEMIC INTERNATIONAL REFERENCE SERIES

The Modern Encyclopedia of Russian and Soviet History 50 vols. 1976-
The Modern Encyclopedia of Russian and Soviet Literatures 50 vols. 1977-
Soviet Armed Forces Review Annual 1977-
USSR Facts & Figures Annual 1977-
Military-Naval Encyclopedia of Russia and the Soviet Union 50 vols. 1978-
China Facts & Figures Annual 1978-
Encyclopedia USA. The Encyclopedia of the United States of America Past & Present 50 vols. 1983-
The International Military Encyclopedia 50 vols.
Sports Encyclopedia North America 50 vols. 1985-
The Modern Encyclopedia of Religions in Russia and the Soviet Union 30 vols. 1987-

SPECIAL WORKS

S.M. Soloviev *History of Russia* 50 vols.
SAFRA Papers 1985-